THE
TECHNIQUE
OF
SCREEN &
TELEVISION
WRITING

Eugene Vale

THE
TECHNIQUE
OF
SCREEN &
TELEVISION
WRITING

A TOUCHSTONE BOOK
Published by Simon & Schuster, Inc.
NEW YORK

First Touchstone Edition, 1986

Published by Simon & Schuster, Inc.
Simon & Schuster Building
Rockefeller Center
1230 Avenue of the Americas
New York, New York 10020

Originally published by Prentice-Hall, Inc.

TOUCHSTONE and colophon are registered trademarks
of Simon & Schuster, Inc.

Manufactured in the United States of America

10 9 8 7 6 5 4   Pbk.

Library of Congress Cataloging in Publication Data

Vale, Eugene.
    The technique of screen & television writing.

    (A Touchstone book)
    Reprint. Originally published: Englewood Cliffs,
N.J.: Prentice-Hall, c1982.
    Includes index.
    1. Moving-picture authorship. 2. Television
authorship. I. Title. II. Title: The technique of
screen and television writing.
[PN1996.V27   1986]   808'.066791   86-13868
ISBN 0-671-62242-0 Pbk.

To My Mother

Contents

Introduction:

The Exciting New Medium

IN THE TWENTIETH CENTURY there was invented a new form of storytelling. Through an ingenious combination of small metal pieces, strips of celluloid, glass in the shape of lenses, electric wiring, a technological breakthrough was achieved that was destined to have tremendous effect upon the minds of millions of people.

In comparison with other forms of art, the origin of the motion picture is peculiar. Unlike the medieval pageants performed on the cathedral steps or the Molière comedies played in the royal palace, "the flicks" came from the primitive hallways of entertainment. The movie was born next to a shooting gallery and raised in the vicinity of a beer hall. Acrobats and peddlers of sexual postcards, sorcerers and snake conjurers, clowns and strong men were practicing their ageless tricks around it. From birth it had many obstacles before it. It needed all the vigor of its lusty nature to survive.

1

The motion picture did more than just survive. Because of its low origin—and surely for no other reason—it was at first ignored or despised by the cultured élite that had all other arts in hand. But soon it could no longer be ignored. The laughter in the nickelodeons became louder and louder, filling the country. The motion picture swept onward with the elemental force of an avalanche. In terms of numbers, it soon reached the largest audience of all times. Indeed, for many in today's young generation, the motion picture has replaced the novel as this century's form of storytelling.

And along the way, it hatched an even more gigantic offspring—television. This descendant not only captured still greater numbers of spectators but assembled them simultaneously across the nation. Whereas movie prints traveled gradually through dispersed territories, a television show could be watched during a single hour by 50 million people.

There are also other differences between motion pictures and television that we shall examine throughout this book. But essentially both have become so similar in their techniques that they are interchangeable in most aspects. This holds all the more true, as the lengths of TV shows have increased from 30 minutes to one hour, and from 90 minutes to two hours, that is, to the time span of the average theatrical picture. To distinguish between films made directly for network telecasts or for movie house release, Hollywood jargon describes them as TV movies or movie-movies. Yet even this separation keeps decreasing, as theatrical movies, destined to be sold to the networks, are already shaped for both the large and the small screens, and are cast with actors who have television appeal.

Beyond that, television has successfully opened the time span for the mini-series—six to twelve hours in length—to be shown on subsequent evenings. They are commonly known as, "Novels for Television."

But despite all these innovations, the pictures and television merely provide additional conduits for the ancient communication between the narrator and his listeners.

Since prehistoric times, when the primitive hunter described his chase at the campfire, the profound human urge to participate in the experiences of others has continued to gather a crowd around the storyteller. The first man knew only his own life and that of the few people in his clan, which were practically the same. Gradually this outlook became enlarged; people who lived different kinds of lives began to meet each other. Wanting information about one another, they began telling stories. By listening to the stranger's tales, the time- and space-bound individual could enrich his own existence. A desire to live another life, or to reach beyond the limitations of his own, arose within him.

Almost from its inception, this need to widen the radius of one's personal view in an ever larger realm of existence grew diversified: it was found that the spoken word need not be the only means to exchange information. The clay figure of a tribal chief could also convey significant content; and the splendid mammoths painted on the walls of caves by our remote ancestors still have the power to evoke long forgotten events for the modern beholder.

As more outlets of expression were developed, their divergent characteristics became more clearly apparent. Each art was discovered to have its own strictures and possibilities; each imposed unique demands upon content and execution. The Greek playwright, dramatizing the murder of Agamemnon, could prolong suspense in the consecutive flow of words, but the sculptor had to arrest tension in the simultaneous, frozen figures of the superb Laocoon statue.

Over the centuries a succession of creators explored, expanded, and perfected the requirements of each art. Great minds from Aristotle to George Bernard Shaw examined dramatic potentials and limitations. On the one hand, it was recognized that certain stories were more suitable for a specific medium and, on the other, that the same story would have to be told differently in the various media.

The unique requirements of the film form are not easily explored. One might say that they are far more complex than those of the theatre. Yet it took the Greek dramatists Aeschylus, Sophocles, and Euripides several scores of years to develop the play from the chorus to its highest form; and it was not until some time afterward that Aristotle formulated its dramatic principles.

In comparison with the slow development of the stage play, the motion picture has made enormous strides since its invention. In the first decades a group of enthusiastic workers was thrilled with each new discovery concerning the nature of this new art. They explored the possibilities of expression inherent in the set, prop, object; they found the close-up, the traveling shot; they invented the sound picture. Most of these discoveries concerned the form of the motion picture, whereas the actual manner in which the film should be written remained in a state of continuous development.

The dramatic concepts which arose from the new form are far from petrified; the best motion picture creators continue to search and experiment. Indeed, what makes this young medium so exciting is that it has not yet reached its final form but is still progressing.

As the rambunctious motion picture infant was coming of age, the legitimate theatre and the novel, descendants of noble ancestry with a hallowed tradition, declined markedly. At the present time, the vigorous upstart and the impoverished aristocrats seem to have met on the same level; if they continue in their opposite directions, the newcomer may soon surpass the others.

All the more astonishing, therefore, is it that for a long time the young titan lacked enough self-confidence to trust his own creativity. For surely this buoyant, vital, and hugely endowed industry could have been expected to attract or develop its own storytellers during the period of its burgeoning growth. But instead of going straight to the authors and playwrights whose original works were successfully published or performed on Broadway, the film industry waited to acquire their writing second-hand. Instead of relying on material directly conceived for the screen, the most powerful, influential, and affluent medium the world has ever known adapted books and plays. Paradoxically, the celluloid giant preferred to stand on feet of borrowed paper.

That incongruous timidity was all the more perplexing because such transfers of content from one form to another are unique in the history of creativity. The composer did not buy and adapt a statue as the basic material for a symphony; nor did the poet find it advantageous to develop an epic from a painting. Why, then, did the film industry, with resources so vast as to dwarf those of any Maecenas or Medici in the past, persist in purchasing its blueprints from its far less opulent siblings?

Certainly, the answer can no longer be found in any disdain of the best talents to devote themselves to a medium that reaches enormous audiences. The immense palette the film hands to the creative imagination is marvelously stimulating. And the squadrons of technicians it furnishes surpass the most exacting hopes of any Renaissance architect.

But the resulting cost is precisely what impedes the enthusiasm of the most fertile creators. Financiers and bankers, accustomed to hard-nosed examinations of balance sheets, are baffled by the unpredictable qualities of such a mercurial product: of two motion pictures costing ten million dollars each, one may reap a ten-fold profit, while the other may lose half the investment.

No wonder that in an industry which is affected by many volatile factors, the yearning for safe footholds led to the futile reliance on established successes. To justify the resistance to original screen material, excuses were cited, such as the insurance derived from "tested" and "pre-sold" work.

Under close scrutiny both these arguments appear inconclusive. The "try-out" in a different medium is scarcely of a nature to inspire confidence. A motor that may have proven its excellence in a Volkswagen will fail pitifully in a Greyhound bus. Likewise, the psychological dissections of even a popular novel or the static confinement of a courtroom drama—though successfully tested in their own media—are not guaranteed to repeat their victories on the huge Cinerama screen or on any moving band of film.

As always, then, the assurances toward which this risk-haunted industry continually gropes dissolve in the light of reality. And their illusory advantages no longer outweigh those of the screen original to such an extent as to exclude it from consideration.

That motion pictures based on originals written directly for the screen can be as successful as the adapted hybrids, even among high-budget productions, has been proven by many top-grossers. Considering the prevalence of pictures based on material from other sources, the record of originals is very good indeed.

In any event, the shrinking supply found in other media coerces a greater responsiveness to the screen original. The number of Broadway productions has substantially decreased from a high of over two hundred in the twenties. And the raw materials furnished by books, while not reduced in quantity, provide less usable themes as undramatic "anti-novels" abound.

Now that the celluloid giant is beginning to trust his own imagination, material written directly for the screen finds a wider market. And the great number of television episodes demands originals to feed the ravenous hunger of the networks. As a result, formerly untapped creativity will be attracted to these hugely important media that reach audiences in the hundreds of millions.

Precisely because the completed product is addressed to such multitudes, the difficulties during production and the uncertainties about the reception by the public cause a lingering insecurity among executives. They pass their lives working with material that is harder to clasp than mercury and more unpredictable than the weather. Thus, the industry is afflicted with an incongruous inferiority complex—despite the fortunes spent on boastful advertising.

In a weak moment, a producer will admit that the reasons for success or failure of many pictures remain a mystery to him. Executives may bring out figures to prove that a perfectly awful picture "cleaned up," and that one which won general acclaim "is dying in the neighborhood houses." Upon insistent questioning, however, a studio head may concede that some pictures that win general acclaim are also successful in the neighborhood houses.

Consequently, the secret of success lies not in some superficial appraisal of good or bad, but in some inner dynamics of the story. A picture that appears to be terrible may still have some hidden merits which lead to its success, and an outwardly wonderful picture may have some invisible deficiencies which contribute to its failure.

Puzzled and worried, some producers have resigned themselves to the belief that a hit picture is a matter of luck. They consider movies a more hazardous game than roulette. Many writers and directors are similarly rattled by the strange behavior of their work. A treatment of a story that reads perfectly well may present insurmountable obstacles in its transformation into a screenplay. A scene that reads well may sound terrible when it is shot. It is easy to sympathize, therefore, with the screenwriter who rushes to his producer, exclaiming enthusiastically: "I've got an idea! It's a great idea, and if you don't like it ... it's not exactly what I mean."

What, then, is the answer to the riddle of success? Can it be found by experience?

When the motion picture was a new form of art, it progressed by experimental methods. The industry groped its way forward. Each picture represented a poll: the public put in its aye or nay, and the industry discarded or developed techniques according to their success. But because there are too many other variables involved in the audience acceptance of a picture, this trial-and-error procedure could not adequately illuminate the inner workings of the film medium.

How can we learn to look through the surface and see what goes on underneath?

When you open the dramatic works of Shakespeare, you find a number of words on white paper. These words were arranged in a certain order about four centuries ago. Today, they still have the almost unbelievable power of making us cry in certain places and laugh in others. Because they were arranged in such manner as to contain emotional stimuli, they have the effect of making us feel sympathy or hatred, of filling us with pity or horror. If such a transmission over hundreds of years can take place, if generations and generations of audiences consisting of different kinds of people are able to experience the same emotions, surely there must be laws and rules which effectuate such an amazing feat.

And if there are such laws and rules, it is likely that there are craftsmen who have mastered them. Indeed, when we consider the creations by some of the best screenwriters and directors, we find that they have a very consistent "track record." This very constancy proves that they are not just *lucky*. Nor can their success be explained by talent alone. No, the unvarying quality of their work also results from a deep knowledge of film and TV.

Frequently, the question is asked whether or not writing can be learned. The answer is twofold. Talent is prerequisite, but the talented person can and must learn how to write. Indeed, the degree of talent one has cannot be determined until the craft furthers its expression.

Let us set out to explore the mysterious dynamics of these fascinating media. And along the way we might heed the advice given by the masterful artist Delacroix to a flamboyant young painter: "First learn to be a craftsman; it won't keep you from being a genius."

PART I

THE FORM

IN THE FIRST JOY over the invention of moving pictures, it was believed that this unfettered form of storytelling was an art of limitless freedom. One could go everywhere with the camera. One could bring railroads to the screen; film battles, ships, coal mines. One could make long pictures and short pictures; adapt novels and plays and short stories, epics and dramas. Rarely was it acknowledged that the motion picture might have its own form, imposing its own artistic restraints upon the creator's imagination.

As a book on playwriting tends to be a compilation of facts—facts which were assembled during hundreds of years of playwriting and play-analysis—so a book on screenwriting must concern itself with the "finding" of facts. The one looks into the past, the other toward the future. The proper method to employ, therefore, is one of pragmatic investigation. Thus we intend to start on the ground and to proceed systematically through the entire material. We shall discard all aphorisms or fragmentary thoughts. We shall not take anything for granted, even though it may have been in practical use for a long time. Instead of making statements on the basis of experience, we shall endeavor to derive and prove them.

Moreover, we shall carefully refrain from expounding any aesthetic theories. It is not the purpose of this book to advise *what* to write, but merely *how* to write. We shall touch the content of the story only insofar as it is limited or conditioned by the characteristics of the motion picture. Attempts to prescribe general artistic theories are likely to fail since they are bound to be personal opinions, subject to the changing moods of the time; moreover, they infringe upon the creative imagination of the writer.

Indeed, no inhibition is intended by exploring the dramatic laws that pervade this extraordinarily fluid medium. To illuminate them more clearly, we may emphasize a specific rule without, in each case, enumerating the possible exceptions which creative freedom may allow to the individual writer. And after defining a term, we shall not continually repeat all its expansions or qualifications. For instance, by storytelling we may mean more than a mere plot. A Chekhov play tells a story about its charac-ters without rushing them through a series of suspenseful incidents.

In the same way, every filmmaker is apt to give his script a different style, according to his own artistic vision; but each of those treatments will contain the bones of a dramatic construction. While it is true that many experi-enced writers create "oblivious" of any theory, it does not mean that their work does not embody the elements of structure. Someone who wants to learn a language must learn its grammar; someone who knows the language speaks it the way it is prescribed by grammar even though he is not conscious of it. And the master dramatist may effectively break the rules of grammar to characterize, for instance, the dialog of an illiterate peasant. There is no doubt that innovators like Ingmar Bergman, Fellini, Kurosawa, Buñuel, are well grounded in basic techniques, whether or not they choose to disregard some of them to achieve original effects.

In what way, then, does the screenplay differ from other forms of expression?

Suppose your mind has been stimulated by a gripping story which cries out to be made as a motion picture. How do you go about organizing the still formless content in the best possible adaptation to this new medium?

To learn how others have done it, you might go to your neighborhood movie theatre. And as you are watching the film unspool, you observe not only your own reactions, but you sense that the spectators around you are also responding to what they see on the screen.

The screenwriter may have wanted you to feel suspense, or sadness, or compassion, or he may have tried to arouse your laughter. You may comply without knowing immediately why. But sometimes you may laugh in a supposedly sad scene and be bored in a merry sequence. Besides, you may have a great many reactions which are unwanted by the writer. You may feel that the picture does not move, you may be interested in parts, or you may get very tired toward the end of a picture which is actually short.

And after leaving the movie house, you may have a wide variety of feelings, ranging from satisfaction to dissatisfaction, from tenseness to relaxation, from happiness to depression. You may have the feeling that you have been fooled or that you were taken for "a ride." You may think that you have been sent away before your interest has ceased to exist. You may have the impression of being let down.

Why did the writer fail by causing the unwanted reactions? And did he succeed in other areas by pure chance?

By now you might be tempted to conclude, along with many experienced filmmakers, that those ornery pictures are absolutely incalculable and unpredictable creations. The contrary is true. In the following chapters, we shall try to analyze the reasons for certain reactions on the part of the spectator. We will find that they are provoked by certain causes and that these causes always have the same effects. The constancy of this behavior can be generalized in dramatic laws.

Going home from the movie house, you are eager to get to your typewriter, for you can certainly do better than the writer of the inept horse opera you just saw. So you thrust the white paper into the typewriter, fully prepared to write FADE IN in the upper left-hand corner. But before you type the first letters, you hesitate in order to choose the very best opening scene. Perhaps none springs to mind that would seem excellent enough to be retained. Or else several possibilities fight each other to a draw. Meanwhile the hesitation grows more prolonged than you expected.

The page remains blank.

You sharpen one pencil, then two. You check the typewriter ribbon, which happens to be in splendid working order. Suddenly, you are inspired by the memory of a great motion picture you once saw. But gradually the comparison to your own beginning leaves you more hesitant than before.

And the page remains blank.

Instead of feeling dejected, be kind to yourself. Give

yourself a break—by not attempting to rush directly into the final screenplay. Consider the completed motion picture you recently admired as the end result of many intermediate steps. After all, you would not endeavor to leap up to the top floor of a skyscraper: you are more likely to enter the building, cross the lobby, and then ascend floor after floor, whether by elevator or afoot. The attempted jump would get you nowhere; the laborious and protracted climb will surely lead you to the top.

By not demanding overly much of yourself from the very beginning, you can let the basic idea ripen and mature. You will develop it in stages, from outline to shooting script. And at each progression you will have a chance to shape and perfect it. The grasp from one draft to the next is no longer beyond your reach.

You can now give your imagination free rein, because you are no longer apprehensive that your first concepts will be subjected to harsh criticism. There will be plenty of time later on to improve and delete. Indeed, the closer your work approaches its final form, the more your critical faculties will come into play and gain in ascendancy over the spontaneous invention that you permitted to flow over the dams in the beginning stages.

Most great artists have had the ability to balance their creative energies with comparably outstanding self-criticism. Without it, their most powerful projections would have been dissipated. But in the creative process, the critique should not be too stringent too soon. If the inhibiting reflex is released simultaneously, often by fear of disapproval or ridicule, it will have a stifling effect. So permit yourself the joy of the initial fantasies and fancies, knowing full well that you will have to shape or correct them subsequently.

And suddenly the white paper in your typewriter is not blank anymore.

Instead of writing FADE IN, you might jot down: "What I have in mind is the story of a boy in trouble, who sets out to . . . ."

To do what?

As in a crossword puzzle, you will fill in your own reply. And from each answer, you will find that new questions arise. By meeting their demands for clarification, you will not only flesh out the sketchy story idea with which you started, but you will end up with more material than you can use. An embarrassment of riches, however, is easier to resolve than the awesome void of the blank page.

Here, then, is the plot of this book: A person wants to know how to write a screenplay. And the first question he asks is: "What is a motion picture?"

DEFINITIONS

What is a motion picture?

The motion picture is basically a story told to an audience by a series of moving pictures.

This definition lets us distinguish three elements:

1. The story—that is, what is told.
2. The audience—that is, to whom the story is told.
3. The series of moving pictures—that is, the means by which the story is told.

The novel or the stage play also tells a story. How do they differ from the motion picture?

For years this difference was a much discussed problem. Since all three can tell the same story, the variation cannot be in *what* is told. Nor can the difference be caused by the audience, because the human being to whom the story is told may be the same in all three cases. Consequently, the difference must lie in the form. The story itself is affected by the form. Not that it can be changed, because the events represented should be true to life and not true to form. But since the manner in which the story is presented differs, not all stories can be told in all forms.

Our initial task then is to start modestly with an examination of the physical characteristics, for they determine the means by which the picture expresses itself. From these means of expression we can proceed to the manner in which the motion picture can tell its story and to the effects which this manner has upon the motion picture audience. And last, we can investigate the quality of the story material with respect to the possibilities of expression and the audience to which it is addressed.

These considerations lead to the division of the present book into three parts. The first part is "The Form." Its purpose is to investigate the physical characteristics of the motion picture with regard to its means of expression. The second part is "The Dramatic Construction", it examines not only the manner in which incidents of real life should be represented by the specific form of motion pictures, but also the effects of this representation upon the motion picture audience. And the third part, "The Story," investigates the content of the story material and the practical application of all our findings to the motion picture script.

Chapter 1

The Film
and TV Language

The sole purpose of any language is to tell something. Style, rhythm, the beauty of word arrangements, may be developed artistically; still, the language is never self-sufficient, but remains in the service of what is told.

Thus the motion picture language must not be judged by its esthetic values alone, but by the service it renders to the story. The motion picture language is not the ultimate goal—instead, the story is our ultimate goal. The best use of the motion picture language is not the one that plays artistically with the motion picture means, but the one that tells the content in the best possible way. All other efforts can be compared to the senseless though interesting sounding combination of words by Gertrude Stein or to the babbling of an idiot whose words do not make sense and consequently are no language.

We shall investigate the motion picture language from the point of view of its expressiveness. In the perfect fulfillment of its duty lies its beauty.

Space

If we were to consider the celluloid strip before us in complete ignorance of further facts connected with motion pictures, we would find that it has a definite length. We might think of unrolling the reels of the picture and spreading the celluloid band over a mile and a half of road. From this we derive the conception of space. For within this limited length we have to tell the motion picture story. We might think of going up and down the road and laying out our scenes, our events, our climax, our solution.

The word "space" is appropriate for the motion picture since its length can actually be measured by the yardstick. The novel does not know the conception of space in this sense. Its story can be told with less physical limitation. The author can end his work when he feels that he has said everything in the best possible way. But the theatre knows the powerful restraint which space puts upon its story because the play has a definite time of performance.

Excepting a few protracted pictures shown with an intermission, the motion picture form limits us to an average length between 7,000 and 10,000 feet of film, unrolled in about 80 to 120 minutes. While this represents a greater variance than is allowed by the exact time-slots in television (30, 60, 90, 120 minutes, less allocations for commercials), the limitation of space in motion pictures affects the creative aspects in many ways.

Whether our story is short or long, whether we would like to stop earlier or later, we cannot fit the length of the motion picture to the length of the story, but we must fit the length of the story to the space available. Thus space becomes the first factor determining our choice of story material.

Moreover, space forces upon us one of the essential demands of motion pictures: economy in storytelling. No matter how much money a producer is willing to spend on the physical production of a motion picture, his writers are forced to economize words, for the space allotted to them remains limited. They may conceive expensive sets, but their writing must stay economical, for the time limits are not as variable as the costs.

Consequently, the writer will have to plan his one and a half or two miles of space in a very careful manner. The more he has to tell, the thriftier he will become in the use of the footage within which he must complete his story.

The conception of space does not concern only the writer of the script; it also affects the spectator. Of necessity, the entire picture must be unrolled for the spectator in one uninterrupted sitting. The spectator cannot pause to rest. Thus the story should be such that he will not get tired, despite the fact that it must be absorbed in its entirety. Nor can the spectator ponder certain passages if they are unclear: the story proceeds relentlessly. Nor can the spectator "reread" certain passages that present difficulties for the understanding.

Picture

In the beginning the motion picture consisted of one strip of celluloid on which the photography was recorded. This was the silent picture. With the invention of the talking picture a second strip was added, running parallel to the first one. This strip recorded the sound.

Together they tell the story to the audience. Together they contain the means of expression. In order to find them, we can ask what we see in the picture and what we hear in the sound.

It is a good thing that the silent picture was invented before the talkies. The fact that the pioneer filmmakers had to get along without sound taught us that we could get along without the help of dialog. Aided by a few captions, the early motion picture was able to make a story clear—silently. Consequently, the means of expression lying in the picture strip are sufficiently expressive to tell a story. This is all the more astonishing because it is unthinkable that we should be able to understand a stage play without dialog.

The camera records sets, props, object, and actors; and these elements can be shown in different lighting. With the exception of some titles, the silent picture had no other means of expression; therefore these elements were able to reveal sufficient information.

The same elements exist in the novel and in the stage play, but there they are not capable of revealing sufficient information. The explanation is that the novel cannot represent them pictorially. And in the theatre the amount of these elements is smaller than in the motion picture. For instance, the camera shows us many more sets than we see in the stage play. The difference in number is so considerable that the set becomes an autonomous part which must be studied specifically. Through the greater number of sets in the picture, we have also a greater number of props. Furthermore, the close-up, through the enlargement of detail, gives the prop a greater importance than in the theatre. Also the objects are seen in action—a train passing, a plane crashing, or a river overflowing. The stage presents the actions of men, whereas the picture presents actions of men and objects. And even the motion picture actor gains new importance: First, he can be shown in actions and reactions which could not be represented by the stage. Second, the close-up reveals clearly his expression, which is hardly visible to the theatregoer who is separated from the actor by a distance.

Although the set, the prop, the object, and the actor exist in the novel and the stage play, they all gain new values and importance in the motion picture because of its specific form. The difference is so great that even experienced novelists and playwrights must carefully examine their new capacities for revealing information before adapting their material to the screen.

The Set: By "set" we usually mean the walls of a room. But in the motion picture we must enlarge upon this conception. We must define the set as any kind of surroundings or background. It can be a living room or a mountain range or the wide open spaces.

The importance of the set results from its connection with locale or place. The set can reveal that we are in a sauna, a library, or a bedroom. Thereby the set gives us a number of important facts. Furthermore, the set of a living room can be luxurious or simple, ugly or beautiful, old-fashioned or modern. It can thereby reveal wealth or taste or even the period in which it was built.

The Prop: The prop can either be a part of the set or a part of the actor. In either case it reveals a characterization. If we see vegetables lying in baskets, the set is characterized as a market. If we see evening gowns hanging in a shop window, the store is characterized as a ladies' dress shop. The quality of the gowns can characterize the shop as youth-oriented or sedate.

If the props are part of the actor, they help to characterize his personality. A man who wears glasses needs them to see better. Or he may use them to conceal his identity. (But that is a contradiction and represents a specific effect.)

There are props connected with certain actions. If we see a man on the street with a fishing rod, we assume that he goes fishing. A tennis ball carries the characterization of a tennis player, or even the intention to play tennis. (Probably the most famous single prop bearing a characterization was the jigsaw puzzle in *Citizen Kane:* it revealed the boredom of the life the Kanes were leading.)

It is tempting to say that the prop in the motion picture takes the place of the adjective in the novel. The novelist may say "an elegant woman." The screenwriter may show her in a mink coat. The novelist may say "a messy room." The screenwriter may show empty cans on the floor.

The Object: The difference between object and prop must not be defined too strictly. Both are things without life, but we can say that the object has the possibility of action. We can consider a car, an airplane, a ship, a volcano, a torrent, or even a rain cloud as an object capable of action. This potentiality is important. It is enough for us to see how a man takes a gun from his drawer in order to understand his intention to shoot somebody.

But beyond that, a dramatic or even an emotional charge may be attached to the object. For instance, a police officer loses his gun to a killer through his own fault. Subsequently, his pal is shot with that same gun. The identity of the weapon powerfully motivates the officer's haunting self-reproach.

The Actor: The looks of the actor already reveal a characterization. An actor can look like a villain or a kind person, like an intellectual or a moron. Beyond this constant characterization, the actor can express momentary and changing moods such as fury, pain, resignation, submission, love, jealousy, or fatigue. At times, such expressions let us understand either a happening which took place before or an intention which the actor is about to execute. At times, it may be enough to show the actor's reaction. One close-up of a man who sees his rival kiss the heroine is enough to expose an important dramatic conflict. If his painful expression turns into resignation, we know that he intends to give up the woman. If it turns into jealousy, we know that he intends to fight for her.

Although the dress of the actor could be considered a prop, it must be mentioned here because it adds so much to the characterization. Consider the information given by a medical smock, a Red Cross uniform, a Salvation Army dress. But civilian dress also gives us information: it can be expensive, elegant, neglected, poor, soiled, or clumsy; it can be evening gown, sports clothes, or overalls. It can be modern or period costuming. Beyond that, an elegant dress can be torn, a coat unbuttoned, a collar open. Together with other information such dress can tell an entire happening.

The Lighting: Lighting can tell us whether it is dawn, daylight, dusk, or night. The different hours of the day have different effects upon us, as we shall see in the chapter about time.

A change in lighting can indicate that a door or a window shutter has been opened. It can indicate that a lamp has been lit; it can indicate that the spotlights of a car are approaching or that a searchlight is directed to a person.

Lighting is of utmost importance for conveying the mood of a picture. But it can reveal only a limited amount of direct story information.

Sound

We should not consider the invention of the sound film as an important revolution, but simply as an addition to the already existing means of expression. The vital function of sound, overshadowing all its other applications, lies in the dialog.

The Dialog: The possibility of letting the actors speak seemed to make the motion picture equal to the stage play. But the dialog in the motion picture has a different role and different values. You can read the dialog of a stage play and understand the whole action without further explanation. But you could not confine yourself to the reading of the dialog in a screenplay if you wanted to understand the happenings. The difference is that the dialog in the stage play is the principal means of expression, while in the picture the dialog shares its role as a source of information with all the other elements which were mentioned before and which are yet to be investigated.

This raises the question of how big a part the dialog should play in the telling of the story. Soon after this new field was opened, there were great disputes among the moviemakers as to the use of dialog. Both extremes were advocated: utmost limitation of dialog or the fullest use of it, as in the theatre.

People speak in real life and therefore they should speak in motion pictures. It would be senseless to despise the use of dialog. But it must be put in its proper place within the frame of the whole.

Two considerations will help us to determine its function. We must realize that dialog is by far the easiest way of exposing facts. It is the simplest source of information for the lazy writer. Therefore he is tempted to exaggerate the use of dialog and to neglect the other elements. This leads to the one extreme.

As an extreme it should be avoided. Although dialog is the simplest way for the writer to convey facts, it is not the easiest way for the spectator to receive them. The spoken word is difficult to absorb. Every orator and every listener to public speeches and every student in school knows how tiresome it is to listen to a long speech. Soon the power of concentration dissolves. Dialog is more interesting than the long speech, inasmuch as two people are speaking; the quicker the dialog changes from one to the other, the better is monotony avoided. But even so, our capacity to absorb through the ear is limited. Therefore, although it is a tempting outlet of information for the writer, it is also a dangerous one, because the audience may get tired and then refuse to understand.

One picture is worth a thousand words. It is a peculiarity of the modern human mind to be fascinated by the visual effect while easily growing tired of listening. The impressions which we get through the eye have an almost hypnotic power over us. It is easy for a spectator to leave during a speech, it is possible for him to leave a stage performance, but it is difficult to drag him out of a movie house even though the picture may be awful.

For this reason it may be wise for the writer to depend more on the visual sources of information than on dialog. Demosthenes, who stuttered, learned how to speak by putting pebbles in his mouth. The writer who wants to learn how to use dialog in the motion picture should try to make his story understandable without the spoken word. In this way he will learn how to handle the other means of expression to the fullest extent. Later he can set this rule for himself: dialog should be used when all other means of expression are exhausted and cannot contribute any further. Dialog should be the last resource. Then it will be in its right place. Moreover, there is a very practical consideration which imposes utmost economy of dialog: audiences in foreign countries where a different language is spoken will be bored by talkative pictures.

Noise: Dialog is not the only function of sound. There is another one which we might call "noise." Any kind of action is accompanied by a certain kind of noise. It would be implausible to have a gun go off on the screen without hearing the noise of the shot. It would be implausible to see a train without hearing the noise of the wheels on the rails. This in itself is not interesting because it is so obvious; but the reverse process is well worth studying. A certain kind of noise represents a certain action. If the noise is specific enough, we can conclude to the action producing it. The noise of a gunshot is distinctive enough; we do not have to see the gun. The noise of the railroad cars is distinctive enough to make us realize that a train is passing without showing the train. Noise not only accompanies the picture but has a life and importance of its own.

We must keep in mind that the field of the picture is limited. The sound, however, being independent, can and must give us information beyond that sector. In this respect noise is valuable: it tells us more than we can see. To give a simple example: An actress walks from the stage to her dressing room. Nothing can be seen but the hallway through which she walks. But we hear the noise of applause. This noise exposes an enthusiastic audience. The noise is dimmed and becomes loud again at certain intervals. What else could it expose than the raising and the lowering of the curtain? Our immediate purpose is to show the actress going to her dressing room. But without losing any time, without any special effort, we give an enormous amount of information; we indicate that there is an audience in the theatre, that this audience is enthusiastic, that the actress is successful; the realization that the curtain goes up and down contributes to the characterization of stage and theatre. We can add new elements by showing the reaction of the actress to this noise: she is grateful for the applause, or she is tired of it, or she is triumphant.

Thus sound is valuable because it can contribute to the story without taking up any space. It helps the action without slowing it up or hindering it.

In *I Want To Live* Robert Wise proved his masterly use of the film medium by an uncannily expressive handling of noise. After Barbara Graham has been convicted, the newspaper man who had taken her side leaves the penitentiary. Looking back, he expresses his anger at society by shutting off his hearing aid. Suddenly all the street noises have ceased, and the audience no longer hears the click of the car door or the starting of the motor.

One of the very important functions of noise is connection. Scenes can be cut into different shots. But the sound remains continuous. While we can turn our eyes upon different objects, our ears will always hear the same noise. If the lens represents the dividing element, the microphone represents the connection principle. In the store of a tailor, for instance, we can have ten shots, each one showing something different. But the noise of the sewing machine will be continuous. Dialog is an excellent means of connection. No matter which actor is being shown, the dialog remains continuous. No experienced editor will change from one shot to the other at the end of the dialog line. He will put the end of the speech upon the other person's face. If he failed to do that, he would disrupt the action. He also knows that it is dangerous to change shots during silence.

The celluloid band which carries the picture can be cut and changed at liberty. But the sound track must be handled delicately because it is continuous.

Background Music: An integral part of the sound track, but not of the story, is the background music. Film composers are seldom consulted when the screenplay is being written. Instead, the finished picture is presented to them with the request to compose music to fit the story, a procedure which is not always to their liking.

The average moviegoer absorbs the background music subconsciously, hardly ever becoming aware of what he hears. Upon leaving the movie theatre, he may not even remember the underlying main-theme unless it was brought out by an actor who sings it, as the piano player does in *Casablanca.*

Nonetheless, background music contributes substantially to the presentation of the story. Even though its presence scarcely penetrates the consciousness of the spectator, its absence, at times, would be felt harshly.

Some years ago, the composer's branch of the Academy of Motion Picture Arts and Sciences tried out the following experiment: sequences of several pictures were shown (1) together with their background music, (2) without it, (3) and then the background music was played alone. The effect was surprisingly strong: when run without underlying music, some sequences lost half their meaning and expressiveness; when the sound track alone was run off, a great deal of the story content was conveyed to the audience, even though they saw nothing.

Thus background music may also be considered a source of information in the motion picture. Its information is not direct, however, as is that of noise or picture. We might say that it expresses information in a third dimension, namely, emotion and mood.

In this sense, it comes close to having the power of revealing, if not the thoughts, at least the feeling of the actors, thereby overcoming one of the crucial lacks of the motion picture form. In *Butch Cassidy and the Sundance Kid* Burt Bacharach's music actually contributed to the characterization of the leads. In *Rebecca* Joan Fontaine walks through all the rooms which were once inhabited by the former Mrs. De Winter. This silent sequence, before the music was added, was not expressive; but after the picture was scored, the addition of haunting, mysterious, frightening melodies made for a gripping effect.

The expression of emotion and mood by music is so strong that it can actually supply story information. This fact is frequently abused in mediocre pictures. A sweet, syrupy violin tremolo indicates or betrays that a love scene is to follow immediately. A man approaches a house, ambling along without any premonition, but the audience is informed that something terrible is going to happen by a wild, furious crescendo of background music. Inasmuch as these instances do not reveal emotions of the actor or of the audience, but of the director, they should be considered wrong.

Here are two correct examples: A woman enters her home and finds a letter on her desk. Upon opening it, she sees that it is from her husband, who was missing in action. Before the audience knows of the letter's content, a few sharp chords accentuate the feeling of surprise and shock. Or a woman is told by the man she loves that he is going to marry a young girl. The camera moves in close so as to show her emotions. At the same time the music swells to a powerful crescendo, so much that it drowns the dialog of the man in the background, which at this point is no longer important. Thus the crescendo of the background music has the same effect of intensifying the emotion as the close-up of the camera.

A further function of background music is the connecting influence upon a series of shots or even scenes. For this reason, an entire sequence of disconnected flashes or shots can be based upon a strong melodic theme, letting them flow, so to speak, on a continuous stream of music. We may remember that the change from shot to shot represents an incision, whereas the sound is uninterrupted.

Sometimes a classical composition is actively integrated into the film, as is the Mozart piece throughout *Elvira Madigan*. But on the whole, background music has no independent life, but is composed to serve the story. Consequently, orchestration effects are more useful than melodic material. The same audience which loves to hear the harmonies of Beethoven or Schubert on the concert stage would be disturbed by them were they used as background music. Modern music with its tendencies toward tone poems and program music is better suited for the task of serving the story. The abstract music of Johann Sebastian Bach, complete in itself, could not be forced to supplement the contents of a scene, whereas Debussy's *La Mer* or *Clair de Lune*, when played in a concert hall, evoke scenes and pictures in our mind.

The merits of the motion picture score are determined by its functional services rather than by its qualities as a concert piece. Nevertheless, many of the great contemporary concert composers have written motion picture scores.

Chapter 2

The Sources of Information

WE HAVE LEARNED how each element reveals information. We can now proceed to investigate the multitude of information which can be expressed by a combination of elements.

Combination

It goes without saying that there is such an infinite variety of informational combinations that we cannot hope to classify them. But we can bring to the fore various principles which will help us learn the use of these sources of information. Even an old and experienced literary writer must learn from the beginning the method of expression in motion pictures.

The only comparison we can give is to the cartoon. There we have a similar combination of elements with the purpose of telling us something. There may be the set, props, object, the expression of the actor, and, underneath, a line, which can be considered the equivalent of dialog.

The combination of elements must be understood as follows: a set, for instance, can reveal the "place." Several props in connection with the set may reveal characteristics such as beautiful or poor, luxurious or dirty. The action of an actor can reveal his relation to the set. For instance, a man who is asleep in a bedroom reveals that in all probability it is his own. A man who offers drinks to other people in a living room demonstrates that it is his home.

Having thereby effected a relation between elements, the combination begins to reveal new information. If we know that a large mansion belongs to a certain character, we know that he is affluent. If we show the charred ruins of a house, nothing more is expressed than that the house burned down. But if we show the expression of an actor sifting through the ruins, we assume that it is his house or the house of a friend of his. Thus these elements give information about each other.

If the different sources of information are exposed at one time, the combination is simultaneous. But the combination can also be consecutive; that is, one fact may be combined with one which was exposed previously or which will be exposed at a later stage.

Once information has been given, it remains valid throughout the story, or until altered by further information. If we learned that a house belongs to a dentist, we continue to believe this until we are informed that he sold or rented it or that it has been destroyed.

Because of the constancy of information, we assemble a certain amount of knowledge during the course of the story. This knowledge, piled up through previous information can add new meaning to new information. Or the new information can add to the previous knowledge.

For instance, we see a man stepping into a car. If we know already that he wants to catch a plane, we conclude that he will drive to the airfield. Or to give an example for the reverse process: we see a man taking a gun from a drawer. We do not know whom he wants to shoot. Later on, we see him enter the home of his enemy. We understand why he took the gun along.

Furthermore, the constancy of information may continue to represent a combination of elements for us regardless of the fact that we see only one of them. If we learned that a child always played with a certain toy, the presence of the toy in a strange place will indicate that the child is there or was there. If the child is dead, the object may still represent the child to his mother.

When new information relieves the first one of its validity, we understand that a change has taken place. A change can only occur through a development or through an action. Thus the motion picture can reveal an entire development simply by indicating a change. For instance, we see a field and afterwards we see a house in the same place. Or a young couple moves into a new house. There is a large double bed in their bedroom. Later we see two single beds instead of the one. Still later, there is only one. The development, implied in this change, is the weakening of their love and their final separation. Or a husband talks to his wife at breakfast. Years later, he reads the newspaper. Or a man steps into a car which is standing before his house. In the next scene he comes out of the car, but this time the car stands before a bank. The change of locale implies the action. The novelist could have expressed this action by a simple sentence: "He drove from his house to the bank." The screen writer has to make use of the visual manisfestation of a change of sets.

The means of expression at the disposal of the novelist

are altogether more facile. The screen writer is severely hampered by the difficulties of the motion picture language. He must constantly search for new combinations to express his story developments. Only through the most poignant use of all the means of expression can he achieve his goal. Let us not forget that the motion picture requires a much fuller and richer and more varied story than the stage play. Not with respect to its content, but with respect to the amount of information given. There are more incidents, more side-actions, more places, more characters, more bit players. In order to fulfill these demands, we must give more information. With the exception of dialog, the motion picture possesses no easy or direct means of expression. Therefore we must carefully study the meaning, purpose, characterization, potentiality of set, prop, object, actor, lighting, noise.

Duplication

School teachers tell their pupils that they should never repeat anything in their writing. They may be right as far as elementary writing is concerned. But as soon as the difficulties of understanding grow, repetition becomes very useful. In playwriting repetition is allowed because it is not easy for the audience to understand the play. An old stagecraft axiom states: Tell every important factor three times to the audience if you want to be sure they understand it. The same holds true for public speaking. Every great orator—beginning with Demosthenes and Cicero and Marc Anthony in Shakespeare's *Julius Caesar*— has applied repetition in his speeches so as to facilitate understanding.

The motion picture has a way of repeating itself which cannot be called repetition. Because it has different means of expression, and because each of them can express the same thing in a different way, it should be called duplication rather than repetition.

Duplication is the use of different means in the motion picture to express the same thing. At first we might be reluctant to use duplication because we think that it is a waste of space, a grave violation of the demand for economy. But there are cogent reasons which speak for duplication.

The fatigue of concentrated attention during the whole run of a picture is very considerable. Sometimes our ears do not pick up certain parts of the dialog, sometimes our eyes get tired, sometimes we have difficulties in following and understanding the plot. In all these cases we shall be grateful if certain facts are brought back to our attention by duplication.

Duplication also may be used to remind us of information which was given to us previously. The audience is liable to forget facts even though they may have been very clearly established at the beginning. If these facts are important enough, it may be advisable to bring them back or to remind the audience of these facts throughout the picture. If we were to do that by the same means of expression, we would have repetition, with its effects of boredom and waste of space. But by expressing the same things in different ways we have duplication, with its agreeable effect of variation.

This reminiscence through duplication of information requires careful handling, for the audience must be reminded of the right factors at the right time. For instance, if it has been established that a man has a brutal character, it may be a correct reminiscence to duplicate this information concerning his brutality just before his wife wants to ask him for a favor. If you have a love scene between a rich girl and a poor boy, you may remind the audience of youth and beauty, or when you have a scene of dispute between them, you might bring out the contrast between poverty and wealth. The pertinent reminiscence of facts may improve the strength of the scene considerably.

Duplication may also be used to elaborate on certain information. Anyone who has seen pictures in small neighborhood houses knows of women in the audience who suddenly exclaim: "See, now he is angry," when the actor makes a face angry enough to scare a bull. "Now he laughs"—when the ham giggles his head off. Even though their desire to fully understand the implication of a situation is absurd in such extreme cases, we must take it into serious consideration for other less obvious examples. We must keep in mind that the picture moves fast and that the audience has little time to lean back and think to the end what it is being told. For instance, the word "wealth" alone is not expressive. Even the novelist will sometimes arouse our imagination by elaborating on the word. He will enumerate what wealth means: good food, beautiful clothes, butlers, comfort. Likewise, if the screen writer tells us only that a certain artist is admired, it does not mean very much to us, especially since we have no time to force our imagination to realize what this word implies. It would be advisable to express this admiration in a few "touches" or incidents.

Of course, duplication can also become a dangerous instrument. If a man comes from the street dripping wet and somebody asks, "Is it raining outside?" duplication becomes an idiocy. If a person is bleeding and the writer in his dialog asks, "Are you hurt, dear?" the question does not make much sense. Yet the question may have looked meaningful on paper because the writer was considering only the one means of expression and overlooking the visual exposition of facts.

Coordination

No other art has as many means of expression as the motion picture. Sculpture has only the plastic form, music has sound, painting has color and line, the novel has the word. Even the theatre, which comes closest to the motion picture in this respect, has primarily only dialog. Therefore a play can be understood by reading only the dialog, whereas the motion picture script will not make sense if you consider only its dialog. As a matter of fact, it needs experience and concentration to read the script of a motion picture which intends to make use of all the means of expression.

The playwright is the primary creator in the theatre, because his writing, or his dialog, is practically the only essential means of expression. Producer, director, and actor are essentially his assistants. But in the motion picture, where the dialog represents only one part of the final creation, the use of many different means of expression demands the imposition of a coordinator, who guides and directs and chooses the right employment.

Usually the director is this coordinator. He is, in some ways, both the arranger who orchestrates the writer's composition and the conductor who brings the score to life.

However, there are no precise lines of demarcation between the writer's and the director's creations. Many a famous "director's touch" was invented by the writer and can be found in the screenplay. Conversely, many a screenplay bearing only the writer's name contains the creative suggestions and inventions of the director. Ideally what is captured on celluloid should be the result of a collaborative effort. And although there is much rivalry as to the relative importance of the screenwriter and the director, neither can hope for a successful picture without the very best contributions of the other. In the final drafts of a screenplay, they often join to discuss the most effective use of the means of expression. Sometimes a speech may be deleted because the director feels that a close-up of the actor would render words superfluous. Then again a line of. dialog may be added to cover an actor who crosses the set.

Occasionally, at that stage, errors arising from an unintentional juxtaposition are discovered. Since each element reveals information independently, a combination of elements may give wrong or contradictory information. For instance, we would be surprised if we saw a man who was introduced as a professor of biology working in a drugstore. The same may be true of a newsboy delivering papers from a Rolls-Royce, a diver plunging into an empty swimming pool, a man in a wheel chair sitting at the starting line of a hot-rod race.

If such a contradiction of information is an inadvertent error, then it is simply absurd. Yet it can also be used to achieve a comic effect—for instance, by showing the drained pool only after the man has started his dive. But if the visual paradox is based upon some specific cause of which we have not yet been informed, then it must be explained: the newsboy's bicycle broke down and a customer lent him the Rolls-Royce to finish the route.

Unfortunately, many pictures are filled with contradictions of information which are confusing at times and occasionally detrimental to the values of a scene. However, contradiction should not be confused with contrast, which is one of the important effects in simultaneous combination of information. In a famous shot in the picture *M,* which Fritz Lang directed, a mother whose child has not retured from school cries down the stairway the name of her child. The shot shows the stairway; we hear the cry of the mother. The sound stands for the anxiety of the mother; the silent stairway represents the failure of the child to come home. This is effective coordination. If we had watched the mother cry and only afterwards in silence seen the stairway, the effect would have been weaker.

Practically speaking, there will always be one main fact which gives a purpose to the shot or to the scene. But at the same time, we can use other sources of information to add further information. We should not be satisfied with the sole expression of the main-purpose, but we should try to put minor developments or less important information into the same space. For instance, the set exposes some sort of a store. Several props indicate that it is a pawn shop. A young man enters. His clothes betray that he is hard up. He carries a guitar. The tenderness with which he holds the instrument reveals his sentiments toward the object. At that point, we make use of dialog; he says that he needs money because his pal is sick. Still we are not satisfied with this exploitation of the scene. We show how the man behind the counter counts money while he is listening. This additional side-action betrays the avarice of that man. In this way we can triple and quadruple the content in the same space. We must spread information thickly over every inch of film.

In concluding this chapter about the various means of expression, it must be made clear that these sources of information should not be confused with symbolism. Symbolism is a very dubious form of pictorial coordination. The difference could be stated in this way: To show an innocent girl with a lily is symbolism. The realization that the lily stands for innocence is a complicated process for which the average moviegoer never has time. To show the girl in a simple white dress and pigtails would be a correct expression of facts. The realization is subconscious. To show a football player and in the next shot a bulldozer would be symbolism. But to show a football player reacting to a bulldozer advertisement could be a natural revelation of his thoughts.

Chapter 3

Enlargement and Composition

UNTIL NOW, we have considered the celluloid band in its entirety. However, as we proceed we find that the space of the picture is subdivided into smaller units which in turn consist of smaller parts which are assembled from still smaller entities. This cutting up of the whole of the space brings the danger that the smaller units will fall apart. Consequently, we must search for ways and means of connecting the divided parts.

At this point, however, we are not ready to examine the subdivision and connection of the story structure. We shall confine ourselves to the investigation of the purely technical and mechanical subdivision of the celluloid band. And here we find that the smallest entity is the picture frame. There are 16 frames to the foot, which means that the entire motion picture consists of about 120,000 to 170,000 frames. If we take the celluloid band in our hands, we realize that each one of these little pictures is different from the other. Each succeeding picture shows a progress from the foregoing. Even though this is a purely technical characteristic, it teaches us that the story must progress incessantly and relentlessly just as these little pictures progress.

An indefinite number of these picture frames forms a shot. A shot is defined by a change of the camera set-up. As long as the camera set-up is not changed, we have the same shot, although the things which are being photographed may have changed. And as soon as the camera set-up is changed, we have a new shot, even though the thing which is photographed in the new set-up may be the same.

The number of picture frames to the foot is mechanically determined. But the footage of film in a shot is undefined. Furthermore, it is a matter for our decision at what distance to place the camera, in which direction to photograph, and at what time to end the shot. We must investigate the principles which will guide these decisions.

First, it is necessary to understand that the field of the camera is limited. The photographic lens cuts out a certain segment of the whole. This is a vital difference in comparison with the theatre. Although the theatre is limited in its possibilities of representation, it exhibits those events fully. Everything that happens in a certain room or in a certain set is shown to us simultaneously and completely. The picture, however, might show us parts of the room or parts of the set. The camera, which cuts out a certain field, does not show us the whole but only part of the whole. Each shot shows a certain section and the next shot may show another section.

The question, What section should be shown? can be answered in the following way. Since the camera picks out a section of the whole, it must pick out the section which is important. Consequently, the motion picture does not give us a realistic representation of events, as in the theatre, but a selective rendition: only those things that the creator judges to be important are shown to us.

Because we are unable to see the whole and decide for ourselves what is important, the motion picture creator must choose for us and show us what he judges important. It is as if he were to say, "Look here, this expression or this action or this object is essential." It is as if he were to point out various elements, thereby accentuating them so that they attain a special meaning to the story. He can further emphasize them by arranging them in space in such manner that the objects in the foreground seem disproportionately larger than the ones in the background. This is due to the distortion of the lens, a common joke with amateur photographers who take snapshots of their sleeping friends by positioning the camera at their feet, which then appear much larger than their heads. In the motion picture this distortion of the lens can be used for emphasis. For instance, a glass of liquor in the foreground which, although small in reality, will fill half the screen. Then, in the background, a habitual drunkard will appear little in comparison with the glass which exerts such power over him.

Since the motion picture director has this power to select the essential, the audience assumes that everything he shows is important. But from this can also result a wrong accentuation, if the director shows a sector which is actually unimportant. Unlike the theatre audience, which automatically concentrates upon certain parts of the stage, the motion picture spectator will not try to decide for himself what is important, but will trust the selection of the director.

Inasmuch as this is the principle which guides the handling of the camera, we must ask, What is important?

To show what is important means to show elements which reveal information. Knowing that the actor is not the only source of information, we must not limit ourselves to the actor. If a gun is important, we must show the gun; if a flat tire, we must show the flat tire; if a rustic setting, we must show the rustic setting. If it is the actor's eyes, we must show his eyes. Depending upon the size of the element which is important, we must come closer or go away with the camera in order to adapt the field of vision to the size of the element which is being photographed.

Since many elements may be expressive, several of them may be important at one time. Then these elements must be combined in one shot. The fact that elements, although of contrasting or different value, are combined in one shot binds them together; we can call this the composition of various means of expression in the same shot. Contrary to the conception of composition in painting, composition in motion pictures is not so much an aesthetic as a functional matter. It is mainly the combination of various elements revealing information.

As the story progresses, the interest will shift from one actor to the other, from set to object, from prop to actor, or from one combination of elements to another. It will not be possible that the same shot can continue to show everything that is important for too long a time. Hence, we have to change the set-up. The smooth handling of the camera means the continuous following of the shifts of our interest. If we delay a shot while interest has progressed, the audience feels disturbed. If we want to see a certain action and we are shown the expression of an actor instead, we feel disturbed. Sometimes the action is less important than the reaction. At times the expression of the actor who is talking is less important than the expression of the one who listens.

If we fail to show the elements in which the audience is interested and which are important, we have the effect of hiding something. This can simply be a mistake, or the director can gain a new effect by making use of the limited field of vision. For instance, we may be able to gather from the reaction of one of the actors that something is happening. But if we are not shown immediately what is going on, in hiding this important element from the field of vision, we arouse curiosity. Later, this factor can be revealed as the entrance of another person, as a gun threateningly pointed at the actor, or as a fire newly started.

This hiding of objects, by excluding them from the visual field, is particularly interesting with respect to sound. We can either show or hide the instrument which causes a sound. We can hide the person who caused a noise by opening a door, or we can hide or show the person who fired a shot.

The camera must be compared to a pair of eyes. Generally, they are the eyes of the storyteller. This being the case, they should be placed where they can see and thereby show us the essential things. But at times the storyteller can identify himself with one of his actors. That is, he can sneak into the soul of one of his persons and look out through the eyes of this actor. Then he can shift to the soul of the other actor and look out from there. Let us assume we show a man entering a room where he sees a scene of horrible devastation. The camera then shows us the scene from the point of view of the actor. Or if you have dialog between an actor who sits in a chair and an actor who stands before him, you can photograph one shot upward, as the sitting actor would see the other person, or a different shot downward, representing the view of the standing actor. But you can also photograph both actors from the side; in that case the shot would be seen through the eyes of the storyteller.

In the beginning of this chapter it was said that the motion picture coordinator could choose the kind and length of his shots. He is not entirely free in his choice, however. He should adapt them to the demands of the story in accordance with the principles which were outlined in these pages. Many a director has indulged in extravagant shots. No matter how interesting and perfect they may be from a technical point of view, they are rather a disadvantage than a benefit to the story. In the picture *Citizen Kane* there is a shot where the camera comes through the roof of a night club. From a technical point of view, the shot is beautifully executed; from the story point of view, the shot has no sense and no meaning. In the same picture, however, there is a shot whose brilliant composition has become famous; there is a glass with poison in the foreground. In the center a woman is dying as a result of the poison; and in the background is the door through which Kane enters—he who is the reason for her attempted suicide.

Technically speaking, the different kinds of shots are classified as follows:

CLOSE-UP (CU)   Camera shot at close range.

CLOSE SHOT   Position halfway between medium and close-up.

TIGHT TWO SHOT   Head of two subjects.

THREE SHOT   A group of three actors.

MEDIUM CLOSE SHOT or MEDIUM CLOSE   One of the most frequent designations in a shooting script.

MEDIUM LONG SHOT or MEDIUM SHOT   Halfway between a long shot and a close shot.

LONG SHOT   Full, over-all shot of complete set or landscape.

FULL SHOT   Camera shot to include all characters in scene.

MOVING SHOT or DOLLY SHOT or TRUCKING SHOT or TRAVELING SHOT   A shot in which the camera moves, usually along with subject.

DOLLY BACK OR PULL BACK   Move camera away from the actor or object.

DOLLY IN   Move camera toward actor or object.

REVERSE ANGLE   A shot made by focusing camera exactly opposite to its original position.

POINT-OF-VIEW SHOT or P. O. V. Camera duplicates on actor's field of vision.

PAN   Slow swing of camera for panoramic view.

PAN DOWN or UP   Camera moves down or up along subject.

PAN TO   Camera direction to follow movement across a set or to give panoramic view of set and then focus on character.

PROCESS SHOT (STOCK SHOT)   Filmed scenes made previously on a process stage, clips from which are projected on a rear screen behind action being photographed. Nowadays, also front projection.

SPLIT-SCREEN   Images from two cameras filmed or transmitted in one frame simultaneously.

ZOOM   Quick change of focal length in lens from long shot to close shot or vice versa.

INSERT   Usually a close-up of object inserted to explain a segment of the action.

Each kind of shot is capable of showing us a different assembly of facts revealing information. The long shot is capable of showing us the total of all the factors, the complete set and all the people and all their actions therein. However, they are seen from the distance, so that details are not clearly visible.

The full shot brings us nearer. It is still capable of assembling all the factors of set, objects, props, actors, and their actions.

The medium shot does not show the whole but only a section. It shows only a part of the set, it shows not a whole group of people but just some of them. The moment we lose the representation of the whole, the camera points to certain parts, as if it were to say: this is important. The total is simply an imitation of life. But at this stage, the principle of selection begins to work. We can assemble factors of different meaning. For instance, a jockey, his horse, a gambler, and the finish line in the background. Or a policeman, a gangster, and a broken safe.

The close shot points to the detail. It can be part of the set, like the bullet hole in a wall, or even part of an object, like a flat tire, or a prop, like a letter or like the nervous tapping of an actor's fingers.

Still closer is the semi close-up or two shot. It is used when we want to show the faces of two people. And last we have the close-up. There we bring the expression of an actor to the last row of spectators in the largest movie house, a fact which has made the movies so popular as a democratic art. The legitimate stage exhibits the actor's expression only to the expensive seats.

The purpose of the traveling shot is to follow the shifting of our interest without interruption, that is, without the change from one shot to another. This confines the use of the traveling shot to cases in which we actually have a shifting of interest and in which the camera is able to follow this shift.

It can mean that the reaction of the face of an actor suddenly becomes more interesting than the group of people or the set behind. It can mean that the interest shifts from one single object to the entire set. Or that the interest stays with a person who moves on. In that case the camera may travel along. But in any case, the movement of the camera must depend upon the story happenings and not upon the director's fancy.

The same principle guides the use of the panoramic shot. We should not turn from one object to another unless there is reason for it. We may want to turn from one group of people to another. Or the director may think it necessary to expose the set by a pan shot. For this purpose he can let an actor cross the room and turn after him with the camera, thereby exposing the set. But the crossing of the actor must have a meaning. Sometimes the walk itself can be important. Charles Laughton's manner of walking in the picture *Henry the Eighth* represented a definite characterization. The danger in the pan shot, as well as in the traveling shot, is that they are slow. It is much quicker to cut from one shot to another. Therefore they should only be used if they actually follow a shift of interest.

It must be realized that each shot is a separate thing by itself, whereas the story represents a continuous flow. The tendency of the division into shots is to cut up the story, whereas we desire to obtain a smooth continuity.

For one thing, the change from one shot to the other should not be too great. If we start out with a long shot showing a person entering a room, we should not follow it up with a close-up. The change is so great that it hampers the connection. Instead we should maneuver the camera closer in two or three approaching shots. Thereby, we convey a feeling of intensified action (which by the way corresponds to the development of most scenes: they grow in intensity). The reverse process has the effect of bringing us back from the detail to the surroundings. It conveys the feeling of the circumstances in which a scene has taken place.

Action makes for smooth connection. We hardly realize that we look at two different shots if the first one shows the beginning of an action and the next one its continuation. A person who begins to stand up from a chair in one shot and finishes this action in the next one represents excellent connection. Even the lighting of a cigarette will connect two shots. The reason is anticipation, which leads our perception smoothly to the completion of the action. Anticipation works even more strongly in connecting two shots if there is no action. It is sufficient for a person to look in a certain direction. We anticipate that something has happened there and we anticipate further that the next shot will show this happening.

Since shot follows shot in one continuous flow, the following devices are used for demarcation:

FADE-IN: The slow appearance of the image on the screen. Most pictures begin with a fade-in. In the course of the film they are generally used to indicate the end of a sequence—a division similar to the chapters of a novel.

FADE-OUT: The slow disappearance of the image at the end of a sequence or of the picture.

DISSOLVE TO: A gradual blending from one scene to the next, used when a lapse of time or a decisive change of place occurs. The division created by this device is less marked than the one of the fade-out and does not indicate an interruption of the flow of events.

WIPE TO: Quick replacement of one scene for another in transition.

CUT TO: A direct switch from one shot to the next. Because the transition is so rapid, no time is lost. But it also means that no lapse of time occurred. Therefore it would not be appropriate to show how a man walks to the door and then cut to a shot where he opens it, because he would have needed several seconds to traverse the room. But it would be correct to let him start opening the door and cut to a reverse shot wherein he finishes the action.

MONTAGE: It is next to impossible to give a concise definition of montage. There are too many different opinions concerning its use. Pudovkin said that film did not become an art until montage was invented. Eisenstein conceived the entire picture as a montage. The Russians used it to a considerable extent for symbolical juxtaposition In Hollywood, montage is used primarily to compress developments too extensive to be presented in fully dramatized scenes.

On the whole, the shots chosen for montage must not only be expressive so as to convey information, they must also be adapted to the style of the film: funny incidents in a comedy, emotional in a love story, exciting in an action picture. While being helpful to the progress of the story, montage has no dramatic force of its own. The scenes glide by so fast that the spectator has no time to sink his teeth in.

The employment of these technical devices is not so much the writer's duty as the director's or film editor's. Although the mere sound of these names is awe-inspiring to the novice who believes that the mastery of these terms would make him a screenwriter, they are of minor importance to the knowledge of screenplay technique.

EXT. or INT. denote that the scene takes place in an exterior or interior setting. Although it may be filmed inside a studio stage, where a garden or a balcony has been built, the differentiation is primarily significant for the cinematographer.

DAY or NIGHT, without any intermediate moods like dawn or dusk, remains rather archaic usage. The scriptwriter, in descriptive passages beneath the shot headings, indicates the nuances.

The following sample pages from a screenplay and a film television script demonstrate that the externals have become identical.

1. FADE IN:
   INT. COAST GUARD, "SEARCH AND RESCUE CENTER"— FULL SHOT—DAY
   A functional room, with shortwave radio set, teletypes, maps, instruments. There is tense activity. A teletype keeps ticking. One of the PHONES RINGS. *LT. WINSLOW,* 29, picks up the receiver.

LT. WINSLOW
Coast Guard, Miami... That's right,
Admiral. It's too early to determine
the exact direction - but she *is*
picking up speed.
(hands teletype to
Ensign)
Yessir. We've already sent warnings
to all ships in the Straits of
Florida.

CAMERA PANS to the radio operator, *BOB PERKINS*, 34, as he contacts a ship.

BOB
Yacht Magnolia, this is Coast
Guard, Miami, over.

2. *EXT. LUXURY YACHT "MAGNOLIA"—LONG—DAY*
Despite the approach of the hurricane, the sleek, beautiful 150-foot yacht is still under a sun-lit sky. From the distance, the costly pleasure yacht appears to be no more than a small shell in the gigantic expanse of the sea, a minute blister of willful life that traverses the waters swirling from horizon to horizon.

BOB'S VOICE
(filter)
Magnolia, do you read me, over?

3. *INT. YACHT, RADIO SHACK—MED. CLOSE SHOT—GARY—DAY*
Under the plaque "MAGNOLIA" we SEE *GARY* at the shortwave set, his haggard face reflecting tension.

GARY
Magnolia. Go ahead, Bob.

BOB'S VOICE
(filter)
Hurricane approaching at twelve miles
per hour.

CONTINUED:

120. CONTINUED:

INSPECTOR
It's easier for you, Colonel, to
protect a fortress. You don't
have to patrol a whole city.

COLONEL'S VOICE (O.S)
Did you cancel all leaves—?

121. *CLOSE-UP—INSPECTOR*
INSPECTOR
Even so, I don't have enough men
to guard every building.

122. *MED. CLOSE PAN SHOT—COLONEL,
CAPTAIN AND INSPECTOR*
While the "ALL CLEAR" signal BLARES and
reverberates between the slopes, they emerge from
their cover.

COLONEL
(squints in the sun)
He won't dare to plant his sticks in
broad daylight.

                    INSPECTOR
So if he waits until dark—
    (gravely)
—still doesn't give us much time.

                    COLONEL
No...No, it doesn't...
    (strides ahead
    energetically)
We'd better have a go at—at—
    (slows down)
—at finding a needle in a
haystack.

123. *THREE SHOT—THE INSPECTOR, CAPTAIN,
COLONEL*

                    INSPECTOR
Maybe the captain can pin him
down—before midnight. The
blackmailer is likely to wait
until his deadline has passed—
    (to Colonel)
—and the Captain has promised
to make the drop.

                              CONTINUED:

Chapter 4

The Scene

THE SCENE is the next subdivision of the entire space of the motion picture. Its length is not determined by any physical necessities but solely by the needs of the story. It can be composed of many shots or only of one or two.

The story is an uninterrupted flow of developments. But the scenes of a motion picture represent only certain events from among this continuous stream. We must consider the motion picture a story of which certain events are told and others are not told. The former are contained in the scenes, and the latter take place between scenes.

The scene can be defined as a section of the entire story in which a certain happening occurs. Now every happening occurs at a certain place and at a certain time. Consequently, place and time become elements of major importance to the motion picture.

The novelist is bound neither to time nor to place: he

can go backward and forward in one sentence; or, in describing the thoughts of one of his characters he can take us to many places without actually settling down to a scene.

The theatre, however, is closely tied to the conception of the scene. But its number of scenes is so limited that place and time cannot become a major influence. Let us assume that the classical play has about three to five scenes and that the average motion picture has about thirty scenes: we realize at once that place and time gain a new importance in the picture since their effects are multiplied.

A scene in the motion picture is not determined by its content of action, nor by entrances and exits of actors, but by a change of place or a lapse of time.

With regard to time, we must consider its two aspects in the motion picture: the running time of the scene and the lapse of time between scenes. The running time of a scene is identical with actual time; but the length of the lapse of time is not defined.

In view of the new significance of place and time in the motion picture, we shall examine each factor separately.

Place

The important role which place plays in the motion picture results from the fact that the camera can go to any location in this world. Without any delay, it can show a scene in Africa, following it up with one in Asia. It can show a scene in an airplane and the next one under the earth in a coal mine.

The theatre is limited in this respect. It cannot go to the places where certain events occur, but must try to bring these events into places which can be represented on the stage. The amount is limited through the technical restrictions and the difficulties of shifting the scenery. Because it cannot go to the places where certain people are likely to be found, but must force these people to appear in a limited number of sets, their entrances and exits, as well as the entire story line, seem very often artificial.

The motion picture is free in this respect. But soon our joy over these immense possibilities is dimmed by the question, to which places should we go with the camera?

As in the decision concerning the choice of shots, we can say that we should go to those places where something important occurs. If we don't, it may be disturbing to make reference to some important event which has taken place somewhere else without actually showing it. This is a vital difference between the picture and the theatre. Very often, a certain event—for instance, a dispute between two opponents—can occur without any necessity for a definite place. In that case the writer is confronted with the problem of choosing the right place for this event.

The freedom to go anywhere results in the demand for the best choice of place.

We must realize that certain characteristics are connected with every place. These characteristics affect the events which occur there. Consequently, the correct choice of place means that these characteristics add to the events; an indifferent choice of place means that they have no relation to them and faulty choice of place means that they contradict them. Actually, we find an indifferent choice of place in most mediocre pictures, faulty choice in bad ones. The good picture, however, makes the correct choice of place an essential contribution to the values of its story.

In *Born Yesterday* William Holden sets out to teach Judy Holliday the workings of democracy. The stage play could only dramatize his efforts by dialog and by props— the books he gave her to read. But in *opening up* the picture, that fine master George Cukor actually showed the pair amidst the monuments of democracy, such as the Lincoln statue and the Capitol dome. Thereby the lesson was visually represented. However, George Cukor emphasized to me that in opening up the stage play a proper balance must be preserved—lest the cohesion of the drama be disrupted.

The characteristics of place consist of:

the *type*—(for example: office, ranch, hospital)
the *kind*—(crowded or new or cheap)
the *purpose*—(art museum: to exhibit paintings; factory: to manufacture goods; jail: to imprison people)
the *relation to one or more persons*—(A wants to buy a certain house; B waits in the library of his enemy; heroine's dressing room)
the *location*—(restaurant in a summer resort; shack in the desert; hotel room in San Francisco)

Each of these characteristics can strongly affect a scene.

The type of place can influence the action. For instance: amputation of a leg aboard a small ship.

The kind of place can characterize the owners: tasteless furniture, indicating newly acquired wealth.

With regard to the purpose of place, we find that a business conference should be held in an office, that work should be done in a factory. But beyond that, the purpose of place has no effect upon the spectator. For a long time it was thought that the insertion of night club scenes would help to entertain the motion picture audience. It is true that the purpose of the night club is to entertain its guests. But it is not logical to conclude that a night club scene will entertain a motion picture audience.

The contradiction of the purpose of place and event is frequently amusing. Let us assume that two people try to talk business in an overcrowded subway. The purpose of the subway is to bring people to their destination, not to provide privacy. This contradiction can result in many funny incidents since the two businessmen are trying to be undisturbed while the other passengers may interfere with their discussion. Or, another contradiction: a cow in the kitchen, instead of in the stable.

The relation of a place to a person may set an entire scene in a different light. For instance, a detective sips a drink at a bar. If we know that this bar is owned by a gangster, the scene gains meaning.

The location may be important not only by itself, but also in relation to the location of another place. The lover may be in New York and his girl friend in San Francisco, or they may live next door to each other. If a man drives from one place to another, the location of the two places lets us understand the distance between them and consequently the approximate time at which we can expect his arrival. This may be important because it can be an hour, a week, or a month.

Knowing these facts about place, we have to learn how to apply them to the story.

Let us choose a place for the following scene: A man informs the father of a girl that his daughter has just eloped with someone whom the father despises.

Indifferent choice of place: the father's office. The place has no connection with the scene. As a consequence, the scene will stand entirely on dialog.

Correct choice of place: The street in front of the father's house. The man calls the father to the window, informing him that the daughter is no longer in the house. All through the scene, the house, from which the daughter has fled, stands as a silent witness (*Othello*, Act I.).

Here is another example: A father is informed that the hit-and-run driver who ran over his little son is his next-door neighbor. This information can be given to him:

a) at the police station, where the aspect of criminal prosecution will be stressed;

b) at the hospital, where the boy is undergoing critical surgery, thereby emphasizing the emotional impact on the father;

c) in his backyard, where across the hedge he sees the neighbor's children playing happily while his own youngster is on the verge of dying.

In each instance, the dialog can be identical. Yet a different content will be projected. The father may even be shown with his back to the camera, and still everyone in the audience will grasp the thoughts that pass through his mind. His face need not express his emotions: much of the burden will be taken away from the actor and put upon place.

We know that a theatre has curtains, spotlights, sets, seats. We know that a hotel lobby has an information desk, telephone booths, various exits, and elevators. If the place is correctly chosen for the action of a scene, it follows with necessity that these props or objects can be put to active use in the scene. The benefit is twofold: first, we gain added material for the scene, and second, we get a more vivid realization of the place if the props or objects are typical. Goethe said, "The vivid feeling of the circumstances and the faculty to express it, this is what makes the poet."

The famous barber scene in Charlie Chaplin's *The Great Dictator,* represented correct choice of place as well as full exploitation of its values. The barber is a very human necessity and therefore contrasts the conceit and superhuman manners of the dictators. Having placed the scene in this locale, Charlie Chaplin made use of the fact that barber chairs can be screwed higher and higher. Thereby he gained an almost philosphical effect for his story.

It is clear that the realization and the feeling of the place depend more on the exploitation of the factors connected with it than on the realism with which the set is built. This realism is necessary, however, because the camera has destroyed the "symbol substitute" of the theatre. In former centuries it was enough to hang a curtain on stage to represent a wall; a chair could symbolize a fountain, a bench a bed. The imagination of the spectator would trans*form these symbols into reality. From the* motion picture we expect more realism because the sharp-eyed camera gives us a photographic representation of the world.

We should not conclude, however, that very elaborate sets contribute to the dramatic values of the motion picture. To the contrary, they attract attention and therefore distract us from the story. They, by themselves, are not interesting to us because they have no life. They only interest to the extent that they characterize the human beings living or acting in them.

Some places have atmosphere and others have not. Artists like Ingmar Bergman have been wonderfully successful in evoking the mood of a locale. To capture the atmosphere of a place goes beyond mere technique; such concepts are too volatile to be defined. But it may be offered, nevertheless, that any place used or frequented by a characteristically distinct group or class of people is likely to have atmosphere. For instance, a place which sells utensils to fishermen who have been fishermen all their lives has atmosphere. However, if it is only a section in a department store, selling utensils to businessmen who go fishing on Sundays, it is likely to have no atmosphere.

Time

In the examination of place we were guided by concrete appearances and material facts. But now we have to study an element which is entirely abstract. Time is invisible, which has led many a screenwriter to think that it can be disregarded. But time, though invisible and abstract, has many concrete ways of assisting or damaging the motion picture narration.

The fundamental difference between place and time is that place remains more or less the same while time never stays the same, not even for a second. The bedroom is the same after a day or after a week, but time has progressed from minute to minute. Because place, generally, remains constant throughout the story, it represents a connecting principle, while time, which always progresses, represents the forward movement and change.

On the other hand, we can have many different places which are separated by distances. No matter how great the distances between them, the time is the same for all of them at a certain given moment. The period of one hour is the same in all these different places. Because time is identical for different locations, time represents an excellent means of linking dispersed places together.

This means that an action which occurs at a certain time in one place can stand in a relation to an event which occurs at the same time in another place. The means of connection is the identity of time. For instance, a wife flirts with a young flier at home while her husband recites Hamlet on stage.

Time always moves and this movement is always forward. The novelist can at liberty describe events which took place in the past and which are to happen in the future. But the scenes in the picture are assumed to represent a forward movement.

This flow can be altered by flashbacks, and now also by the relatively recent innovation of the flashforward. Both have to be handled expertly to avoid confusing the audience. A quick and salient exposition should mark the reversal or jumping of time. However, protracted or frequent flashbacks tend to slow the dramatic progression; unmotivated jumping of time is likely to rattle the audience, thereby breaking their illusion that they participate in the lives of the characters. The resulting loss will not be compensated by admiration for the virtuoso effects on the screen.

The total time represented by the motion picture story is unlimited. It can vary from two hours to two hundred years. But it must be realized that within each scene one second of running time represents one second of actual time. A scene which lasts five minutes represents five minutes of actual time, no more, no less. In other words, in a picture which covers in two hours a period of two hundred years, we see only two of the thousands of hours contained in this long space of time. The rest is contained in the lapse of time between scenes. Whereas the running time of a scene is identical with actual time, we can cram a period of five or ten years into the split second needed to change from one scene to another.

This means that a scene which continues for too long will appear slow because the uninterrupted flow of time will appear slow in comparison with the periods we can traverse in the lapse of time. The screenwriter can interrupt his scene by interposing another one. Later he can return to the first scene. But he must realize that in the meanwhile time has progressed. He cannot take up the first scene where he has left it, but must take it up at a later moment which as a minimum represents the time that passed in the interposed scene. It can be longer however, because the time which passed between scenes is not determined.

Now the length of the lapse of time has an effect upon the story. One of the essential effects of passing time upon our minds is the fact that it makes us forget. It heals wounds, it makes us smile at past angers. One hour after we have been insulted, we are still furious. A year later, we may have forgotten the incident altogether. If two scenes are separated by a lapse of one day, all the happenings of the foregoing scene are still acute and vividly represented in the mind of the spectator as well as in the minds of the actors. If a year has passed during the change from one scene to the other, the events are still vividly present in the spectator's mind, because he lived only through one second, but not so in the minds of the characters represented in the story. For them the long lapse of time has effaced the momentary effect of fury, anger, joy, or sadness. Only the most fundamental emotions and situations can survive a long period of time. A picture with long lapses of time between scenes becomes epic instead of dramatic. It can only become dramatic sporadically, that is, in those blocs of scenes which are not separated by long intervals of time.

We spoke of the purpose of a place, but with regard to time we should rather speak of its customary use. The twenty-four hours of the day are divided into certain sections and customarily used in a certain manner. The day is primarily used for work and other normal activities, the evening for rest and pleasure, the night for sleep. This routine is universal for all mankind. Therefore it forms an excellent basis for dramatic effects, particularly if it is contradicted.

For instance, a man is asleep in his bed at night. His action is normal. But if a man is asleep in daytime, his action stands in contrast to the customary use of time. This discrepancy may imply that he works on a night shift, or that he was kept up during the night because of some special happening.

Another example: A man wants to inform someone of most important news. If he makes his visit in daytime during office hours, there is nothing to show the specific importance because the time is normal for such purposes. If the writer wants to stress the importance of the message, he will have to do so entirely by dialog. But the skillful writer will choose night as the correct time. If the man breaks into a house at night and wakes the other man, he must have a very important message. Otherwise he would not have found it necessary to disturb the other man's sleep. We do not need a word of dialog to stress the importance of the message.

A clerk who sits in the office in daytime represents a normal action. The same clerk in the same office at night represents a discrepancy. Something is wrong: either he is catching up with some work or he wants to falsify figures or he is trying to confuse a computer—as Peter Ustinov did in *Hot Millions* (screenplay by Ira Wallach and Peter Ustinov).

A scene of jealousy can take place at any nondescript time. But if the jealous woman stays up most of the night until the man returns from an unexplained errand, time adds heavily to the quarrel.

Every action requires time. Every development needs a certain amount of time. Every accomplishment implies a certain lapse of time. To bake a cake or to boil water requires a certain amount of time. And if you find the water boiling, you know that it must have been heated for a certain time. The measure of time contained in an action depends upon the kind of action. Some require more, some less. This means that you can foresee how much time will be needed if you know what action has been started. It means also that you can estimate how much time has passed if you see the accomplishment of an action.

In my screenplay *Hurricane Carla* an SOS called several ships to the rescue of a fishing boat. The time limit was defined by the sinking vessel. The time required to reach the survivors might be longer than the deadline. The suspense was contained in this question: Will any of the ships arrive in time to rescue the drowning people?

Almost every action picture contains this problem: Will the hero arrive in time to save everything? For instance, a saboteur wants to blow up a dam. He must plant the dynamite, prepare the explosion. The protagonist has to drive to the dam. Which action demands less time? The same problem exists when a train drives toward an undermined bridge while a guard rushes along the rails to warn the engineer. Or when a jockey who has been delayed rushes toward the stable while the other jockeys are mounted and prepared to the start.

Thus time has very powerful effects upon the story.

Exposition of Place

Each scene occurs in a certain place and at a certain time. From this we can derive the rule that the audience ought to know the place and time of a scene.

For one thing, the omission of this exposition would impede our understanding of the scene because we would lack the knowledge of two vital factors. Also, we would be deprived of all the advantages which place and time can contribute to the scene were we unable to recognize them.

Thus the exposition of place and time becomes an essential problem to the motion picture. The novelist, with a few words, can identify the place where an event occurs. For instance, "He went to the museum." "He slept at Jack's house." The theatre has no direct means of exposing place and time for its scenes. But the program informs us exactly where and at what time each scene occurs: "Act 1. The dining room at Mr. Clayton's house. Act 2. A few hours later. Act 3. Evelyn's Beauty Parlor."

Except for titles, which are hardly ever used today, the motion picture lacks even this primitive exposition. Furthermore, we find that the average picture has about thirty scenes as compared to the three to five of the stage play. This multiplies our difficulties. It is obvious that any kind of exposition takes up space. If we have to expose place and time for about thirty scenes, the space available to the motion picture begins to dwindle before our eyes. No wonder that many a writer in his desperation or through lack of knowledge of the requirements of the motion picture neglects the exposition of place and time.

Let us investigate, therefore, the manner of exposition. The information can be given to us beforehand, at the very beginning of the scene, or later during the course of the scene. Each of these methods is practicable as long as we know the effect of this timing upon the story and the audience.

In the first case the place where a following scene is going to occur is prepared beforehand. When we actually arrive at this scene, we already know where it is taking place. For example, one man says to another: "Let's go to Dick's house." The effect of preparation of place upon the audience is the arousing of interest. The spectators expect to be shown a place for which they have been prepared.

Several methods can be used to expose place at the beginning of a scene. In most cases the set can be easily identified. All that the director has to do is to show the complete set in a long shot at the beginning of a scene.

If a prop or an object is typical enough, it can be used to expose place. A menu can identify a restaurant. A photograph with an inscription can identify the home of a friend. Surgical instruments can identify a hospital. Such identification is particularly useful if, for economical reasons, only part of a set is built on the stage.

Place can also be exposed through dialog or noise or through the actions of a person.

All these sources of information can cooperate in the task of exposing place. It is even likely that they will, because the camera cannot concentrate indefinitely upon a prop or an object, but will shift from set to actor or from actor to prop and so on. This is particularly important because our full understanding of place depends not only on the knowledge of one factor but of several. Therefore the set can expose the place, for instance, a living room. Then a prop such as a precious marble bust can expose the kind of place, in this case a dignified living room; then the behavior of an actor, such as his offering drinks, can explain that the living room is part of his home. Dialog may be added if necessary.

Now, it is not necessary that all the facts about place be exposed at once, or at the very beginning. The essential factor is the kind of place because it reveals at the same time its purpose. The other information may be given when it is advantageous.

This means that we can give one or two factors through preparation of place. Later we may add others through exposition in the beginning of the scene and complete the details in the course of the scene.

But the total neglect of the necessity of exposing place can have detrimental effects. No matter how interesting the action of a scene may be, our understanding could be hampered until we know where we are. Whether we realize it or not, our curiosity is aroused. We ask, where are we? The writer is allowed to create this curiosity by withholding the information about place in the beginning, but only on condition that he give us this information at a later moment.

A most effective device was used in the picture *Cavalcade*. There is a love scene on a boat. The two young people are standing on deck, making plans for the future. At the end of the scene, they walk away, making visible a life preserver behind them. The inscription on the life preserver is "Titanic." This exposition of place had a shattering effect.

Exposition of Time

It is sufficient to identify a certain place once, because place remains the same. If several scenes during the course of the story occur in the same place, it is only necessary to identify place the first time. Subsequently, the locale will be easily recognized. This means that we are less and less confronted with the necessity of exposing place toward the end of a picture as the same places reappear. The benefit derived therefrom results in our undivided concentration upon the action because we are not distracted by exposition or lack of exposition of place.

Not so in regard to time. Time, which is forever changing, must be constantly exposed.

The need for a precise exposition of time is less severe
than for place. Except for a specifically indicated flash-
back, we know as a matter of course that each consecutive
scene takes place at a later time. Our only question is,
How much later?

The answer can be given in two different ways: either
we expose the time of the first scene and the time of the
second scene separately, whereby we define the lapse of
time between them, or we expose the time of the first
scene and the length of the lapse of time before the
second scene. Obviously, this exposes the time at which
the second scene takes place.

In this manner we obtain an uninterrupted relation of
the time for all the scenes in a picture.

In view of this fact, we need a starting point: we must
know the time of the very first scene. The fashions,
clothes, sets, props will help reveal the year in which the
first events take place. If it is a historical picture, the
costumes inform us about the period. Often it is helpful
to make reference to an event which represents a definite
mark in the flow of time through the centuries. For instance, the invention of the automobile, the Civil War,
the World Wars.

Time, being invisible and abstract, can only be exposed
by its practical manifestations.

Since an action or a development always contains a
certain measure of time, the lapse of time can be represented by the result or the progress of an action or a
development. The result as well as the progress of action
or development can easily be shown in the picture. In
doing this, we expose time.

We can consider the change from day to night and from
night into morning a development. The same goes for the
change of the season. A scene in spring and a scene in fall
will expose a lapse of at least a half year.

The evaluation of time is mostly a subconscious process. In order to understand the lapse of time which is exposed by an action, we must have knowledge of the measure of time necessary for the action. If a man says: "I shall go home after I have written this letter," we have the knowledge that not too much time could have passed when he arrives home. But if a composer says, "I am waiting for an idea," we lack any possibility of evaluating the time necessary, because we do not know how long he will need.

It is important to recognize the connection between time and action as a desired means of exposition as well as an undesired consequence. If we know that it takes a man an hour to get to his office, we cannot possibly let him appear there earlier, even though it may be desirable from a story point of view. We cannot let somebody call for a doctor and have the doctor appear in the very same scene; we would have to interpose a lapse of time and have the arrival in the second scene. This is particularly interesting if we have two different actions, each of which exposes a different measure of time. It would not be possible to let two men, converging upon the same destination, arrive at the same time if different starting points are implied. Things of this sort frequently represent serious obstacles to the story construction and very often— through neglect—result in actual absurdities.

If, instead of the lapse of time between scenes, we want to expose the time of the following scene, expressly and directly, we can do that by dialog. The manner is similar to the information about place. The time of this scene can either be prepared beforehand or exposed at the beginning of the scene or withheld until later in the scene.

The Rhythm of the Lapse of Time

In certain instances, an action or a development taking place between scenes will give us an approximate idea of the lapse of time. But there are many instances when no action or development has been mentioned as having occurred in the change from one scene to another. We are tempted to search for ways and means to bring those lapses of time which are not defined into a relation to those which we somehow exposed.

The time of the first scene and the time of the last scene determine the entire lapse of time of the picture. It may be a period of twenty-four hours, or of several years. Within this total period, the thirty scenes of the picture are dispersed.

We can represent the entire lapse of time of a motion picture story as a straight line:

X_____X

In this line we can indicate the scenes as x. The space between these x's represent the interval of time between scenes. If they were very irregular, our aesthetic feeling would be hurt, just as our understanding would be confused if the scenes in the picture were to follow each other in absolutely irregular intervals.

X x x x x xx x x x x xx x xx x X

Instead, the idea of a certain pattern is suggested to us. This does not mean that in a story extending over a period of thirty years, the intervals between scenes ought to be one year each. There are different patterns to follow, and these patterns are a natural result of the story and the length of time it covers. If the total time is a period of a few days, a pattern of equal intervals may be very practical. If the period is long, we may establish several blocks of scenes with equal intervals between the blocks and equal intervals between the scenes within a block. Another pattern might have steadily growing inter-

vals between the scenes. Or it may start out with long
intervals which grow steadily smaller. We can even use
two different patterns with the same picture. Here are
some graphic representations of such patterns:

```
X       X       X       X       X       X
XXXX    XXXX    XXXX    XXXX    XXXX
X       X       X       X       X       X
X       X     X       X       X     X       X
XXXXX   XXX   X       X       X     XX      XX
```

Obviously, these examples do not exhaust all the possibilities of patterns. But just look for a moment at the
difference between the irregular arrangement and the
aesthetic impression which results from the patterns.

Some kind of rhythm is absolutely necessary to carry
the imagination of the audience along. If the spectator
gets used to a certain pattern within the first quarter of
the picture, he will anticipate the lapse of time between
scenes for the rest of the picture. His understanding will
go along smoothly.

If the author fails to establish this rhythm, he faces a
dilemma: either he spends so much space on specific exposition of time for each scene that he has not enough
space left for other things, or he disregards the necessity
of exposing time and thereby throws the audience into
complete confusion.

Looking back upon our own lives we find that the
outstanding events took place in a certain rhythm of time.
Events like birth, first efforts at speech, first day in school,
graduation, first job, marriage, first child, divided the
time of our lives into a certain pattern. If we consider the
intervals between these happenings in measures of time,
we find that the intervals at the beginning are much
smaller and that they grow gradually. The longest intervals are in the second half of our life, with death being
the final event.

Chapter 5

Selection of Information

We have learned by what means the motion picture reveals information. Now we can proceed to investigate the function of information.

It is necessary to understand that a story is a series of items of information. The storyteller informs the listener about persons and events.

Because of the differences in their forms, the novel, the stage play, and the motion picture handle their information differently. Though it is difficult to derive any rules for novels, because there are so many different kinds, it can safely be said that the novel has the possibility of giving total information with regard to a story. This means that the novel can—and frequently does—tell us all about its persons; it can inform us about their characters, their pasts, their thoughts, their doings. Some novels even give us a description of the period, the background, the history, the customs. One remembers the gigantic canvas painted by a novel like *Gone with the Wind.*

76

As for the stage, it is only in dialog that the playwright has a certain choice in the information which he wants to convey to the audience: he can let the actors talk about things that have happened or that will happen. But it is not possible for him to withhold information about events which occur in the course of the scene which is represented.

The information of the motion picture, however, is entirely selective. Of course, to a certain extent, both the novel and the stage play select information. But selection plays a far greater part in motion picture writing.

We have seen that the camera cuts out certain sections of the whole, thereby selecting certain information. We have seen that the motion picture does not represent the entirety of a story, but that it only represents certain scenes: it selects parts of the entire story. From among the wealth of facts, the motion picture chooses certain facts which are to be told, others which are to be implied, and others which are left untold. This being the case, we must learn what to select.

First it must be realized that the choice of information is only partially free: it depends not alone on the judgment of the writer, but is also determined by the requirements of the story. Almost any information the writer decides to give will require additional information which we might describe as the need for explanation. Thus the writer must supply sufficient factors to give the audience a full understanding of the story. He must avoid leaving any necessary factors uncertain or vague.

Aristotle said, "So long as the plot is perspicuous throughout, the greater the length of the story, the more beautiful will it be on account of its magnitude." It is self-evident that if the writer strives for such magnitude, he will have to tell about more persons and happenings than if he writes an empty story. Nevertheless, the motion picture enables him to do this since it does not require

total information; by expert selection, he can tell a complicated story with the same amount of information used in
an empty story, the information of which is badly selected.

In order to select the right information, the writer
must first know the total information about all the main
characters and happenings. Although, in the final form,
the story is only partially told, it is not possible that the
writer conceives it partially. If he were to do that, he might
choose the wrong information. His selection would be
faulty.

Since the writer cannot give all the information pertaining to a story, he must choose information which is
important. There is no general rule to define what is
important. It differs from one story to the other. If the
story tells about a husband leaving his wife, it may be
important to know, not that he likes to play tennis, but
that he does not want to give her any money for support.
However, in another story, the characterization as a tennis
player may be of vital importance. If you apply for a job
in an aircraft factory, you will have to fill out a different
form than if you want to open a new bank account, because the management of the factory and the bank are
interested in different facts about you.

In reducing the total information to that which is important, the good writer can tell a story in a smaller
amount of space than the writer who is not capable of
picking out the essential facts.

With regard to one happening, the writer may give too
little information or the correct amount of information or
too much information. We shall see that the correct
amount is not identical with the amount necessary to
understand a scene. In order to exploit the values of a
situation, we must not only make it understandable but
most effective.

Let us assume we have a scene in which a husband leaves his wife to get a divorce. He tells her that he is going to see his attorney. He walks out of the room. Although the meaning of this scene is clear, which may have led the writer to believe that he gave sufficient information, the scene is not interesting. We have too little information.

But let us assume that the story has given us more information pertaining to this scene. Previously, we may have learned that the wife loves the husband very much. The scene gains in strength. If we know that the husband leaves his wife because of another woman, the feeling of jealousy is introduced. If we know that the husband leaves his wife without any money for her support, we get angry at him. If we know that she is about to have a baby, we pity her. If we know that she married him against the will of her parents and has abandoned security in order to be with him, we feel sorry for her. In the first case, in which we have no additional information, the scene leaves us cold. But in the second case our emotions are aroused. Yet the actual scene may be played in exactly the same way. The same words can be used, the same action, the same actors. The scene without all the additional information can be perfectly understandable. But the spectator who has all the other information before he sees the scene will be much more deeply impressed than the spectator who has not.

Let us consider another example—a silent scene which in itself is absolutely clear. A man loses a thousand dollars in a gambling spot. So what! There is nothing particularly interesting in this scene. If the man is a millionaire, he can well afford to lose the money. But if we know that the man is poor, and that he lost his last dollar, drama is introduced. If we know that the thousand dollars were intended to pay for an operation to save the life of his sick youngster, tragedy is made clear in a scene though not a single word is spoken. Let us be certain about this: it is not the losing of a thousand dollars which makes this scene interesting. It is the information pertaining to this action which carries the interest.

Nor is it always necessary to have a great deal of information in order to change and improve the effect of a scene. Sometimes a simple word like "only" can have an important dramatic value. For instance, a young girl is killed by an automobile. Friends bring the news to her mother. If we are told that the child was her daughter, we feel deeply sorry. But how much greater is the tragedy if we are told that the victim was her "only" child.

From this we can conclude that a story which reveals too little information cannot be interesting, or moving, or dramatic. But too much information has equally bad effects. For one thing, too much information about one event prevents us from giving sufficient information about others. Furthermore, too much information necessarily entails the unessential—that which is not important to the understanding or to the appreciation of the scene. Too much information prevents the events from being perspicuous. It spoils the dramatic effect.

Having found the right amount of information, we can proceed to the next question, At what moment in the story should certain information be given?

In the beginning of the motion picture we don't know anything. During the course of the story, information is accumulated, until at the end we know everything. At least we should know all the essential facts.

Information can be accumulated because we accept each factor as constant until new information specifically relieves the old information of its validity. This constancy of the information has two results: For one thing, the task of information is much greater at the beginning of the story than toward the end. Since we start from scratch, we are desirous to give as much information as possible right at the beginning. Because, until the spectator has accumulated a certain wealth of knowledge, he is unable to experience emotions.

Consequently, the first part of every story is devoted to the exposition of facts which prepare the dramatic situations that are to follow. It is no easy task to supply all the primary information without becoming slow or boring. By the successful solution of this problem one can recognize the experienced writer. Luckily for many a bad writer, the audiences start out with an initial good will which helps to overcome a tedious "first act."

The second effect of the constancy of information could be described in this way: even though certain information may not be needed until much later in the story, it can be given earlier, since it will remain valid until such time as it is needed. Professionally this is called the "planting" of information. The advantage is that the information may be planted wherever it is convenient while the fruit may be gathered at a later stage. For instance, it may be established that a man becomes vicious when he is drunk. If we show how another man gets him drunk at a later moment, we realize the danger in which the second man is placed—we reap the fruit of the early planting.

In the beginning of the story, the writer will plant such information as will be useful at a later moment. In the latter part, however, he will not attempt to introduce any new factors, but will try to employ those which he has already given.

At times, however, the writer may decide to give the information at the precise moment when it is needed. This can be called the revelation of information. The information about one factor in close connection with another factor may result in a strong effect, particularly if they stand in contrast to each other. For instance, just before a man is getting married, we are informed that he has lost his job or his money. The effect of this revelation is produced by the right timing. Were this information planted, it might lose its power.

If the writer fails to plant information or if he fails to reveal it when it is needed, he is withholding the information. This should not be confused with failure to give information, which is a fault for which there is no excuse or purpose. It results in our inability to understand a happening, or in our being deprived of evaluation and emotions because we do not have sufficient knowledge of the facts.

The withholding of information invariably arouses curiosity in the spectator. To be curious means to be eager to know. Therefore, the writer can arouse the interest of the spectator by making him curious. But at the same time he must be aware that he may destroy our full understanding of the event at the time it takes place with the result that many emotions and feelings are lost.

So far, we took for granted that all the information was truthful. But the story can also supply us with misinformation. In principle, the spectator is a trusting soul. Therefore he may be led to believe in the wrong things. For instance, he may think that a certain person is a murderer, whereas in reality this person is innocent. Or he may be led to believe that a crook is a distinguished citizen. However, it is necessary that such misinformation be finally corrected by the true information, no matter how late. If the writer chooses the best moment for such a revelation, he can gain very powerful effects.

In reviewing this chapter, we find that the selection of information can make the story more interesting than it actually is. Because we do not give all the facts, but only the essential ones, the story becomes more poignant and effective. Because information may be given at its most decisive moment, the surprise may shock the spectator. Because information can be withheld, the spectator can be made curious. Because the spectator may be led to believe in misinformation, and because the revelation may be given at the appropriate moment, a new effect will be gained which does not lie in the actual series of events, but in the method of telling them. Therefore a story can appear more interesting to the audience than to the writer who has the knowledge of all the factors at all times.

Chapter 6

Division
of Knowledge

THE PREVIOUS CHAPTER has not exhausted all the functions of information. Until now, we have only considered the information which is to be given to the spectator. But we must realize that there are different actors in the story, that each of them may have a different knowledge about events which take place, and that their knowledge may be different from that of the audience.

This division of knowledge is complicated, but must be understood. Let us assume A killed B. C may have been present, and therefore he has the same knowledge as A. But D and E do not know anything about it. The spectators may have seen the actual murder and in that case, they have the same knowledge as A and C. Or they may not have seen it or have heard about it and, in that case, they are in the same position as D and E.

This division of knowledge multiplies the needs and effects of information. C may have the correct information, while D lacks all information and E has misinformation. Furthermore, the audience and C may have the correct information while E has misinformation. Or D and the audience may lack all information while C has the correct information. Or the audience may be misinformed, while the actors know the truth. There are more combinations possible—and each of them has a certain effect upon the story.

If we assume that C is a detective, he may be the only one who knows the man who committed the murder, while none of the other actors or the audience know the murderer. Or let us assume that the murderer prepares a deathtrap for the detective. The audience has seen his preparation and knows of his plans, while the detective does not. Therefore, as he is merrily walking into the trap, the audience which has the information would like to warn him, and is altogether aroused. But it may be the case that the audience as well as the detective does not know about the trap. Then the audience as well as the detective will be equally surprised when he is caught.

The difference between withholding information from an actor and withholding it from the audience could be described as follows: until an actor has received the information about a previous fact, he cannot start any action in connection with this fact. The action is held up until he has received this information. But the action can progress even though the audience may be left in the dark. It simply has the effect of making them curious.

We can see a thief stealing a car. It is not possible for another actor who was not present to chase after the thief unless he has been informed about the theft. If we fail to give this information to the actor, and if he still acts as if he knew about it, the audience will ask, How does he know about it?

This can be exploited in another direction: the audience assumes that a certain actor does not have certain information. He acts as if he did not have this information. Suddenly he reveals that he had the knowledge all the time.

Then again, an actor may know things which the audience does not know. Or the spectator has knowledge which the actor lacks. Or they both know the same thing. These three possibilities divide the manner of revealing information in three ways.

In the last instance, the information is given to the audience and to the actor at the same time. They both may see a certain event, thereby gaining the same knowledge. Or a certain factor may be told to an actor and at the same time to the audience. The second instance—the spectator has information which the actor lacks—makes the revelation of this information to the actor necessary. The disadvantage and danger of this revelation is that the audience gets impatient when facts which it knows already have to be told to an actor. We shall be bored by this revelation of information to the actor if we have seen these happenings in previous scenes. The only case wherein this revelation can become interesting is when the reaction of the second actor is of particular interest. In order to circumvent the boring effect of such repetition of information, the writer will search for indirect ways of giving the facts to another actor. Frequently, he implies that the information is given to the actor in the lapse of time between scenes.

The first instance, where the actor has the information which the audience lacks, contains other obstacles. How can the author find a way to tell the audience something which his actors know already? The actors can hardly tell it to each other again in order to let the audience partake of their knowledge. Sometimes the writer finds an actor to whom the information can still be told and sometimes it can be implied by certain dialog or certain actions. But very often this method entails strenuous efforts.

The last result of division of knowledge is the misunderstanding, particularly important because of its comic effects. This misunderstanding is nothing but the "quid pro quo" of the old *commedia dell'arte*. For instance, one actor may think that another actor is the brother of a woman whereas in reality he is her husband. Or a victim may believe that he is talking to a detective whereas he is actually talking to the head gangster. Shakespeare's *Comedy of Errors* is such a series of misunderstandings as a result of this division of knowledge. If the audience shares in the error, then the effect is produced only when the truth is revealed. But if the audience knows the truth while the actor labors under the misunderstanding, the spectator can enjoy the situation. The play *Kiss and Tell* is almost entirely based on a misunderstanding. The parents believe that their daughter is pregnant, whereas she is only covering up for her married girl friend.

Comic effects through the misunderstanding occur frequently. We may believe that an actor is talking about his wife while he is actually talking about his horse. Most of the laughter aroused by the routines of vaudeville comedians is a result of misunderstanding made possible through a division of knowledge.

The division of knowledge requires the full attention of the writer. If it is handled correctly, we gain new effects, which make the story more interesting than it actually is.

Chapter 7

The New Styles of Scriptwriting

By INVESTIGATING the physical characteristics of the motion picture form, we arrived at the conceptions of space, picture and sound, means of expression, enlargement and composition, the scene with its components of place, time and the lapse of time, the selection of information, and the division of knowledge. The enumeration of these factors is sufficient to prove that the motion picture is a new and original form of storytelling, as different from the others as the opera from the short story, or the stage play from the novel. Hence we must cease to consider this new form as a slight variation from existing methods of storytelling. Instead of burdening it with rules and prejudices from other arts, we must concede to it an independent life and shape. To stress this point even further, it may be advantageous to compare the physical characteristics of the three principal forms of storytelling.

At times, their similarities are overestimated; then again, their differences are exaggerated. There are comparatively few writers who are equally familiar with each of these media. The preference of a writer for a particular form does not necessarily result from his greater experience in handling one or the other medium. It is also determined by his temperament, which may prefer a specific form.

The chart on the following page facilitates a clear evaluation of the differences between the three forms. Though this chart takes into consideration only the physical characteristics, it must be kept in mind that their differences determine the more vital differences between the dramatic structures of the novel, the stage play, and the motion picture.

If we balance the findings of this chart, it becomes clear that the form of the novel is rather shapeless, allowing the author much liberty, whereas the stage play is very restricted, subjecting the playwright to a rigid structure. As for the motion picture, the chart seems to indicate that it is a child of the novel and of the stage play, incorporating some of the characteristics of both and, in some instances, creating new ones.

From the novel it has the freedom of time and place. From the theatre it has the definite length of performance, the representation of events, the lack of expressing the thoughts of the characters as well as of the author, the lack of descriptive, explanatory and connecting sentences. As in the theatre, its audience must understand the story in one sitting.

Among the new characteristics, we recognize the sources of information of the motion picture which differ from the novel and the stage; the greater amount of scenes, as compared to the theatre, but restricted with regard to the novel; the problem of the selection of information; the decisions with regard to enlargement; the use of the lapse of time.

CHART OF COMPARISON

	Novel	Theatre	Picture
Length:	indefinite 1-10 volumes	120-150 min.	80-180 min.
Presentation of events:	narrated	represented	represented
Amount of scenes:	unlimited	limited appr. 3-10	restricted appr. 30
Number of Characters:	unlimited	limited	moderately limited
Use of time:	free	free	free
Progress of time:	complete liberty forward, backward	forward flashback	forward flashback flashforward
Lapse of time:	not essential	not essential	important
Choice of place:	free	limited	free
Use of dialog:	at liberty	total	partial
Thoughts of characters:	described	withheld	withheld
Thoughts of author:	described	lacking	lacking
Connection between scenes:	descriptive	unnecessary	lacking
Exposition of place and time:	descriptive	through program	no direct means, except titles
Exposition of motives:	descriptive (psychological)	through events	through events
Enlargement:	lacking	lacking	important
Time at audience's disposal:	unlimited	one sitting	one sitting
"Rereading:"	possible	impossible	impossible

Regardless of partial similarities, the motion picture is a new form, independent of the novel or the theatre. Not giving a definition, but merely an illustration, we could say: the motion picture is theatre carried to every location that might be chosen by the novelist. This expresses the fact that the motion picture must be dramatically conceived and may yet be epic. To find the right measure is the great difficulty of screenplay writing.

The author who begins to write for motion pictures should not believe that he approaches a perfect form of art. His illusions about the great freedom of motion pictures are soon destroyed. He must realize that he has to deal with an invention which was born with great advantages together with great deficiencies. He will be torn between both extremes. He will find himself in a constant dilemma between his wishes and his resignations. These possibilities and limitations hold and confine each other. They battle with each other in every scene.

The motion picture offers many possibilities, which, because they exist, demand to be exploited. But the peculiar form of this new art contains many obstacles which obstruct the successful fulfillment of all its possibilities. Although it has many means of expression, it lacks some of the most essential ones. Although it has freedom of place and time, it has difficulties of exposing place and time. Although it has the possibility of introducing many characters, it lacks the essential means of characterization: description of thoughts. Although it can show many events, it has difficulty elucidating them because it is not aided by descriptive or explanatory sentences. Although it has the possibility of selecting scenes, it has difficulty connecting these scenes. Although it can tell an extensive, varied story, it is limited by space.

All the more reason for the writer to study its nature carefully so as to learn how to overcome its limitations.

PART II

THE STORY

SINCE WE KNOW by now "with what" the picture tells a story, we can proceed to investigate "in what manner" it must be told. This "manner" is the dramatic construction.

It would be wrong to assume that only the drama requires a dramatic construction. The word "drama" is taken from the Greek word *dran,* which means merely "action." Consequently any form of art which tells a story requires some kind of dramatic construction, be it a comedy or an adventure story, a drama or a psychological tragedy, an opera or a ballet, a painting or a pantomime, a symphony or a poem, a short story or a stage play.

Stories are in the minds of many people, and they may be good stories, based on personal experiences. But most of these people lack the conscious or unconscious knowledge of the manner in which such stories have to be told. The vivid impression of an event, or the impact of an experience, or even the honesty and sincerity of the

95

storyteller are not sufficient to enable him to report the story. Attorneys, judges, doctors know how difficult it is to extract the facts of a happening even from a person who has no intention of hiding anything. To the contrary, in spite of the greatest desire to tell everything about a case or a sickness, a person may be unable to make the story understandable because of a lack of "dramatic construction."

All of us know instances where a joke, told to one group of people, causes a burst of laughter, and on another occasion, the very same joke told by another person produces embarrassed silence. Yet it is the same joke; the difference between making people laugh and leaving them bored lies in the way this joke is told—it lies in the construction.

The very same story in a treatment by two different writers can be intensely interesting in one case and flat and boring in the other. Yet if we were to summarize the actual happenings and characters of both stories, we might find that they are identical. The difference lies in the respective qualities of their dramatic construction.

At this point, we must define the difference between the story and the dramatic construction. The story is the actual happening. The dramatic construction is the way in which this happening is told. The story is varied and rich as life and the world. The dramatic construction consists of a limited number of rules which are applied in order to get certain effects. The story springs from the imagination of the author; the dramatic construction results from his technique. The story is the creation; the dramatic construction is the form into which this creation must be poured.

Sometimes the two are confused. It is thought that a story can be dissected scientifically in accordance with certain rules. This is impossible: the story is the free, unchained, and imponderable outgrowth of the creative mind. But the dramatic construction can be defined almost mathematically. Its laws can be applied to a variety of stories. If, however, we were trying to find rules for the story, we would have to create as many different laws as there are different stories, that is, millions. But the basic principles of the dramatic construction are few.

Some people believe that the dramatic construction is the important thing; but a clever dramatic construction without a good story is like an empty shell. Others despise the dramatic construction as something artificial and think that the story alone is important. But the story without dramatic construction is chaotic. It is like a world before God created order, and because of its chaotic state the story misses its primary purpose, which is to be understood by the person who is listening to it.

However, dramatic construction is not identical with plot. In Aristotle's definition, plot is the organization of the incidents of the story. But dramatic construction, reaching beyond this limited function, embraces a larger field. It adapts the facts of the story to the form in which they have to be expressed, arranging them in such manner as to achieve the best possible effect upon the mind of the spectator. Thus dramatic construction is actually dependent upon and conditioned by three factors: the form, the happenings of the story (identical with reality), and the peculiarities of the spectator's mind.

Of these factors we have so far only investigated the first one: the form. It is sometimes assumed erroneously that the dramatic construction pertains merely to the organization of the incidents of the story. But since each form of art has different physical characteristics, which bring the incidents in a different relation to themselves, a specific dramatic construction is necessitated for every form of storytelling. To prove this, we could take one story and tell it in the different forms of art. Try, for instance, to tell the story of *Scheherazade* in the following arts: painting, symphonic tone poem, novel, stage play, opera, ballet, motion picture. It is evident that the story would have to be constructed differently, in each case, even though we might leave the facts unchanged.

First to point out this interesting phenomenon was Lessing in his eighteenth-century treatise *Laokoön*, where he investigates the differences between painting and epic writing. He finds that the painting exhibits the objects simultaneously whereas writing is consecutive. Painting shows everything in juxtaposition whereas, in writing, word follows word and page follows page. From this he deduces that the painter is able to depict a warrior in full battledress, whereas the writer commits a mistake if he were to describe this warrior by saying: He has a helmet on his head, a shield in his left hand and a sword in the right one. Strangely enough, few writers are aware of this mistake and wonder why their descriptions become boring, a result which stems from their wrong attempts to evoke a simultaneous picture in a consecutive form of art. Lessing explains that the writer must use action which is always consecutive in order to arrive at the same image which the painter can evoke by simultaneous exhibition. He proceeds to give the classic example, from Homer, the first and perhaps the greatest of all epic writers: instead of saying that the warrior wears a helmet, a shield, and a sword, Homer describes how the warrior lifts up the helmet and puts it on his head, then takes the shield from the wall and thereupon grips the sword. The resulting image in our mind is the same in both cases; but Homer uses consecutive action, adapting his method of telling to the consecutive progress of words.

The influence of the physical form upon the manner of telling the story is most obvious in the stage play, so much so that the conception of dramatic construction originated in the theatre. Indeed, the physical limitations of the stage impede the flow of the story to such an extent that the dramatic construction becomes of utmost importance. It is true that the motion picture is liberated from the restraint of the theatre. Because of the freedom of place and time, the story appears to be more natural as it is less afflicted by the rigidity of the form. But although its dramatic construction is less obtrusive, it would be entirely wrong to assume that it is less important. To the contrary, in spite of being more abstract, it is perhaps even more stringent. And it is more difficult to define and apply its laws.

Chapter 1

Characterization

A STORY TELLS ABOUT MEN and their doings. Some people are more interested in "men"—that is, in human characterization—while others are more interested in their "doings"—that is, in their actions. Some novelists are satisfied when they have given a complete description of a character in the few hundred pages of a novel. Some picture producers are solely interested in action and despise characterization as "psychological stuff." Both elements, however, are necessary for the motion picture story.

Action by itself does not exist. Somebody must act. This somebody is the human being; consequently, we must be acquainted with the human being in order to follow and understand the action. On the other hand, it is not possible to understand the human being unless he acts. He comes to life only through action. Even though the preponderance of characterization or action is a matter of taste, the motion picture should not neglect or disregard either of them.

100

In creating the story, the writer may use characterizations of people whom he has known or invent new characterizations. These invented characterizations, however, are frequently most unreal. To prevent such impossible concoctions, the writer needs a deep understanding of human nature; he needs a knowledge of psychology.

The behavior of a human being, though seemingly unpredictable, is never accidental. And the structure of the human character is a conglomeration of many factors; thus it is seldom simple and clear; but in spite of its complexities, which, at times, let it appear illogical, it is nevertheless, consistent. A human being will act or react upon certain causes in a certain way. Not always are these patterns obvious. Since they are the result of complicated processes of the mind, they are frequently most surprising. For instance, a friend tells a woman that her husband died in an accident. It might be expected that she would cry; but instead she may start to laugh, even though she is actually shattered by the tragedy of her husband's death. Often, the assumption of an apparently logical reaction is wrong, whereas another one, seemingly farfetched, is correct. All we need in order to explain the mysterious behavior of a human being is a deeper knowledge of psychology.

But psychology, a science about which thousands of books have been written, embraces so extensive a field that we cannot even attempt to incorporate any part of it in this volume. It is a prerequisite for any writer. It continues to be the object of ceaseless study, be it by methodical learning or personal observation. Without the knowledge of human nature, no writer should dare to approach the task of writing a story about human beings.

This knowledge, however, will not yet enable him to create a vivid motion picture characterization. Both a professor of psychology and a man with deep insight into human nature may be absolutely incapable of communicating a well-conceived characterization to a motion picture audience. For this the writer needs the knowledge of dramatic characterization.

The problem then is not alone to conceive a plausible, lifelike characterization, but to convey this characterization to an audience. Indeed, it is no easy undertaking to arrange our words and events on paper in such manner as to evoke the impression of living human beings in the mind of the audience, making the spectators believe so strongly in their reality that they become their friends or enemies within the short space of 120 minutes.

Judging by the average motion picture, this form seems to represent greater obstacles to successful characterization than any other form of art. By way of contrast, we find that the novel has by far the best and deepest characterizations. Just remember the uncanny presentation of human characters in the novels of Dostoevski, the powerful figures in Balzac's novels, the vivid appearance of human beings in Hemingway's writing, or the relentless probing of their minds in *Ulysses*, by James Joyce.

This advantage of the novel over the motion picture does not result from its greater length, but from its form, which permits the description of the thoughts of its characters, thereby gaining something like a third dimension. Furthermore, the novel renders the thoughts of the author, enabling him not only to describe the characters, but also to explain their motives and actions.

Since the motion picture is deprived of all of these expedients, characterization becomes a very difficult task. We must understand that the many faulty, uneven, nebulous or even blank characterizations in the average motion picture are not merely an oversight on the part of the writers and producers, nor are they intentionally created to please any imaginary bad taste of the audience; to the contrary, some of the most successful pictures are painstakingly careful as regards the characters. No, the difficulties of characterization inherent in the form of pictures are so great that only the writers who master dramatic construction are capable of bringing characters to life. The others will either go amiss or—which happens more frequently—resort to the stereotype. By reminding the audience of a universally known stereotype like the cantankerous Irishman, the formal butler, the crooked lawyer, the absent-minded professor, the irascible millionaire, the dashing newspaper reporter, the wisecracking girl friend, they arrive without any effort of their own at some kind of a workable characterization. It goes without saying that this is a poor "ersatz" for the power of a true character.

Driving the writer even closer to the stereotype is the fact that the characterization created by him is performed by an actor who, by his mere appearance, reveals a character. Many a producer depends solely upon the looks of his actors for characterization; he may say "Write me a Robert Redford type, or some kind of a Jill Clayburgh." But this is in no way sufficient for a characterization—aside from the fact that the exposition of characterization by the looks of the actor may be contrary to the exposition of characterization by the story.

The novel gives us its persons in a more or less vague way as to their appearance. No matter how sharply the novelist designs his characters, each reader will form his own idea of the looks and behavior of these persons. Each reader will make them come to life in his own imagination, reconceiving them and recreating them. The same character which originated in the mind of the novelist will reappear in a million different shadings in the minds of a million different readers.

But the picture shows to everybody the same portrait of an actor who performs a part. The close-up is absolute, ultimate, clear, final. There is no freedom for the imagination. There is no room for subtle shadings. The face is universally the same. Consequently, the actor is chosen for his appearance, which must reveal the same character as his role exposes, or the part must be written to fit the actor's looks. This dilemma is further aggravated by the fact that the same actor played other parts before, teaching us thereby what character his looks reveal. The same actor with very little change in make-up may have played a stupid detective or a simple sheriff or a Roman Senator or a kindly priest. It is logical that the average picture has little ambition to add subtle touches to its characterizations. The result? Stereotype characterizations in the writing of most scripts.

In spite of all this, the difficulties of characterization, while considerable, are not insurmountable. This is proven by the fact that good pictures contain good characterizations. We now proceed to investigate the problem of dramatic characterization.

First we must understand the difference between characterization, character, and characteristic: characterization comprises all the facts about a human being of which character is only one. And characteristics are the single factors of which a character consists.

In order to understand a human being, we must know sufficient facts about him. Therefore, after the writer has a characterization completely in his mind, he must expose its facts to the audience. There are certain facts with regard to a characterization which need to be told in order to lift it from a nebulous state. We might call them the obligatory facts. Indeed, most vague characterizations which do not seem to come to life are impaired because one or the other of the obligatory facts has been omitted.

We find first that it is necessary to know the approximate age of the individual, for the different ages have considerable influence upon the behavior of the human being. An old man and a young one will react differently toward business, toward love, toward all sorts of problems. A young girl will behave differently from a middle-aged or an old woman. Therefore the knowledge of the age of a human being will imply a great amount of information with respect to the characterization. This knowledge can easily be exposed through the appearance of the actor or the actress.

Every human being has a position in the world. We might call it his occupation, if we do not confine the meaning of the word to profession. For we must realize that the housewife, or even the married woman who does not do anything else besides being married, represents an occupation. To be a playboy means to have an occupation. And a dropout is sharply characterized through the lack of occupation.

A man can be a laborer or a professor, an artist or a business man, an actor or a scientist. A woman can be a dancer, a housewife, a lecturer, or a sales girl. The type of occupation characterizes the human being to a great extent. The laborer is apt to lead a different life from the scientist. The commercial artist does and knows different things than the wine merchant, and the tobacco importer's life is distinctly different from the life of a farmer.

The simple knowledge of a person's occupation, that is, the person's position in the world, is capable of revealing a great deal of information. It was the trend of the last decades to stamp a human being as a factory worker, or as a bourgeois, or as a middle-class merchant, or as an intellectual. But though contributing to the characterization, the occupation does not reveal final information. For the human being remains an individual irrespective of his occupation. However, it would be equally wrong to describe the character of a human being without stating his occupation.

The next important factor concerning the human being is his relation to other human beings. People do not stand alone in the world. And if we find a solitary human being who does not seem to have any relations to other human beings, this lack is a most revealing factor.

Primarily, we find family relations with father, mother, husband, wife, sons, daughters, brothers, sisters, uncles, aunts. Beyond this, we find relations of friendship or enmity, relations between neighbors, relations which are formed through identical jobs, relations between employees of the same office, or between boss and employee, relations between salesman and client. It is useless to try to define all possible relationships. The fact remains that in a city with thousands of inhabitants, each of them has relations to some other individuals. And the same individual may have many relations of a different kind: a man can be a father and a husband and a son and a brother and an employee, all at the same time.

The relation is important because it reveals information. For a father is supposed to have a different attitude toward his children than toward strangers, and the married man is supposed to act differently than the bachelor. But beyond that, we must recognize that the moment such relations exist, the personalities of two people come into contact because they are connected by the relation. This being the case, they are capable of revealing information about each other. For instance, an employee who knows that he works for a gangster. What else could he be but a dishonest person? Or two partners in the same firm. One of them is known to be a crook. Unquestionably it reflects upon the other if he is informed about the crooked business. Or a man is married to a lascivious woman.

This does not necessarily mean that he is a lascivious man himself, but it reveals a number of facts about his character which have to be specified by other information: for instance, he is terribly in love with his wife, although her behaviour is torturing him.

It is absolutely necessary that all these obligatory facts be given to the audience in order to achieve a vivid characterization. But beyond this necessary information we shall expose further facts, the choice of which is determined by the principle of selecting information: What is essential? It is obvious that different facts may be essential for different stories.

For instance, it may be sufficient to say: a wine merchant. But then again, it may be advantageous to state: a sly wine merchant or a charitable one. We should never say a millionaire. Instead, we should describe him as a millionaire stockbroker or a millionaire wildcatter.

At times, it may be advantageous to elaborate on the information which is revealed by the simple factor of occupation. For instance, an executive. This occupation implies that he is responsible for decisions regarding his business. Nevertheless, it might be stated specifically that he is a busy man. Or if you characterize a man as being old, we understand all the information which old age implies. Nevertheless, it may be advantageous to elaborate that he is tired or alert.

Other information may be considered essential with respect to a certain story. For instance, the past of a person. It might be essential to know that a famous actress was raised in poverty, or that a criminal was beaten in his youth, or that an old tramp was handsome. In other instances it may not be essential to know the past of an actress or the background of a criminal, or the degradation of a tramp, particularly if this past has no direct reference to their present actions. The future plans of a person may be equally important to the characterization since it makes a difference whether a drug store clerk intends to continue in this occupation or whether he is studying engineering in night school.

Such additional information may be an elaboration or duplication. But it may also reveal contradictions of the general information revealed by one of the factors. If we know that a man is old, we expect him to be weak and tired. Instead he may be vigorous and youthful. Nevertheless, he is not a vigorous and youthful man, but a vigorous and youthful old man.

The occupation of a playboy would indicate that he does not work. Nevertheless, we may find him working in a shipyard. But this does not mean that he is a shipyard worker; instead, he remains a playboy working in a shipyard, with all the implications derived from such a contrast.

And now we come to the most important factor of the characterization, which is the character of the human being. While there are millions of laborers, the individual character distinguishes one laborer from the others. While there are tens of thousands of professors in the world, one professor is distinguished by his character from the others.

But the motion picture cannot describe a character as the novel does. We cannot say he is brutal or dirty or stingy or powerful or nervous or cowardly or jealous or beautiful or ugly or intelligent or stupid or good or bad, for the author has no words of his own in the motion picture. He would have to let one of his actors give such a description; but there might not be any truth in the actor's statement, for he, himself, may be bad or stupid so that we cannot trust him.

Instead of describing it, the motion picture must prove the character of an actor. It must make the characteristics apparent by manifestation. We conceive the character as being in a state of latent existence, coming to the fore only through a person's actions. In order to make the character manifest we must show the character in action.

Characteristics determine our decisions with respect to certain actions. For instance, a human being is not good or bad, but will act or react "good" or "bad." Because the person acts good or bad, we call the person good or bad. As long as a man does not act or react, he is neither good nor bad, although the characteristics are latently existent and would become manifest the moment he has to make a decision with respect to an action. A characteristic like stinginess means that the person does not want to spend money. This can only become apparent when a demand is made upon the person to spend money. Likewise, a coward and a gutsy type can only prove themselves if they have to decide whether to run away from danger or run into it.

This leads us to the most important deduction with regard to the dramatic exposition of character. Although the motion picture is unable to describe characteristics, it can present actions. Since characteristic and action are inseparably connected, the audience can conclude from the action to the characteristic which determined it.

For instance, a teacher who writes a letter during a bombing reveals a calm character. A man who starts to cry when he is slapped shows little courage. A crook who sets out to rob an old widow of all her money reveals a rather sordid character. People who act or talk stupidly reveal their stupidity.

When we speak of action, we do not limit ourselves to the narrow meaning of "doing something." We consider thinking, feeling, or speaking actions equal to stealing, kissing, or sleeping. In this sense dialog can become most expressive for character, since to speak in a certain manner reveals the likes or dislikes of a person.

Furthermore, in order to deduce the characteristic which determined the action, it is not necessary to see the action in its actual execution. To expose the result of an action or the intention to do an action is sufficient. This opens a wide range of possibilities for revealing character. For instance, when David decided to fight against Goliath, he proved his courage before he even got into the struggle. Obviously, not all decisions are subject to free will so that they cannot always clearly indicate a characteristic.

Sometimes an unimportant side-action is capable of revealing more information about a character than blood-and-murder events. For instance, a man kicks a little dog on his way into a house, or a woman tries to get her dime back after completing a call from a pay telephone. Or consider this example: a big industrialist stops on the street to pick up a penny. This seemingly irrelevant detail can reveal a wealth of information. It can indicate that he was born poor, that he remembers his childhood when a penny meant much to him. It may reveal that his love for the penny formed the basis for his prosperity. The novelist could describe the tycoon's character at length, but the screen writer must search for an expressive action in order to expose the character. And some of the greatest writers have used the smallest details to reveal the deepest characterizations. Nothing a person does is too irrelevant to betray a characteristic. Consider graphology, which bases its analysis of the character upon the small points and circles and lines which a man jots carelessly upon a piece of paper.

The second important deduction from our findings proves that the character of a person is exposed not only by his own actions, but also by the actions and the attitudes of other people with regard to him. For instance, we may show the fear people experience of a brutal person, or the respect they have for a powerful man, or the admiration they show for a great artist, or their disdain for an incompetent person. The charm of a beautiful woman may be exposed best by the reaction of other people to her beauty: by the jealousy of other women and the admiration of men. We can even go so far as to say that it is necessary that a beautiful woman attracts attention in the story, and, if she fails to do that, although she appears to be beautiful, the characterization is faulty.

In this manner the characterization of a person can be revealed by the reactions of other people even before the person is introduced to the audience. This indirect method is one of the most effective means of characterization. However, we must keep in mind that it is an indirect method: the spectator does not see for himself what sort of a character the person in the story has, but sees it through the eyes of other persons in the story, and their eyes are colored according to their own characterizations. For instance, if a person speaks critically about another one, we might assume that the other person is really bad. But if we know that the person speaking critically is bad himself, we might even reverse our opinion to the belief that the other person is good. If a man whom we know to be a villain dislikes a woman, it does not necessarily mean that the woman deserves dislike; to the contrary, she may be very good, because the one who dislikes her is bad. If we use contrasting reactions of different people toward one person, we create a disputed and therefore more interesting characterization.

At this point, we must distinguish between characteristics and passing emotions. To be furious is not a characteristic, but a passing emotion, for we cannot imagine a furious character. To have a good time does not mean that we have a joyous character. To make a bitter remark may be incidental; but if a person continues to make bitter remarks, it would appear that he has a bitter character. If someone is continually sad, it means that one of his characteristics is sadness, whereas a happy person may be sad occasionally under the influence of a tragic event.

The continuous attitude distinguishes the characteristic from the passing mood. Therefore, constancy is the essential attribute of the character. Not that the character is not subject to changes. But these changes are never rapid. For we must realize that the character is a product of many years of life, beginning with early childhood. It is crystallized over a long period of time. Even an unpredictable character must continue to act in an unpredictable manner. We would be very astonished if this person were to suddenly settle down to normal actions.

This constancy of the characteristic complicates our task of exposing the character through action. For it is obvious that a person performs many actions in the course of a story. Since all these actions reveal characteristics, they must be chosen so as to reveal a consistent characterization.

Of course, the human character does not consist of only one characteristic like stinginess or stupidity or mildness. Instead, it is a conglomeration of characteristics: a person can be good and intelligent and stingy. Another one can be gay and jealous and experienced. Therefore several actions during the course of the story may establish several characteristics of one person, rounding out the portrait.

But once a characteristic has been established, we are forced to believe in its continued existence. If subsequent actions reveal a contradiction, the character becomes inconsistent and appears confused. This is further complicated by the fact that the reactions of the other people with regard to a certain character must be consistent. To achieve this consistency is even more difficult, for we must take into consideration the different characters of the other people. For instance, it is not possible for a brave man to be afraid of one who has been established as a weakling, since this unexpected fear would create the contradictory impression that the weakling is dangerous.

It becomes clear how easily one can fall into the mistake of creating an inconsistent character in a motion picture. To some writers the people of the story are not so much human characters as simply persons who execute actions. Many a writer, pressed by the needs of the story, distributes his actions planlessly to different persons, disregarding the fact that each action reveals a characteristic, and that different actions attributed to the same person reveal a character which cannot possibly exist. The good writer, however, will create a certain characterization in his mind; thereafter he will ask, By what actions can I make this character manifest? He will choose various actions until all characteristics have become manifest.

This completes our examination of the nature of dramatic characterization. Our way is cleared to study the practical application of our findings to the motion picture script.

Since a characterization consists of many facts, the writer must determine each fact in such manner that, in combination, they form a perfect entity. Once he has chosen some of them, the rest which still have to be invented must fit them.

Moreover, the mutual interplay between characterization and action must be kept in mind. The action exposes the character, but once the character has been established it determines all further events. The writer cannot invent characterization and story events separately. If he were to do that, he might choose a most sympathetic characterization for his hero without realizing that the actions which the hero performs make him appear as a coward or as a dishonest or stupid person. Instead, if the writer is primarily concerned with unfolding certain characterizations, he must search for an adequate plot. If the series of events is his primary interest, he must conceive his characterizations to fit the action. Otherwise, they may be very different from what he intended them to be.

Furthermore, he must realize that certain situations have an entirely different effect upon different characterizations. Imagine a scientist and a rock musician falling in love with a stripper. The rock musician is apt to know how to handle the situation while the scientist may be utterly confused. On the other hand, the scientist may feel very secure if he is confronted with a chemical problem while the musician may be thoroughly helpless. Consequently, the writer should choose the right characterization so as to exploit in the best possible way the situations he is preparing.

Once the leading characterizations are chosen, they determine the quality of the entire story. You cannot hope to build a comedy like *You Can't Take It with You* with characters from *Wuthering Heights,* nor can you develop a spiritual story like *The Song of Bernadette* with characters from a prison-break drama.

We would go wrong, however, if we were to choose similar characterizations within our story so as to obtain a certain mood. To the contrary, the characterizations must be of wide variety. Because the story brings up many demands, this variety must be satisfied by a variety of characterizations. Shakespeare inserted comedians into his saddest tragedies because he needed a variety of effects and did not want to make his tragic persons funny. It is the preponderance of a certain element that creates the mood.

By all means, we must try to prevent too close a similarity between characterizations in a story, because it is confusing. Instead, we should create contrast, which makes each characterization appear more vivid.

This differentiation has the same effect as the color scheme in painting. Let us assume that a painter has a blue color in one of his paintings. He is satisfied with its quality, but wants to give it more importance. He can achieve that by surrounding it with a different type of blue, or with contrasting colors. In both cases the original blue gains a new quality, although it has not been changed.

In the same way the characterization of a very stingy, avaricious person gains strength by contrast with a very generous drunk. A thief can be shown up in comparison with a very honest man. A beautiful woman of about thirty years of age appears in a better light if she is with a very old woman whose life is almost over, or with a young girl, whose life is just about to begin.

The picture *How Green Was My Valley* has a masterful color scheme. It is a picture with very little plot, but its characters are beautifully blended. For one thing, it represents three generations of men: the father, an old man; the sons, who are in the prime of their lives; and the youngest son, who is still a child. Then you have the mother, an old woman; the daughter, a romantic character; the wife of one of the sons, a realistic character. From these result different types of love. There is the love of the mother for her children, there is the love of one of the sons for his wife, there is the romantic love of the priest for the daughter, and there is the juvenile love of the youngest son for his brother's wife. Also, there is the old and loyal love between father and mother. From this perfect choice of characterizations, the picture proceeds to show the impact of life upon those different persons. The old father is resigned in his relation to the coal mine, the sons revolt, and the sensitive child is almost crushed in his first contact with the school, but then he learns to fight. The happy marriage is destroyed by the death of the husband, the unhappy marriage goes to pieces through incompatibility of characters. Every little happening mirrors itself in this variety of characterizations. It is like a ray of light falling upon the many facets of a diamond.

In this color scheme, the bit parts are hardly less important than the leads. The choice of characterization of bit parts distinguishes good pictures from bad ones: in general, you can judge from their quality the ability of the writer and director. Not that we think the singing cabbies and the wisecracking soda fountain boys and the severe butlers are excellent characterizations of the bit parts. But some of the smaller characterizations can contribute to the main characterizations by what they say or do in relation to them, or simply by the "color scheme." A secretary should not be "just a secretary." If she works for a very important man, she may be overworked and nervous; if she has a position which demands little work, she may be bored, which can be expressed by having her read a novel or knit a sweater. A chauffeur should not be "just a chauffeur." If he works for arrogant people, he may be a snob. If his boss is democratic, the servant can express this characterization, by his attitude, even before we meet the boss. An illustrious astronomer who is always deep in his thoughts appears more vivid if contrasted with a very realistic scrub woman trying to clean up his study. The shady past of a woman can be exposed through the slight touch of confidential intimacy with which the maître d'hôtel of a restaurant, where she used to go, greets her. The important fact about the characterization of the bit part is that the person or the reactions of the person must be very typical because we have little space or time in which to design a more complex character.

By careful comparison of the first and second folios of Shakespeare's works, one finds numerous instances where he developed the bit parts with extreme care. In the first version they may be mere personages who have to be present so as to execute actions. Later on, he gave them deft touches of dialog; with a few lines he characterized them with incredible vividness.

Our last problem is to examine in which manner all the information concerning the different characterizations should be conveyed to the audience. Every characterization consists of many facts which have to be exposed, and such exposition takes up time and space. That is why many a producer and writer is tempted to neglect these "psychological studies," claiming that they hold up the progress of the story and make the picture slow and static. There are, however, ways and means by which to overcome this dilemma.

If we had to expose all the facts of a characterization at the very beginning, it would indeed slow up the picture. Instead, we can disperse this exposition over the entire story, adding information whenever convenient and feasible. We prefer, therefore, to speak of "perfection of characterization" instead of terming it exposition, it being a gradual and continuous process.

It is obvious that we should begin with the revelation of those factors which are most urgently needed to understand and follow the events of the story.

If the appearance of the actor does not reveal his occupation, we should take care to expose it as soon as possible. Not that this fact is more important than the character; but it is needed at an earlier stage since it reveals so much information about a person without which subsequent events may not be understandable.

Furthermore, we must recognize that factors of a circumstantial nature are subject to very rapid and very thorough changes, whereas characteristics change slowly. A person can lose a job, or become poor, or acquire a fortune, or a divorce in a very short period of time. But this same person's character cannot be transformed from good to bad, or from simple to intelligent in the same amount of time. This being the case, we are forced to reveal facts of a circumstantial nature immediately, because they are fluctuating, while we can take our time with the definition of the character. It is necessary to reveal first that someone is an affluent stockbroker before we can add that he is thrifty. If we were to proceed differently, the understanding of the story developments would be hampered.

There is one more advantage to the perfection of characterization: in adding continuously new touches and new information about a person, we constantly hold the interest of the audience. The process of perfection can' be compared to the work of a painter who begins with the outline of a portrait, adding more and more details until the face appears lifelike.

We are allowed to proceed differently, but only if we understand the consequences: they are identical with those that were examined in the chapter on selection of information. We can plant the information or we may reveal it at the needed time, or we can withhold it, or we can give misinformation. Moreover, we can create division of knowledge. To illustrate this, we can imagine the case where a man is shown spending a great deal of money, without betraying his occupation or the reason for his wealth. Or we can give the information that a man is a surgeon whereas he is really a cattle thief. Or the audience knows an actor to be a tennis champion while another actor does not know it. In *Oedipus* the man kills his father and marries his mother before finding out that he is the son.

No matter which method we choose as the most desirable for a particular story, we must see to it that the characterizations are perfected at the end—which means that all the factors have been exposed. Unfortunately, many pictures "get stuck" after the primary facts like sex, age, or occupation have been exposed. The result is deplorable; the picture becomes dull and flat. All the interesting situations are impaired, leaving both plot and action insipid, because the spectator is not interested in the type but in the individual. He does not care about the "dentist" but about Mr. X who is a dentist.

By way of contrast we find that great writers distinguish themselves through the excellence of their characterizations. The success of writers like Eugene O'Neill, Bernard Shaw, Arthur Miller, George Kaufman, Moss Hart, results largely from their mastery of characterizations. The benefits from their adroit choice of characterizations reach beyond the facts discussed in this chapter. We have not yet mentioned the most important necessity regarding the choice of characterizations: to choose combinations that will result in action. But before studying this, we must first know the nature of action.

Chapter 2

Transition of Action

FUTURE, PRESENT, PAST

GRAMMATICALLY, every verb can be conjugated in the fundamental tenses: past, present, future. I killed, I kill, I shall kill. A noun, however, is not bound to time. "House" or "dog" or "anger" cannot be conjugated.

A verb represents action. Therefore action can be conjugated in the three time dimensions.

Dramatically speaking, past, present, and future exist together in the motion picture story.

This is a fundamental realization. It would seem that because the happenings are shown in actual execution we are only concerned with the present. This is a false im-

120

pression. Past and future form a very important part of the story.

A person can say in the picture: "I committed a murder." Or he can be shown in the process of committing a murder, or he can say: "I shall kill him." Consequently, we are in a position to represent not only the present, but also the past and the future.

These different times have different effects upon us and arouse different emotions: the anticipation of a horrible event arouses fear in us; when we actually see it, it fills us with terror; and when it has happened, our only emotion is sorrow. Similarly, a good thing which is expected fills us with hope; when it actually happens, it gives us joy and afterwards satisfaction. It is not possible to experience fear or hope with regard to something which is happening or has happened, but only if it is about to happen or going to happen. Nor can we experience terror or pleasure because of something which will happen in the future, nor can we feel sorrow or satisfaction before something has actually taken place. Therefore the past, present, and future of the story are most important.

Time progresses from the future into the present and thence into the past. Therefore, all action progresses from the future into the present and into the past. I shall kill him, I kill him, I killed him.

Such being the case, it is not possible for us to consider only one of these stages. The three are linked together: before doing something, I must have the intention of doing it, an intention desires its execution—that is, an action—and after an action has taken place, it exists as a result. From the result we can conclude that an action was necessary to achieve it, and from an action we can conclude that an intention to do it must have preceded it.

For this reason, different actions may exist in different stages of time at one moment of the motion picture story.

A hears that B has killed C. The murder is an action in the past. A takes the revolver from a drawer. This is an action in the present. A has the intention to kill B. This is the intention to do an action in the future. Consequently, all three times exist at one moment in the same scene.

It is necessary to recognize certain factors in the nature of these three times. An action which is planned for the future registers in our mind as an impending event. Knowing the progress of time from future into the present, we expect that this impending event will, at a certain moment, come into the present, that is, into actual execution. But there is a two-fold uncertainty connected with this transition from future into present. For one thing, the extent of the future is limitless, we do not know at what time the event which is planned will move into the present. It can happen within a split second if we decide to slap somebody's face. Or it can take two years until we get a chance to do it. But even the split second represents a plan for the future, that is, an intention to do it preceded the action. The second uncertainty is the fact that an intention to do something can be frustrated. Even though we may have the intention of slapping somebody, we may never have a chance to do it.

The present dissolves both uncertainties. If we see the actual happening, that is, the execution of the intention, we know automatically at what moment the future moved into the present. Furthermore, our doubt of the fulfillment of the intention is removed because we see the actual happening. The present does not represent an actual stage of being; it is only the line where the future moves into the past. While the extent of the future is limitless, the present is not even the fragment of a second. If we drop a hammer, we have had an intention to drop it which inch by inch moved into the result, that is from the future through the present into the past. Generally speaking, the present is so quickly gone that we do not have time to conceive or understand an action in its actual execution. We must have previous information of what people want to do in order to understand what they are doing. The knowledge of the future must precede the event so as to make it perspicuous.

Just as the future, the past is limitless. An event moves further and further into the past, and consequently further and further away from us who are always staying in the present. Therefore it becomes less and less interesting. The fundamental difference between past and future lies in the fact that an event, once it is removed to the past, can never again reach the present whereas an impending event can move into the present.

For these reasons, the past of the motion picture story is fairly uninteresting to us. It is valuable only as motivation for future intentions. The present is so short that it does not give us a chance to conceive or understand a happening. Consequently, the future in the motion picture story remains as the fundamentally important time.

The general belief that the present is the essential time stems from a misconception: we are interested in the future with regard to its moving into the present. Nevertheless, our interest remains in the future. And the two uncertainties connected with the future (if it will move into the present and at what time) are not a disadvantage, but to the contrary, an incentive to our interest.

The foregoing investigations about past, present, future, are difficult to understand, but they are absolutely necessary. Not only did we find that the future is the most important time, but we shall see later that the future in the motion picture is more important than in any other form of storytelling. This is a new knowledge, but without it no good motion picture writing is possible.

MOTIVE, INTENTION, GOAL

Having understood the relation between past, present, and future, we need the knowledge of further facts in regard to action.

Let us, for example, imagine that a man is killed. It is logical that there must have been a reason for this action.

A motive for action will result in an intention to act. Before we do something, we must have the intention of doing it.

An intention always desires the attainment of a goal. In the above example, the goal would be the death of the other person. Every action has a result, therefore every intention must have a goal. It is not possible for an intention to exist without a goal.

The motive invariably comes before the intention and the intention before the goal. We shall investigate them in the order of their appearance.

The Motive

No action is possible without a cause. There are actions of objects and actions of human beings. A stone falling down from a mountain is the action of an object. But if a man kills another one, we have an action of a human being. The actions of objects are caused by physical laws while the actions of men are caused by the human will. We speak of the cause for the action of an object, and of the motive for the action of a human being.

The connection between cause and effect is direct. But the motive as the cause for a human action is less obvious.

It took modern psychology to show that any action—even the most accidental and unimportant doings—have their motives, which may be found in the distant past or in the subconscious mind. Without a motive no human being will do anything.

Now, we must ask, what constitutes a motive? What makes a human being act?

A human being will act to remove pain. If he feels no pain, he will be satisfied to remain in the painless state— he will not act. Therefore the motive is pain.

The human being feels pain when he wants something and does not have it or when he does not want something and has it. These two different types of motives might be called affinity and repulsion. Affinity is the desire to be united with something, and repulsion is the desire to be separated from something. Affinity means that the human being wants something, and repulsion means that the human being does not want something. Affinity could be described as "love," and repulsion as "hatred."

The lack of something wanted as well as the presence of something unwanted is reflected by pain. The human being acts to acquire something which it wants or to eliminate something which it does not want.

If it acquires the thing it lacks, the pain ceases to exist, and consequently the motive for action is destroyed. If it repels the thing which it does not want, the pain ceases and consequently the motive for action.

If a man is hungry, he feels pain because he lacks food. Hunger is pain caused by a lack. From it results the intention to eat. If a man is tired, it is because he lacks sleep. Fatigue is pain caused by a lack. From it results the intention to sleep or rest. One might say that the man "loves" food or that he "loves" sleep.

But if a man is freezing, he feels pain because of the presence of cold. Freezing is pain caused by the presence

of something unwanted. From it results the intention to
get warm. If a man is hot, it is because of the presence of
heat. To feel hot is pain caused by the presence of something unwanted. From it results the intention to cool off.
You might say that the man "hates" cold, or that he
"hates" heat.

We must not believe that pain has to be inflicted before
constituting a motive. We may be afraid that we shall be
hungry and so we work to avoid being hungry. The motive for our action is not pain which has already been
inflicted, but the fear of pain. Our action will try to
prevent the pain which may be caused to us in the future.
We might say that the fear of pain is already felt as pain.

The principal affinity in our lives is love between two
people, and the principal repulsion is the hatred between
enemies. Love must be understood as the desire to be
united with somebody we lack. Plato in his *Symposium*
tells the following story about the creation of men: man
and woman were once one human being with four feet
and four arms. Later, a god cut them into halves, one part
being man and the other part woman. Since that time
each half has been searching for the one from which it
was cut.—This tale is interesting to us because it conceives
man as lacking the woman and vice versa. The intention
to overcome this lack is felt as love. It is the desire to
eliminate a pain which is caused by the separation of man
and woman. Love is not a state of being, but an unceasing
struggle to eliminate pain. When the lovers are united,
the lack and consequently the pain-motive cease to exist.
Since this is never fully possible for any length of time,
the tie between love and pain, constantly deplored in
poetry, is thus explained.

Enemies, however, want to repel each other. In this
case the pain is not felt because of the lack of something,
but because of the presence of something unwanted.

Therefore the motive comes into existence by bringing the enemies together.

Pain caused by the forces of affinity originates from separation of the parts which "love" each other, while pain through the forces of repulsion comes into existence by bringing together the parts which "hate" each other.

The Intention

In order to understand the full meaning of the intention, we must give a very comprehensive definition.

If we put a pot with water on the stove, we might say that the fire has the intention to boil the water. If we drop a stone from a mountain, the stone has the intention to fall. If a train drives at a speed of seventy miles an hour, it has the intention to continue at this speed while the law of friction has the intention to slow it down.

With respect to human intentions, we find a great variety: there are conscious and unconscious intentions, there are intentions to act or intentions to react, there are voluntary or involuntary intentions. They can be direct or indirect, obvious or subtle. We must discard the belief that the only type of intention is the conscious and voluntary intention, the volition where a man wants something and knows that he wants it.

Here are some examples for the latter type: Someone wants to go to New York, or a woman may want a divorce. A banker may want to make a million dollars, or a thief may want to steal cattle. A girl may want to have her back scratched, and a boy may want to play football. Although the exertion of the human will, the conscious intention, is the most valuable dramatic intention, we cannot limit ourselves to it.

If a man is hit, he has the intention to bleed. A man in a burning house has the intention to run away. It must be understood that in bleeding we do not have the intention to act, but the intention to react. The man who runs from the burning house does not voluntarily do so but is forced to do it.

Although the amount of possible intentions is as inexhaustible as life itself, and although these intentions widely differ from one another, there are certain principles which hold true for all of them.

An intention always leads into the future. Everything that leads into the future is an intention. No event can take place in the future unless somebody or something intends it to happen.

An intention comes into existence through a motive. The intention always wants to attain a goal. The goal is always identical with the elimination of the motive. Therefore, the intention becomes extinct as soon as the goal is attained.

But there is nothing in the nature of the intention which guarantees its success. A motive invariably results in an intention; the intention invariably sets a goal; but this goal may or may not be attained. The intention may be fulfilled or frustrated. If a man wants to go to New York, the goal is set. But it is not certain whether he will get to New York or not.

Of course, an intention which is not opposed must necessarily reach the goal which it set out to attain. If the man wants to go to New York, he will get there, unless he is prevented. It is possible, however, that the path of the intention is obstructed by difficulties; then the intention can be frustrated.

In any event, the intention must be completed. Completion is not identical with the attainment of the goal; it merely means that the intention is brought to an end, by fulfillment or frustration, by success or failure.

The clash of the intention with the difficulty results in a struggle. This is the most important function of the intention. It must be understood that human beings can stand in contrast, but conflict can only result from their intentions. As long as two people are merely together, no matter how great their contrast, no conflict can result. Only when their intentions clash does a conflict arise.

Thus we have found the two reasons which give the intention paramount importance over all other dramatic elements: It is the only means of creating conflict, and it is the only element which leads into the future.

The Goal

We prefer to use the term goal instead of objective. The latter implies a conscious, voluntary intention whereas the goal is set by any kind of intention.

The goal is a result in the future. The intention desires to achieve this result. The goal exists whether it is attained or not. However, a goal cannot exist without an intention. If we intend to go to Wilmington, this city is our goal. But Wilmington is not a goal by itself, it is not a goal through any specific qualities of its own, but solely through our intention to go there. If we do not want to go there, it loses its qualities as a goal.

Cause and effect are directly and immediately connected. But between motive and goal may or may not be a distance. This distance is the length of the intention. If a man gets slapped and hits right back, the length of the intention is very short. But if he plans to puncture the aggressor's tires instead of hitting back, the distance between motive and goal is longer. A day or a week may pass before he can fulfill his intention. In both cases, the intention is revenge, but the direction which the intention takes to attain the goal is different. The two components of goal are distance and direction.

If we go on an excursion, we must know two things: either we know the goal and the direction in which it can be found, in which case the distance is a result of the two known factors; or we must know the direction and the

distance and through these two known factors, we find
the goal.

In other words, if we know that our goal is Wilmington, and if we know the direction in which to go, we know
the distance after we have arrived in Wilmington. Or if
we know that we have to go ten miles in a certain direction, we know that we have arrived at the goal after
traveling ten miles.

The most important factor concerning the goal is that
two or more intentions may have the same goal. Several
people may want to go to Wilmington. Several men may
want to marry the same woman. The same goal may be
identical for different intentions.

First, let us assume that a gangster intends to rob a
bank. The police want to prevent it. They have the same
goal. But the gangster's goal is positive, while the goal of
the police is negative.

Or let us imagine that a man desires to marry a girl,
while her father wants to prevent him from doing that.
Again, we have a negative and a positive goal. But if two
men want to marry the same woman, we have opposing
intentions. Still the goal is identical.

It is obvious that the identity of the goal will bring the
different people in relation to each other. It is obvious
that the two rivals for the love of the same woman will
fight with each other. Now consider the other possibility:
Each of them loves a different woman. Each of them has a
separate goal. Their actions can hardly be related to each
other, because their intentions are not focused upon the
same goal. Since their intentions are parallel, the story
falls apart in two separate halves. Connection between
them becomes difficult and painful, almost impossible.

Therefore the focusing of the intentions upon the same
goal is of vital importance to the dramatic story. From it
results contention, conflict, action. Very often, the goal is
diffuse. Then the writer wonders why he cannot lead his
characters into any dramatic situations.

Despite the dangers which two different goals contain, it is very often necessary to use them, mostly in pictures that have an action story but require at the same time a love story. One intention is victory over the adversary; the other must be boy wants to get girl. To avoid the splitting of the story into two separate parts by these two parallel intentions, the author must try and bring them into as close a connection as possible. He will be successful if he is able to unite them in this way: Boy can only get girl if he wins victory over his adversaries. Or he can only win victory over his enemies if he gets girl. Thereby the second goal is eliminated. In the first case the only goal is to get the girl, while the victory over his adversaries is reduced to a necessary condition to attain the goal. In the second case it is reversed.

The same goal may be desired by a large group of people. In that case they are all held together by the identity of the goal. For instance, a football team trains to win an important game. The common goal is to win that game. Or all the members of an underground movement have a desire to defeat the Gestapo. But people living in an apartment house form no basis for successful construction just because they live in the same building. But if the street in front of their house is torn up, and their common goal is to have it repaired quickly, they become united from the point of view of dramatic structure. Or an endangered airplane may join not only the passengers and the crew, but also various people on the ground.

Chapter 3

Disturbance and Adjustment

A HUMAN BEING may be undisturbed; that is, he feels no pain. Then pain may be inflicted upon the human being, which means that a disturbance is created. We must understand that the disturbance is a combination of two factors: the human being and the thing which inflicts pain. After the motive is created through pain, this motive results in an intention, and this, in turn, results in a struggle with opposing difficulties. After the intention has won the struggle, a state of adjustment is gained.

This lets us recognize four stages:

1. The undisturbed stage.
2. The disturbance.
3. The struggle.
4. The adjustment.

THE UNDISTURBED STAGE

No intention and consequently no action can result from an undisturbed state of affairs. There is no pain inflicted upon any person. Therefore the person has no motive for any action. Before the disturbance occurs, the story cannot be a series of incidents, but remains a description of circumstances.

No fully undisturbed state of affairs is possible. We are born with continuous disturbances like hunger, thirst, cold, and others. These motives result in the average actions of our lives. However, a story does not concern itself with the average and common actions, but with the specific disturbances and intentions. This does not mean that we should only tell about outstanding people and their outstanding actions; but it means that we should only tell about the specific disturbances and intentions, even if they are of average people.

The story may begin with the undisturbed stage, or with the disturbance, or sometimes during the struggle. Often it may be advantageous to begin with the undisturbed stage in order to show the contrast between this stage and the disturbance. If you begin with the undisturbed stage, the exposition of the disturbance becomes much simpler. For instance, you show the happy life of a family before visitors from outer space intrude. But should you want to begin with the disturbance, you have to imply an undisturbed stage: You begin with the accident of a husband, and imply that he lived happily with his wife.

THE DISTURBANCE

The human being must be disturbed in order to get into action.

A person is disturbed when something or somebody inflicts pain. Thus it is clear that a disturbance is a combination of two parts: one part is capable of "loving" or "hating" and therefore can feel pain; and the other part is this somebody or something which arouses such love or hatred.

In order to create a disturbance by a combination of two such parts, their characteristics must either repel or attract each other. To satisfy this condition, two prerequisites must be fulfilled: first of all, the two component parts must have distinctive characteristics because nonexistent or vague characteristics will neither repel nor attract each other. This, however, is not yet sufficient. There may be combinations of distinctive characterizations, which, nonetheless, remain indifferent to each other. Therefore the second prerequisite to create a disturbance is to match the characteristics of the two component parts in such manner as to produce affinity or repulsion. Thereby the writer creates the basis for a disturbance and for the resulting struggles. But he has not yet created the disturbance itself. Take for instance the combination of a man and a woman who love each other. The component parts are attracted to each other. If they are happily married, no disturbance exists. Or a man in New York and a man in Chicago dislike each other. We have repellent characteristics. But if no relation between them exists, they will not feel disturbed.

The final step in creating a disturbance is to separate

the parts with affinity or to force together the parts with repulsion.

It is comparatively simple to separate the parts with affinity. For instance, a man likes money and has none. Or a man likes a woman whom he cannot get. But no disturbance exists if the man who likes money is wealthy, or if the man who likes the woman is married to her.

It is more difficult to cause a disturbance through repulsion because the repelling parts must be forced together. If they are not, any resulting action may be compared to shadow boxing. As long as the two fighters remain in their corners, they cannot do more than look threateningly at each other. Only when they meet in the ring can they begin to fight.

We all know examples of family members who love each other as long as they are living in different cities. But if they are compelled to live in the same house, they begin to fight with each other in the most violent manner. Many a husband is dearly beloved by his wife as long as he is on a trip, but as soon as he returns, the quarrel renews.

There are different kinds of forces or relations holding together parts with repulsion. For one thing every human being, by reason of his birth, has a relation to the outside world, that is, the circumstances surrounding him. If circumstances and character are in accord, there will be no disturbance. But if they are not, a disturbance is created. For instance, a professor of biology works in a drug store. An innocent man is in jail. A thief is employed as sales manager in a jewelry store. A peaceful man goes to war, or an ambitious man rises from low origins. There can be a jealous woman in a harem or a courtesan in a cloister. In all these cases we find a discord between characterization and circumstances; a disturbance is the result.

Next we find that relations exist between various people. There are family relations like parents and children, or marriage; there is friendship, or the relation between boss and employee, between people working in the same office or traveling on the same train.

These relations can either be disturbed or undisturbed, depending on the accord or discord of the people within the relation. A loyal husband and wife form an undisturbed marriage. A philandering man and a faithful woman represent a disturbance if they are married. If they are not, there is no disturbance because there is no relation between the repelling characterizations. Or a hard working son and a lazy father form a disturbance. Likewise a thrifty boss and a squandering employee. Or people living in the same house with a tenant who plays the trombone. But they will not care if a tenant in another city plays the trombone.

Finally, a relation can be created through somebody's intention. In that case it is his intention to force himself upon you. It may be that the other person's intention is agreeable to you—then there is no disturbance. But if he does something which you don't like, there is a disturbance. A relation exists if a man wants to steal a thousand dollars from you. The relation continues as long as you fear he will take the money from you, or, in case he has taken it, as long as you want to get it back.

Now it is clear that we must keep the disturbance in effect as long as we need action, that is—for the entire length of the dramatic story. But the very nature of the forces of affinity and repulsion is such that they desire the elimination of the disturbance; this notwithstanding the fact that they are the preliminary requirement to cause a disturbance. In other words, the forces of affinity desire to form a relation between the parts which are attracted to each other and which are separated; and the forces of repulsion desire to break a relation which holds together the parts "hating" each other. Therefore we must take care that they cannot achieve their goal as long as we need the disturbance for the dramatic purposes of the story.

By now we understand the nature of the disturbance. However, the matter is further complicated by the fact that both affinity and repulsion can exist in the same combination. A boy can love a girl, but she does not return his love. Or they both love each other, but they belong to different factions (*West Side Story*). There is affinity between their characters but repulsion between their circumstances. There may also be affinity between some characteristics and repulsion between others. Many marriages are that way: husband and wife love each other physically, but detest each other mentally.

The very fact that affinity and repulsion exist in the same combination may make a disturbance possible without the help of outside forces. The repulsion prevents the affinity from ending the disturbance by forming a relation while the affinity prevents the repulsion from ending the disturbance by breaking the relation. The disturbance can only end when either the affinity or the repulsion is eliminated.

This is the basis of almost every love story. The author asks himself, Why do they want to get together? And why can't they get together? Within this circle lies the story. Consider *Romeo and Juliet*. Affinity through youth and beauty of the lovers, repulsion through the enmity of their families. Neither repulsion nor affinity remains victorious, therefore the tragic ending of the story, destroying the exponents of repulsion and affinity.

The only two ways in which a love story can be told dramatically are to show how the lovers realize their love, which is simply a slow process of affinity coming into effect, or that the lovers are conscious of the affinity but repulsion prevents them from getting together. The standard motion picture love story begins with the slow realization of affinity and thereafter it brings to the fore repulsion of some kind.

Until now we have spoken only of very simple characters with clear and distinct desires. Of course, characters
are never that simple, they are not all wicked or decent,
nor are they beautiful or ugly. A man may be courageous
and undecided, lascivious and puritanical. The character
can comprise qualities which contradict each other or
stand in contrast to each other.

Different characteristics have different tastes, different
likes or dislikes, different loves and hates. If these characteristics stand in contrast, it may result in a person wanting a thing and not wanting it at the same time. Affinity
and repulsion are within one person. The clash is within
the same human being. It can only be ended by eliminat-
ing the power of one or the other characteristic.

Two people with different affinities, unless they are
held together by a relation like marriage, will simply
separate. But one person cannot separate; therefore if
opposite affinities are in one character, the person will be
"torn." This can be the case with a lascivious and puritanical man: he may be married to a decent wife and love
her and the children very much. At the same time, he
may have a mistress who corresponds to the sensual qualities in his character. Between the two women, the one
man may be torn. Such people are often mysteries to their
friends. The explanation is that they have opposing characteristics and opposite affinities.

Examples for such disturbances are as frequent in real
life as in literature. Goethe in *Faust says*, "Alas, two souls
I have in me."

Robert Louis Stevenson goes even further in dramatizing the conflict of one person in *Dr. Jekyll and Mr.
Hyde*. He creates the same person in two different issues,
which look and act differently from each other.

The institution of the opposing God and Devil is a
dramatization of the conflict in the human soul. It is
difficult to understand that a disturbance through opposite characteristics like good and bad can actually take

place within one and the same character. Therefore, there is the tendency to extend the conflict to two different personalities such as God and Devil.

The conflict between opposing characteristics within the same person is one of the most valuable dramatic effects. It leads up to the test of character. After the opposing characteristics have been established, the person should be forced to a choice. Invariably, this brings about a climactic scene of true dramatic force.

The conclusion from this theoretical examination is that action is not possible without characterization. The stronger an action we desire, the more careful a characterization we must create. There is no alternative: characterization or action. The two are inseparably connected. Moreover, though a script may have distinct characterizations, it may not produce disturbances if the combinations are not well fitted to each other. People who do not want anything from each other or find anything which they do not want, cannot possibly get it or not get it. From disinterested characterizations, although each one might be interesting by itself, no action can result. Very often the writer will simply "create" action. The result is painful and false. The falseness will become apparent in many scenes because people will do things for which they have no cause. This mistake is common with novelists and epic writers who try themselves in dramatic technique. Frequently, they fail to realize that the drama requires not only interesting characters, but also combinations of characters which create disturbances.

Turning our attention to the practical application of our findings, we realize that we must begin the creation of the story by inventing characterizations which will produce affinity or repulsion. This primary effort can clearly be recognized in every successful play or motion picture.

After these combinations of characterizations have been fitted together, we must strictly discriminate between the forces of affinity and the forces of repulsion. Because in order to set them to work, we must keep the parts with affinity separated and the parts with repulsion together. It is not possible to have a person run after something which he already has, nor will a man try to eliminate something which he does not have. In order to keep the parts with affinity separated, we must have the reasons for their separation, and in order to keep the parts with repulsion together, we must have the forces which prevent them from splitting.

Frequent mistakes with respect to affinity result because the writer offers no good reason for the lovers to stay separated. Such writers should go to see their pictures in small neighborhood houses where they may overhear remarks like "Why doesn't the guy kiss her?" Or "Why don't they get married?" Such remarks are very often based upon a true dramatic feeling of affinity which is not obstructed.

Similarly, it is a frequent mistake that the force which holds the parts with repulsion together is weaker than the force of repulsion. In this case the relation would simply be broken. But this may not be the writer's intention: he may need action through enmity. This leads to absurd situations which again are shown up in the neighborhood movie houses. The people there ask: "Why doesn't the guy give up the job?" if they witness a violent struggle between a boss and an employee, the latter being able to get another position, while the boss could get another employee. The force which holds the contrasting parts together is weaker than the struggle between them.

THE STRUGGLE

A story without a struggle can never be a dramatic story. It remains a purely descriptive story. This does not necessarily mean that it is a story about an undisturbed state of affairs—an idyllic story; even if it tells about people who are resigned to the permanent acceptance of a disturbance, it still remains a descriptive story. For the core of the dramatic story is the struggle, the desire to eliminate pain through acquisition or repulsion.

There are millions of different kinds of struggles, but in all this variety the dramatic struggle has its definite requirements. It is a struggle to eliminate the disturbance. The escapades of a drunken rowdy do not represent a struggle; but the persons upon whom he inflicted pain will struggle to regain an undisturbed state of affairs.

As such, the struggle appears as the transition from motive to intention to goal, and underlies all the rules which we found for this transition.

A human being will react differently to different types of motives, and the same motive will have different effects upon different human beings. Consequently, the quality of the struggle is a product of the nature of the motive and the characterization of the human being.

Consider a gangster of given character. He will react differently, that is, he will have different intentions, if you stand on his feet, refuse food to him, threaten him with a pistol, or kill his daughter. The same man with different causes for pain will have different intentions. In the first instance, the intention of the gangster may be to slap you in the face, in the second case to steal the food, in the third to eliminate your pistol, and in the last a terrible vengeance.

Now let us consider the reaction of different people with respect to the same motive. Somebody kills the daughter of a gangster, of a simple citizen, of a detective, of a religious fanatic. It is likely that the gangster intends to shoot the murderer himself, that the ordinary citizen will go to the police, that the detective goes to find the murderer, not to shoot him but to hand him over to justice, and that the religious fanatic puts a curse upon the murderer. Each human being has different reactions to the same motive and different methods by which to eliminate pain according to his nature and the means at his disposal.

But the power of the intention is determined by the strength of the pain which the motive inflicts and by the strength with which the human being is capable of reacting.

Therefore the proportion between the strength of the motive on one side and the strength of the intention on the other is of vital importance. In no event can a weak motive give rise to a strong intention.

At times, however, the strength of the cause may add to the strength of the human being. A man can grow beyond himself, if the cause warrants it.

Now we are ready for the investigation of the transition from intention to goal.

The setting of the goal follows with the same necessity as the intention results from the motive. In any and all cases, the goal is the elimination of the motive. The goal is to regain an undisturbed state of affairs. As such, the goal is clearly defined by the motive. It is not possible to struggle blindly in all directions. If our pain is caused because we want money and do not have it, our goal—as caused by this specific disturbance—cannot be to go swimming or to play the piano, but to acquire money. The piano playing, in this case, could only be a means of acquiring money and not a goal by itself.

Each intention has obstacles to overcome in order to attain the goal. The struggle is a result of intention and difficulty.

It must be evident that without an intention, that is, without wanting something, we cannot possibly have any difficulties. On the other hand, a difficulty does not exist by itself, but only through the desire of somebody to get something. A mountain is not an obstacle by itself, but only if somebody wants to get to the other side. The dramatic story of which the struggle is the essential part cannot exist without intentions and difficulties.

We find three essential types of difficulties: the obstacle, the complication, and the counterintention.

The obstacle is a difficulty of circumstantial nature: in physics it may be the law of friction against the law of continued movement. With respect to the human intention, it may be a mountain which must be climbed or lack of money or failure to understand a foreign language.

The complication is of accidental nature. For instance, a jet is grounded by bad weather, a messenger who wants to bring a message breaks his leg, a thief who wants to break into a house is prevented by the accidental arrival of a few drunks strolling along the street.

The counterintention is the definite intention of another person to prevent the fulfillment of the first person's intention. The counterintention is also called the counterplot. The difference with respect to complication lies in the fact that the counterintention is directed toward the same goal, thereby requiring the frustration of the first intention, while the complication may be the result of the accidental arrival of an obstacle or of the unintentional interference with the first intention by another intention which, however, is directed to another goal. To use the above mentioned examples for complications: the storm is simply a meteorological disturbance without having the definite purpose of forcing the airplane down. But if the jet is grounded because of an attack of the enemy, or because of the work of saboteurs, then you have a counterintention directed to the negative goal while the intention desires the positive goal. The broken leg of the messenger is not a counterintention but an accident. The accidental arrival of a drunk who prevents the thief from breaking into the house does not represent an intention to prevent the thief from fulfilling his plans. But if policemen arrive after the thief has touched off a burglar alarm, they represent a counterintention.

Because it is directed to the same goal and represents a conscious desire to obstruct the first intention, the counter-intention is the most effective dramatic difficulty. The advantages lie in the fact that the struggle gains continually new aspects, and that the chances of victory or defeat are rapidly changing.

In comparison, the complication is less effective; because of its accidental nature, it arouses resentment in the spectator: it is neither planned nor desired by anybody, it could not have been prevented or foreseen by the actor, and therefore it is no real test of the human being's power to execute his will. Furthermore, because it is accidental, it cannot persist; it is a temporary difficulty, since the storm will dissolve into good weather, the leg is going to heal, and the drunk will leave the street. But the counter-intention will only cease to exist when the first intention is fulfilled or frustrated.

The obstacle's disadvantage is caused by its tendency to remain static—its circumstantial nature cannot undergo any sudden changes. The mountain remains a mountain throughout the story. Therefore, while obstacle and complication are satisfactory temporary difficulties, they should not be employed as the main difficulties for an entire story. However, they can be used advantageously to strengthen the counterintention.

Just as the intention, the difficulty is characterized through quality and strength. Not anybody or anything is a difficulty for a certain intention. The quality of the person or thing in relation to the quality of the intention can cause opposition. Only a person or thing which opposes the path of the intention can be a difficulty.

Furthermore, we find that every difficulty has a certain strength. It appears as the power to resist. Therefore it can only become manifest through the clash with the intention.

If you want to smash a window, the difficulty has little strength because the glass has little power to resist. If you want to break through a safe, the difficulty is stronger because the steel offers greater resistance. Although it exists constantly, the strength of the difficulty becomes manifest only if somebody intends to break the resistance. In the same way, the power of the intention remains latent; that is, it cannot exert its force if the goal is attained easily. This does not mean that the intention is less strong if it has no difficulties to overcome. It simply means that its power can only become manifest by virtue of the power of the difficulties which it overcomes or which it wants to overcome. Both the man who wins over strong difficulties and the man who fails reveal strong intentions. It is neither success nor failure in the desire to overcome the difficulties which reveals the strength of the intention, because success or failure depends upon fate, competence, good or bad luck. But the strength of an intention is already revealed by the strength of the difficulties which it attacks.

If a man loves a woman very much, his desire to be united with her is very strong. If he lives in Long Island and she in New York, the difficulties in going from one place to the other are very weak. But if the man is in China and the woman in New York, the difficulties are considerable. In both cases the intention of the man to be united with the woman is equally strong. But in the first case the strength of the intention cannot become manifest, because the difficulties which he has to overcome are small, whereas in the second case the strength of the man's intention becomes manifest. Whether he gets to New York or not has nothing to do with the strength of the intention, which is already revealed by the simple fact that he attempts such a difficult task.

For these reasons, it is not practicable to "talk" of the strength of intentions in the dramatic story; instead their power must be made manifest through the clash with strong difficulties. Many an author is so convinced of the strength of his protagonist's intentions—particularly, if the story is true—that he fails to make them manifest. But the spectator has no proof of the strength of emotions or intentions; he is reluctant to believe the words of the author as well as the words of the actor. He will only believe it when the strength becomes manifest through the clash with difficulties. Even the theatre allowed the hero to proclaim at length how much he loved the heroine; but the theatre is limited in the quantity and variety of intentions. The motion picture, however, with its possibilities of showing many intentions has the duty of making them manifest through the clash.

As such, the struggle is a fight between opposing forces, whether they are attack and resistance or attack and counterattack. Any fight between opposing forces must end in victory and defeat unless the fight is interrupted or ends in a draw. Such an interruption is not permissible in the dramatic story. Victory and defeat are identical with the fulfillment and the frustration of the intention, respectively. The final decision is rendered in the climax. After the climax no change is possible. The climax, however, is not identical with the goal. The climax decides the defeat of one side, after which the victorious side may proceed to attain the goal, which may be attained instantly or at some later date.

Thus we find a number of factors with conclusive relations and proportions between them. We find an interwoven and interconnected system of laws which is easily violated. The resulting mistakes are not easily recognized.

From the motive we can conclude to an intention, from the intention to the goal; therefore we can also conclude from the motive to the goal. From the intention alone we can conclude backwards to a motive and forward to a goal. From the goal we can conclude to a preceding intention and from there to a motive. The only factor remaining outside this circle of logical conclusion is the fulfillment or frustration of the intention.

The difficulty of the material often tempts the writer to overlook or violate these relations. At times, he may show a motive without following it up with an intention. At times, he may show intentions without motives. This is particularly tempting when he needs an intention for a certain story development for which he has no motive. Then again, it happens that, through the developments in his story, motives are created which are not wanted by him. He is not interested in the intentions resulting from these disturbances and therefore is tempted to disregard them. But this is not possible: whether undesired or overlooked, violations of these conclusive relations are mistakes. The writer must learn to respect these laws. In order to find the motive, he can ask, Why would a man act like that? In order to find the intention he can ask, How would a man act if this happened to him? The failure to realize latent motives might be expressed by the somewhat exaggerated example of a man who stays in bed even though his room is afire, which should be sufficient motive for him to run away.

Another frequent mistake results when the writer may have given a motive, but would like the actor to attain a goal which is more practicable for the story purposes. Then he has a motive without resulting intention and goal, and he has a goal which lacks intention and motive.

Furthermore, the strengths of motive and intention stand in proportion. They must be of equal strength. It happens very often that the clash with the difficulties reveals a stronger intention than the motive warrants. Let us consider this example: The boss of an engineering firm sends one of his employees to a factory which is losing money. The engineer goes there. His motive is simple: it is his job, he gets paid for it. Upon his arrival, he finds that arsonists from a competing factory are trying to ruin the machinery. In the course of the conflict both sides get into great danger: they risk their lives. Now let us review the motives: He makes three hundred dollars a week. For that he has to risk his life. It does not make sense. Now let us attempt to improve the strength of the motive in order to make it equal to the strength of the intention. The engineer has tried everywhere to get a job and has failed; he is about to starve when he is offered this assignment. This motive makes sense. If he does not accept the job, he might starve. If he takes it, he is liable to get killed. Or let us try another way: the saboteurs are from outer space. If the engineer risks his life, he does not do it for three hundred dollars a week, but for the planet Earth. That is strong enough to account for a strong intention.

These are the dangers resulting from the interconnection of these laws. But there are also advantages.

If these relations and proportions are so firm and strict that we can conclude from one to the other, we can dispense with showing and exposing each and all of them; it will be sufficient to expose one in order to know the others. This is of inestimable value in telling the motion picture story.

On the other hand, if the writer fails to take into consideration this automatic exposition of the factors between themselves, and hopes to avoid contradictions simply by showing only one or two factors, he could be compared to an ostrich who puts his head into the sand.

Now we come to a very important point: The only exception with regard to these automatic conclusions is the fulfillment or frustration of the intention. But this possible uncertainty underlies equally firm rules. We know that the intention has the desire to attain the goal. Therefore we conclude that it will attain the goal. The only case where the uncertainty comes into effect is when the intention is opposed by difficulties. To be uncertain about the fulfillment or frustration of the intention, we need knowledge of the existence of opposing difficulties.

This has prepared our understanding for one of the most essential facts about motion picture writing. Now we are in a position to transform our theoretical knowledge into the rules for its practical application.

In reality, the transition from motive to intention to goal takes time. If we want to walk from Washington to New York, our undertaking will require a long time. If we want to light a cigarette, the time required is short.

It is our desire to represent those intentions which require a long time as well as those which require a short time. But the motion picture has only about two hours at its disposal while the intention to walk from Washington to New York requires probably two weeks. Nevertheless, the motion picture is able to contain such time-absorbing actions because of the interruptions between scenes. We remember that during the change from one scene to another an undefined lapse of time occurs. Consequently, the transition from motive to intention to goal may have taken place in this lapse of time.

This is a singular advantage of the motion picture because the theatre, which has only few scenes, and thus few lapses of time between them, must nearly always execute the entire transition; it must show the entire development, except for the rare intermissions or exits and entrances of the actors. The disadvantage is twofold: first, it makes the movement of the story slower, and second, the stage has to discard many developments which would take too long to execute.

But the motion picture can make use of our ability to conclude with regard to the transition from one factor to the other by pushing the actual time-absorbing transition into the lapse of time between scenes.

Thus we can decide which happenings should occur in the lapse of time and which should be presented in a scene. Every action, every happening or event, every development to which we can conclude, should be pushed into the lapse of time. It is without interest to us. If something to which we can conclude is shown to us, it has the same effect as if we were told again what we already know. It is as if it were told to us twice, thereby boring us and slowing the progress of the picture.

Only those developments and happenings to which we cannot conclude with certainty are interesting to us, and they should be shown. Now we found that the only factor which is beyond the reach of our conclusion is the attainment of the goal, if we have the knowledge of opposing difficulties. The execution of an intention becomes interesting only if there is a possibility of its frustration. In reverse, this means that in order to be permitted to show the execution of an intention, we must create an opposing difficulty. As soon as this possible opposition disappears, we conclude to the fulfillment of the intention and the picture must lead us immediately to the goal.

Let us consider an example: A man intends to go to Florida. He has the money, he has the time, and there is no doubt connected with the attainment of the goal of this intention.

The picture would be forced to show him immediately in Florida. It would be entirely without interest to show him buying the tickets, going to the station, taking the train, and then arriving in Florida. In order to make it possible to show all these things, we would have to establish that something or somebody wanted to prevent him from going there, because then we could not conclude with certainty that the man's intention would attain the goal.

This applies also to the love story. If a man and a woman with perfect affinity and no obvious difficulties meet each other, there is no doubt that they will attain their goal. The picture would have to show their marriage in the next shot, since we have no doubt of the fulfillment of their intention. All love scenes in between are without any interest. In order to show these love scenes, we must give the spectator a knowledge of some difficulties to prevent him from concluding to the goal.

The opposite case is equally wrong. When we have the knowledge of some opposing difficulties, it would be false if the picture led us immediately to the goal, because then we could not conclude to the attainment of the goal. There is a doubt about the fulfillment of the intention, therefore the execution of the intention must be shown. For instance, a man wants to drive from one town to another. We know that some criminals have prepared a trap on the highway. It would be wrong to show the arrival of the man in the next scene. This is a very obvious example, but there are cases where the intention is confronted with difficulties which are not particularly desired by the writer. If you cross from the living room to the bedroom, there are no apparent or obvious difficulties confronting your intention. But if a man crosses the Amazon jungle, he is confronted with enormous difficulties. It would be impossible to conclude to the successful fulfillment of his intention. The writer is forced to show instances where the intention successfully overcomes the opposing difficulty—escape from hostile tribes or the killling of snakes—or he must prepare beforehand such a safe way of executing the intention that we conclude to the successful attainment of the goal. Or he may tell us afterwards how he was able to overcome the difficulties. But in no event is the writer allowed to ignore the difficulties which oppose an intention.

With this, we have investigated all the rules with regard to the struggle and their practical application to the motion picture story.

THE ADJUSTMENT

The adjustment takes place when the goal is attained.

It means that the purpose of the struggle is fulfilled: the disturbance has ceased to exist.

The disturbance is the point of beginning and the adjustment the point of end. The transformation from one to the other can either be gradual or sudden, which means that in the first case the process of adjustment is slow and distributed over the whole story; in the second case the adjustment is rapid, made possible through a sudden event. In either case the struggle is continuous.

We find only three possible ways of achieving adjustment: either we destroy the forces of affinity or repulsion, or we form a relation between the objects of affinity, or we disrupt a relation between the objects of repulsion.

A relation can be formed or disrupted suddenly and momentarily. We can get married quickly after the difficulties which may have stood in the way have been overcome, and we are quickly and suddenly relieved if our enemy is shot. But in order to annul the forces of affinity or repulsion we must either change the characterization or the circumstances. Circumstances may change quickly or slowly; for instance, we may acquire money in a poker game or lose it in a bank crash, or we may get another job; on the other hand, we may save money slowly. But characterization can only be changed in a slow process. A character may deteriorate in the course of years, or improve in the course of months, a vivacious person may become depressed and a sad person optimistic, a stupid person can learn, and a carefree person become disciplined. But it is not possible that a thoroughly bad person becomes good instantly, nor a brutal person mild, nor a liar a truthful man. For these reasons an adjustment where the forming or disrupting of a relation is involved, or where an annullment of affinity or repulsion through a change of circumstances is needed, can take place rapidly. But where a change of character is necessary, the adjustment must be gradual and slow.

It happens often that the writer is little concerned with

the adjustment until the latter part of the story. This is possible if the adjustment is to take place rapidly, but if it is to be achieved by reason of a change of character, it must be prepared long before. Failure to recognize this results in very silly situations: the writer searches for something which will suddenly change the wicked fellow into a good person. He will search in vain, for there is nothing strong enough to change a character suddenly. But here we remember that a character may consist of two contrasting sides. If this is the case, a certain event may cause the victory of the good or the bad side; however, this is not equal to a change of character but to a victory of one characteristic over the other. For this reason it must be established beforehand that both sides exist in the one character.

A good example of the change of character is Shakespeare's *Taming of the Shrew*. Kate starts out as a wild girl, and is slowly transformed into a mild and subdued woman. But even there we should assume that in all her original wildness is a desire to be subdued, which again is equal to two different sides of one character. The disadvantages of such a slow adjustment lie in the fact that no climax is possible, and that Petruchio's intention to subdue her gradually loses uncertainty because it becomes more and more evident that she will be subdued as her character changes into mildness. This gradual change toward certainty of the outcome diminishes our interest gradually.

Adjustment means that an undisturbed state of affairs has been attained. This undisturbed state of affairs can either be the same from which we started out or another one. It is very dangerous to return to the same state of affairs, because then—even though things have happened— nothing has been changed. The audience will feel dissatisfaction if it is led back to the starting point, like the man in the desert who returns to his own tracks. If nothing has changed in spite of all the forces that were aroused, the

spectator is liable to ask, Why tell this story? If the adjustment is achieved through the marriage of a formerly
unmarried couple, you have a change. Or if the adjustment results from a divorce, you still have a change. But
if you have a story of a married couple, and of a third
person who arrives and threatens to break up the marriage—if this story ends with the outside person being
pushed away and the married couple continuing to live
happily—you have no change. To make this story
workable it will be necessary to show at least that the
married couple fights over little things. Suddenly, real
trouble comes along in the form of a third person. After
this person is eliminated, the love of the couple becomes
stronger and sublimated. There will be some change at
least.

It is interesting to note that in Alfred Hitchcock's picture *Suspicion,* most spectators feel intense dissatisfaction
after the ending. There seems to be no obvious reason,
because it is a happy ending. The explanation is that no
change is achieved through the struggle. Cary Grant and
Joan Fontaine are happily married before and after. This
is further accentuated because the struggle arises not from
a real cause but from a fictitious one. The public resents
having take part in suspicion and suspense for no actual
reason and with no actual result.

This explains the nature of adjustment with regard to
disturbance and struggle. It must be realized, however,
that within the story not all intentions can achieve adjustment. To the contrary, in a story with intention and
counterintention, the one must be prevented from achieving adjustment in order to let the other attain it. Even
though not every intention can be adjusted, every intention must be brought to an end, which can mean frustration, whereas adjustment means that the intention attains
its goal by being fulfilled.

If the writer has brought all intentions to an end, he
has a right to hope that the audience is satisfied, but soon

he will find out that the audience will not accept definite frustration of a good intention, nor will it believe in the final adjustment of a bad intention. Its verdict is likely to be that the story is not at an end because it would only be finished after the good had won.

Therefore an unhappy ending caused by a failure of adjustment that might possibly be achieved at a later time is a false unhappy ending. As long as man lives, he will continue to strive, to hope, to desire an adjustment. We expect the persons whose intentions apparently have been frustrated to try sooner or later to achieve adjustment. We can take such an unhappy ending only as a temporary station. We know that the unhappy person's mind is not at rest, because it still feels pain; and feeling pain, the person will act to eliminate the cause for pain. Audiences are not satisfied because they want to know how the next attempt to achieve adjustment will come out.

The acceptance of a constantly disturbed balance is called resignation. To a certain degree, it may constitute a point of rest and consequently a proper ending for a story. The only difficulty is that no human being is ever entirely resigned, while someone may be entirely satisfied. The disturbance is latent and can be aroused at any time. Therefore the audience refuses to accept the ending as final.

A true unhappy ending exists when the exponent of the good, or one of the lovers, dies. Then it is impossible to achieve an adjustment at a later time. The tragic effect caused by such an unhappy ending is not a result of faulty dramatic construction but of story content. True unhappy endings can be found in pictures like *Camille*.

If both lovers die, we have no real unhappy ending, because then the lovers are united in death. It is interesting to notice that an audience does not resent such an unhappy ending, because it feels that the lovers are not separated. You feel no dissatisfaction at the ending of *Romeo and Juliet* or *Wuthering Heights*. In those stories the lovers are united in death. The explanation of our lack of dissatisfaction from the structural point of view is that no disturbance remains, as it does in those cases where one lover remains alive.

Chapter 4

Main Intentions and Subintentions

IT MUST BE REALIZED that the world and our lives are one continuous chain of causes and effects, disturbances and adjustments. There is no beginning and no end; in these interwoven nets of motives, intentions, goals, we find no absolutely undisturbed state of affairs, at least not for any length of time. Nor can we possibly achieve final and lasting adjustments.

We are born with continuous disturbances; others are forced upon us by other people. But the people who inflict this pain upon us must have had disturbances themselves in order to be moved to action, and these disturbances must have been caused by other people or things and so on. There is an uninterrupted chain starting in the distant past and leading up to the present day. Because of its limitation of space, the motion picture story cannot possibly render full justice to this entire chain of events. Whatever is to be told, must be told in two hours. There-

157

fore we have to decide what to tell, where to begin, and where to end.

We answer this question by saying that we must limit ourselves to showing the outcome of one intention. This includes the exposition of the disturbance and the outcome of the intention, whether it be fulfillment or frustration. It is not possible to end the story before this outcome of the intention is shown, nor is it possible to have the intention attain the goal in the middle of the picture and then continue with another one.

This defines very strictly what the motion picture should tell. It is not advantageous for an ambitious writer to describe the entire life of a person—which generally consists of many intentions—except in cases where an entire life is devoted to one great intention.

Thus we derive the conception of the main intention. The main intention is the one out of many intentions about which the story proposes to tell.

The disturbance causing this main intention must be told, as well as the adjustment. The life of a human being will never attain complete adjustment, but can gain temporary adjustments for some intentions. We may never gain final adjustment for love, but we may have found a woman who seemed to represent adjustment, even though we may find out later that she was the wrong person. We all have at least once succeeded in fulfilling one ambition, even though this success may be later destroyed by the misfortunes of life. It is the duty of the story to single out one disturbance, show the fate of the resulting intention, and end with final or temporary adjustment.

Thus the single main intention becomes the primary subject of our attention. This main intention may be opposed by a counterintention, but the counterintention can still be considered part of the main intention. It can even be opposed by several counterintentions; nevertheless, the main intention remains the backbone of the story. One main intention can be carried by several people: by astronauts in a spaceship. But even in this instance we do not tell about more than one main intention.

In rare cases a story may have two main intentions if they are contained in the same person. For instance, the hero desires the girl and victory over his enemies. While this is still possible, more main intentions destroy the motion picture story. The writer finds that such stories cannot be constructed, because they fall to pieces. Several main intentions are bound to run parallel or follow one after the other. Even though in this latter case, we have only one main intention at a time, the mistake is equally detrimental. Stories with such consecutive main intentions have the forward movement of a rabbit. This occurs frequently in episodic pictures unless they have one main intention connecting the episodes.

From the main intention we derive the conception of the subintention. The nature of the main intention is such that for its fulfillment we may need a number of small intentions.

Here is an example: A young man wants to make a career as a singer. His final ambition is to sing a great role at the Metropolitan Opera. It is impossible for him to achieve this main intention at once. Instead, he will have several subintentions: he may have to start as a singer in a night club. Then he may want to sing with a rock group. From this he may obtain enough money to take lessons from one of the great teachers. After that he is ready to sing in the Music Hall with the hope of being heard by people who can give him a chance in the Metropolitan. He is given a small part in the opera. Thence he moves forward to the final goal: a great role at the Metropolitan.

This necessity for subintentions holds true for real life as well as for the movie script. Mountain climbers will cut up the main intention into various objectives. First they must reach a ledge here and then one further on; then they must scale a sheer wall and cross a ravine. And so on, until they have reached the peak.

But even a simple love story contains the principle of subdivision. The final objective is clear. But there are various subintentions—to attract the attention of the beloved one, to talk to her for the first time, to see her alone for the first time, to kiss her—and from then on the subintentions will depend upon the quality of the final goal.

Life is full of intentions. It is not always easy for the writer to discern between main intentions and subintentions. Strength is no criterion, because sometimes the main intention of a story is merely to plant a garden— which is not very powerful—and sometimes the subintention may be to slaughter a family. We must forget about size and power as standards by which to differentiate between main intention and subintention.

In order to recognize an intention as a subintention we must ask, Does it further the main intention? Every intention that does not further the main intention is an independent intention. It has to be discarded because the story cannot stand too many main intentions.

This is a very important discovery. The theatre is so limited in the material which it can use that it is not confronted with this problem to so great an extent. But the motion picture can represent so many different intentions that the writer is tempted to go off on all sides. Soon he will realize the damage done to his story. He will ask, Out of this maze of intentions, which shall I represent?

The answer is given through unity of purpose. The law of unity of purpose replaces the laws of unity of time and place in the theatre. After we have selected the main intention of the motion picture story, we can ask about all other intentions: Do they further the cause of the main intention? If they do, they are subintentions; if they do not, they are main intentions and must be discarded.

We must keep in mind that the main intention as well as the counter main intention may have subintentions. Each of these subintentions must either further the cause of the main intention or of the counter main intention. All the same rules apply to either of them.

The subintentions are of constantly changing nature, while the main intention remains constant.

If we want to go to New York, this main intention remains the same, no matter what happens. But our subintention may have been to take the plane. The plane takes us from Los Angeles to Fort Worth, where a storm grounds the plane. Consequently, a new subintention comes into effect: we want to take the train. We ride on the train until we arrive at a bridge which was destroyed by a flood. So we have to cross in a boat. Upon arrival on the other side, we take a car. Suddenly we discover that our enemy is lurking on the road. So we make a detour. Finally, we fulfill our main intention by arriving in New York. Among all these constant changes in subintentions, the law of unity of purpose remains in effect: they all further the main intention to get to New York.

Subintentions can lie within different people. For instance, a business man wants to make money. The employees working for him represent subintentions, since their work furthers his plan. But the employee who goes on a weekend vacation fulfills no subintention from the boss's point of view but a separate intention.

Like any intention, the subintention must have a cause and a goal. But the cause for the subintention is not a motive but a motivation. The cause is not pain, like the motive for the main intention, but it is the reason why this subintention will further the cause of the main inten tion. As such, the motivation is completely dependent upon the motive. This dependency results in two rules: the motivation exists only through the motive, and the motivation must have less strength than the motive.

The strength of the motivation cannot exceed the strength of the motive. Let us assume that a man met a woman at a party and flirted with her. After such short acquaintance, the pain caused through separation cannot be very strong; therefore the motive is weak. Consider these two possibilities: the man is in Long Island and hears that the woman is in New York. He will go there because the motivation is even weaker than the motive. It does not require a very strong motivation to go from Long Island to New York. But if the man is in China and hears that the woman is in New York, he will not attempt the trip for a woman he hardly knows, because the strength of the subintention would exceed by far the strength of the main intention. The motive would have to be augmented: his love for the woman must be very strong.

The subintention sets an auxiliary goal. The auxiliary goal lies in the future. It may or not be attained.

If the subintention is characterized by the law of unity of purpose and if the motivation is characterized by the dependency upon the motive, the auxiliary goal is characterized by the law of the concentric direction.

The main intention has the desire to attain its goal in the shortest possible way. We can visualize the main intention as a straight line from motive to goal, because the shortest possible way is the straight line. If we want to go from New York to San Francisco, we will not go first to Miami, then to Chicago, then to New Orleans, then to Alaska and then to Los Angeles. We will take the straight line from New York to San Francisco. Consequently, the auxiliary goals desire to rest on the straight line between motive and main goal. This is not always possible because

the difficulties may demand detours. The counterintentions may change the straight path of the subintention.
But no matter how many detours, the auxiliary goal
must lie always in the direction of the main goal.

It is not possible to go backward, or far off toward all
sides, particularly not if it is unwarranted by the difficulties. A graphic description of this mistake would look like
this:

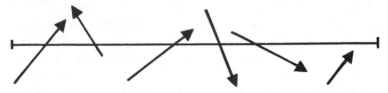

It is obvious how harmful to the progress of the story
such confused directions are. But the law of the concentric
directions, represented graphically, looks like this:

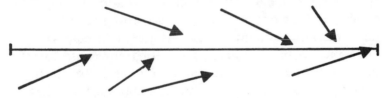

There are football teams which pass the ball to all
sides, but never seem to approach the goal. There are
others which with a few calculated passes push right
through. There are stories which reach out in all directions, but do not lead us anywhere. But there are other
stories in which everything leads to a point. Stories with
concentric direction are tense and powerful. Without,
they are dissipated and tiresome. Besides, they waste so
much time on their aberrations that they have little left
for the main purpose.

The reader should not expect the auxiliary goals in a
story to be very firm and concrete or obvious like the

railroad stations along a route. They are of different strength and appearance; they may appear very rapidly and disappear again. One auxiliary goal itself may be subdivided into various other goals of much less importance and of even less definite appearance. The intention to meet somebody in a certain place sets an auxiliary goal, as does the intention to buy a new dress or to watch the performance of a play. One has said about Van Gogh's paintings that there is not one dull square inch on his canvas. If you look at one square inch of his painting, you will find the same elements which make his entire picture interesting. The same applies for the motion picture story: each little section should contain the same elements of the future—intention and goal—which are desirable for the entire story.

The subintention which can be fulfilled or frustrated, must be fulfilled or frustrated. Any subintention must be led to a definite end. Many pictures violate this law. The error may be more or less grave according to the importance of the subintention. Let us assume a man says, "I am going to bed." There is no apparent cause for the man's intention to be frustrated. Therefore we conclude that he will attain his goal. But if a man declares that he is going to Singapore, and if we see him in the next scene walking in Times Square, we are confused. What happened to his subintention to go to Singapore? Why was it frustrated? When did he decide to go to New York?

Nowadays, such inconsistencies are frequently seen in motion pictures which have been badly cut for television showings. It is possible to eliminate a sequence, but not the preceding dialog that prepares it.

In regard to the auxiliary goal we find other difficulties. At times something is revealed as an auxiliary goal. If this is the case, it exposes the need for a subintention and for a motivation. For instance, a lady in an evening dress in a swank restaurant, a worker in overalls standing in a factory, a man in a bathing suit in a pool, do not all represent auxiliary goals. But if a poorly dressed man goes into a luxurious restaurant, or if a man in overalls appears at a dress party, or the man in the bathing suit stands in Times Square, all these incidents reveal auxiliary goals which require motivation.

Failure to recognize these auxiliary goals and to give the respective motivations results in absurd situations. Sometimes a story may require a person to be in a certain place in order to meet another person or to witness something. If that person in that place does not represent a contradiction of information, we do not need any motivation. It is perfectly natural for the workman to see something happen in the factory. If our story requires that he see a happening in a night club, we need a strong motivation to get him there. Writers suffer from this demand; they must ask themselves, How can I get him there, or how can I make him meet her, or how can I make him see what happens there? It is obvious that the motivation must be in direct connection with the story line because, if it is not, the explanation would lead us too far astray from our story and would completely disrupt the forward movement, even though the motivation may be correct. It is not possible to explain that the man in overalls goes into chic restaurants because of a desire to live above his means, which was caused by an event in his childhood . . . and while he is there, he sees a girl steal something from a man. Such a motivation would be criminal in terms of economy. No, he goes there because he suspects his girl to be in that night club, or because he knows that somebody is to be robbed. In that case, the contradiction of information revealed by the overalls and the elegance of the night club becomes an excellent means of exposing the strength of the subintention.

Chapter 5

The Effect
Upon the Audience

WE ARE NOT JUST TELLING A STORY—we are telling it to an audience. It is therefore necessary to determine how the audience reacts to the manner in which the story is told. For the time being we shall confine ourselves to the effects of the dramatic construction upon the mind of the spectator, leaving the examination of the effects of the actual story content to the third part of the book.

The reactions of the audience are neither unpredictable nor uncertain. The public reacts to certain parts of the story in a certain manner. Knowing this, the writer is in a position to obtain the desired reactions from the audience at his choosing.

Only the novice writer believes that the reactions and moods of the actors in his story will cause identical reactions and moods in the audience. If the characters in the picture laugh and are amused, it does not necessarily mean that people in the audience will laugh and have a good time. As a matter of fact, some of the greatest comedians make their audience hilariously gay without laughing once themselves. Sadness of the actors on the screen does not necessarily make people in the audience sad. Nor will the spectator be fascinated just because the actor is terribly interested in what he is doing. Excitement, shooting, and much movement on the screen do not necessarily excite the audience. The spectators may watch these happenings in complete boredom. On the other hand, silence may put the audience into a state of excitement. The laughter of an actor may make the audience cry, and the sadness of a character on the screen may make them laugh.

The experienced writer knows that the reactions of the audience are not identical with those of the actors. Nevertheless, the reactions of the spectators are not independent: they are caused unavoidably by certain elements in the story.

Moreover, it must be understood that the quality of the story content does not necessarily create interest or suspense. A story with superb qualities may be supremely dull, and a very trite and common story may be intensely interesting.

A correct dramatic construction presents the story content in the most effective manner. It should prevent the spectator from feeling boredom, fatigue, dissatisfaction, and lack of speed. It should cause surprise, hope, fear, suspense, and forward movement.

We must learn so to construct a story that it will arouse, sustain, and steadily increase the interest of the spectator. To achieve this, we must make use of the spectator's capacity and ability to anticipate.

ANTICIPATION

Anticipation is the ability of the spectator to foresee a happening which is to take place in the future.

In order to enable him to anticipate an event which is to take place at a future moment, he must know of something that is intended or planned to happen. For instance, a stone breaks loose from a housetop. The spectator anticipates that it will hit the ground. Or a man intends to go to New York. The audience anticipates that he will reach New York. However, if nothing is intended or planned by persons or objects in the story, nothing can be anticipated.

Notice that we said intended or planned by persons or objects in the story. In no event should the spectator anticipate the intentions of the author of the story. Such false anticipation has done much to discredit anticipation as a valuable reaction. Stories which "telegraph their ending," to use the technical term for false anticipation, are indeed devoid of merit.

But true anticipation, which is caused by the intentions of actors in the story, is of great value to the construction of the motion picture. William Archer in his book *Playmaking* states: "The essential and abiding pleasure of the theatre lies in foreknowledge. In relation to the characters of the drama, the audience are as gods looking before and after. Sitting in the theatre, we taste for a moment the glory of omniscience. With vision unsealed, we watch the gropings of purblind mortals after happiness and smile at their stumblings, their blunders, their futile quests, their misplaced exultations, their groundless panics."

The nature of anticipation is not easily recognized. Although the intention is the preliminary condition for the spectator's anticipation, it does not conclusively determine this anticipation. The spectator's anticipation is a reaction which is merely set into motion by the intentions appearing in the story.

This is due to the fact that an intention is not certain to attain its goal. And it is up to the spectator to decide whether to believe in the fulfillment or frustration of the intention, choosing, so to speak, what outcome he wants to foresee.

In many cases, where the goal—that is, the result in the future—follows with certainty upon the intention, our anticipation will be certain. For instance, the sun "intends" to rise every morning. We anticipate that it will rise every morning. But then again, we may state, "The water will begin to boil—if it is long enough on the fire." The second part of the sentence expresses the uncertainty of our anticipation. Perhaps somebody will extinguish the fire or take the pot away. Then there are intentions which have no chance to succeed, because they are hopeless or impossible. In this case the spectator will refuse to anticipate their success, even though the actor in the story believes in it. If an actor in the story proclaims that he is going to jump to the moon, the spectator will by no means anticipate seeing him there but, deciding for himself, expect to find him in an insane asylum.

This being the case, we need knowledge to decide what the probable outcome of a happening is going to be. And this knowledge is a result of our experience.

Experience, in turn, is proof accumulated through repetition. If the same thing behaves in the same way under the same circumstances, it is logical that it will continue to behave identically. If this repetition is constant enough to take place a hundred thousand times, it can be crystallized into a scientific law of absolute exactitude, thereby guiding our anticipation with certainty.

We expect the sun to rise every morning as it has for many thousands of years. But in the dark past of mankind even this anticipation was uncertain: in pagan times, men still feared that the sun might fail to rise one day, leaving the earth in eternal darkness. After a few thousand years of experience, man is fairly certain that nothing can go wrong with his anticipation of the sunrise. This made it possible for the prophets to base some of their most horrifying predictions upon the contradiction of such certain anticipations: "The sun will stay still in mid-heaven." The prophets who directed their prophecies to simple people knew that the movement of the sun was a well-established anticipation which—if it was broken— would cause the realization of a terrifying change in nature.

Thus we understand that several spectators may have different knowledge with regard to the same happening so that they may anticipate differently, some correctly, some wrongly, and some not at all.

In real life, every person anticipates in many instances a reaction which has become so automatic that he may not even be aware of it. A man who drops a letter in the mailbox anticipates that the post office will deliver the letter to its destination. A secretary who rushes to catch the bus anticipates that the bus will leave the street corner at a certain time.

Our anticipation can be provoked by customary happenings, by legal institutions, by the constancy of psychological patterns, or by mere repetition. But with regard to human behavior, a fact which is repeated four or five times will already induce us to anticipate its recurrence.

For instance, if a person has been established as honest, we anticipate honest actions from him; we refuse to believe that he would commit any dishonest deeds. If we see how a man is beaten, we anticipate that he will react, because we know that we would react, and we know that other people would react when they were beaten. We anticipate further that his reaction will be to defend himself and not to treat the aggressor to an ice cream soda. If someone steals money, he must anticipate being put in jail as soon as he is caught.

The general knowledge of the spectator, which varies in comprehensiveness, can and must be enlarged by information given in the story with regard to a specific person or happening. For instance, you must let the audience know that a father is brutal in order to make them anticipate that he will beat his child who has broken a window.

The information, supplied by the story, will cause us to anticipate as long as it contains the element of repetition. We may remember that the very definition of a characteristic is based on repetition in contrast to the passing mood. Therefore the factor of repetition, whether in regard to a character or event, may be merely stated or implied; it can, however, automatically arise should the same happening be shown three or four times in the course of the story.

If a swindler marries women as a method of obtaining their money, we anticipate after the second or third woman that he will act similarly with any other woman he meets.

Repetition is a very frequent effect in comedy: every time a comedian appears, he asks a certain question. After the third or fourth time, the audience anticipates that he will ask the question. If it was funny, they will laugh before he has even opened his mouth. It is a comedic reiteration of the old Pavlovian dog experiment.

Now it is clear that information given by the story may be replaced or even contradicted by later information, during the progress of events. Consequently, our anticipations are subject to constant changes, being interrupted, transformed, or replaced. For instance, in Neil Simon's *The Out-Of-Towners,* directed by Arthur Hiller, Jack Lemmon plays a young executive flying to New York for an important business meeting. Everything has been prearranged, but nothing goes according to schedule. His plane is detoured to Boston, he misses a train connection, he loses his reservation at the Waldorf Astoria, he is held up and arrested, and on his way home he is hijacked to Cuba.

However, in each instance, an anticipation which is not led to fulfillment must be interrupted and thereby destroyed. The anticipation which is left dangling in the air causes a subconscious dissatisfaction on the part of the spectator.

All of us have experienced the feeling which is created when somebody promises to telephone and fails to do so. The disappointment may not be warranted by the importance of the call, but is simply a result of our dissatisfied anticipation.

Thus it is not practicable to show a train heading toward a broken bridge and in the next scene to show the travelers at their destination. It is not feasible for an actor to intend to steal cattle and then fail to do it without telling the spectator of this change in plans. So long as this change is not made public, the spectator will anticipate that the man will steal cattle. The longer it takes, the more impatient the spectator gets. And if the picture ends without the man having stolen cattle, the anticipation of the spectator is definitely dissatisfied. The following brief explanation on his part might have destroyed this anticipation: "I am going to become an honest man."

There is a familiar joke based upon dissatisfied anticipation. A salesman who is sleeping in a small inn is awakened in the middle of the night by another guest who returns to his room on the upper floor badly intoxicated. With utter disregard for the sleepers, the drunk throws one of his boots to the floor. One hour passes. Finally, the salesman can bear it no longer. He knocks at the wall and shouts: "For God's sake, throw that second boot down, so that I can go back to sleep." Many pictures are full of second boots which fail to fall.

It must be realized that not only the spectator anticipates; the actors on the screen are also in a position to anticipate. The general anticipations, based on universal knowledge, are the same for all human beings: the actor as well as the spectator anticipates that a burning match in the haystack will start a fire. As for other anticipations which are based on specific knowledge, the actor may possess information which is different from that of another actor or from that of the spectator. This was explained in the chapter on division of knowledge. We merely have to add that the anticipations of two actors in respect to the same thing may stand in complete contrast. Or the anticipation of an actor may stand in contrast to that of the audience, which has different information.

This contrast in anticipation is most effective. For instance, a man who is doomed to die makes plans for a new business. He does not know that his illness is deadly, whereas the spectator is so informed. A criminal intends to start an honest life, unaware that his old pals are waiting to kill him. A couple enact a love scene on board the *Titanic.* Their anticipation: a happy honeymoon; the spectator's anticipation: the shipwreck. Or a comic effect frequently used in early movies: somebody carries a pack, not conscious of the fact that it contains dynamite. With complete confidence he lights a match and smokes a cigarette, anticipating that nothing will happen while the spectator anticipates that the dynamite will explode.

Since an event which is planned for the future can move into the present, a relation exists between the anticipated event and its actual execution.

1. We anticipate a certain happening. The event occurs just as it was anticipated. That is: fulfilled expectancy.

2. We anticipate a certain happening. Another event takes place instead. That is: surprise.

Fulfilled expectancy is not necessarily a disadvantage. There will be numerous cases in a story where an anticipated event will take place as it was foreseen. For instance, a man intends to kiss a woman. We anticipate that he will kiss her. He actually does. Or a gangster intends to break a safe. He does.

The danger of fulfilled expectancy is that it is almost a duplication: we are showing the spectator something which he already knows because he foresaw it. Therefore the anticipated event must be shown quickly, if it is shown in fulfillment, or the event must be so thoroughly interesting that the audience will not be bored. In many instances it is interesting to compare the anticipated event with the one which the imagination foresaw.

Surprise is one of the most important effects of any story, whether it is used for comedy or drama or tragedy. Surprise can only be achieved by way of anticipation. We must anticipate that another event will take place in order to be surprised by the actual outcome. If we do not anticipate anything, we cannot possibly be surprised. In this sense, it must be recognized that a perfectly peaceful state of affairs, where absolutely nothing is anticipated, contains a definite anticipation, namely, that nothing will happen. If then suddenly something does happen, our anticipation is surprised.

Such being the case, the spectator must be led to believe in something before he can be surprised. In vaudeville—and no one had better knowledge of dramatic effects than vaudevillians—you will remember with what care a clown prepared his surprise. For instance, a clown starts to jump over a fence. He begins with considerable preparations, making it absolutely clear that he is going to jump. He indicates the great difficulties of this feat, thereby intensifying the anticipation of the spectator. Again and again, he indicates his intention, until the audience anticipates his jumping with absolute certainty. Finally, he walks around the fence. The anticipation of the audience is surprised. The audience is fooled and will laugh. For decades clowns have made people laugh by such simple deception of anticipation. We may also remember the comedian who repeats a funny remark upon each entrance. After three or four times, the anticipation of the audience has become so strong that they will start to laugh upon his entrance. After their anticipation is strong enough, the comedian can surprise them by saying something else, thereby arousing a new wave of laughter.

The same holds true for the drama. For instance, a man has been established as a law-abiding citizen. The audience has been led to believe firmly in his honesty. Suddenly it is shown that he is a criminal. It is obvious that the audience could not be surprised if it had no opinion of the man. Only because the spectator believed in something else could he be surprised.

Charlie Chaplin made frequent use of surprise to cause laughter. In one of his pictures he jumps from a bridge into the water. We anticipate that he plunges into a river. But the river turns out to be a shallow puddle, so that he falls flat on his stomach. In *The Gold Rush* a woman comes smilingly toward him. He anticipates that she smiles at him and is very happy. But the woman passes by and goes to a man who stands behind him. In *The Great Dictator* he prepares to fire an enormous cannon. Again and again, we see the colossal cannon and all his preparations. We anticipate a tremendous explosion and a projectile which will go twenty or thirty miles. Instead, the projectile comes out slowly and falls down at a short distance.

Another effect of anticipation is the delay. Delay is only

possible if we anticipate an event at a certain time. Let us assume that a murderer intends to kill a woman. We know that the hero is to arrive at their house at a certain time. But time passes by and he does not arrive. This delay is extremely effective. If we did not anticipate his arrival, at a certain time, we could not be irritated and excited by the delay. For example, a door opens, and we anticipate that somebody will enter right away; instead, a long time passes before the person enters.

As long as we anticipate a certain event at a certain time, the event may take place too early instead of too late. For instance, a woman thinks that her husband will be absent for a week; instead, he returns after two days and surprises her with another man. Her surprise results from her anticipation that he would return at a later date, while the husband's surprise results from his anticipation that he would find her alone.

Last, it must be recognized that the anticipated event may be pleasant or unpleasant for the spectator. If the anticipated event is pleasant, the spectator will be eager to see it executed. You may have overheard remarks in small movie houses after the hero of the picture has declared his intention to beat hell out of his adversary. Your neighbor may have nudged you and said, "Boy, this is going to be good." You neighbor's enthusiasm is caused by the anticipation of the beating the villain is going to get. He can hardly wait until the motion picture narration gets to this scene. If the hero had failed to make public his goal, your neighbor would have continued chewing his gum in complete boredom, being unable to anticipate something pleasant.

But the anticipation of something unpleasant fills us with fear. For instance, a child has broken a window at home. The father has been characterized as a brutal person.

We fear a frightful beating for the child.

A hopeful anticipation as well as a fearful anticipation can be surprised. The promised beating which the hero was going to administer to the villain can turn out to be a beating for the hero. Our anticipation is surprised. The surprise of a hopeful anticipation can only be disappointment. In the example of fearful anticipation, the brutal father may forgive the child. Again we have surprise. The surprise of a fearful anticipation can only be relief.

In a story with intention and counterintention, the spectator will experience contrasting anticipations: the anticipation of the deeds of the hero, and the anticipation of the deeds of the villain. The first may represent a pleasant and the second an unpleasant anticipation. Consequently, the spectator may experience hope and fear at the very same moment. For instance, the villain is about to torture the hero's girl. We anticipate his deeds and are full of fear. But we also know that the hero is on his way to the house where the villain holds the girl. We anticipate his arrival. We are full of hope, while at the same time we are full of fear. The entire scene before the hero's arrival stands in the shadow of our anticipation of his arrival. The moment he comes in we experience relief, because our fearful anticipation is surprised or destroyed. However, we do not feel surprised because the hero arrived, since we anticipated it. If he were to come too late, our hopeful anticipation would be surprised or disappointed. In order to make either effect possible, we must inform the audience that the hero is on his way to the house.

Thus the screen writer must arrange the story information in such manner as to cause anticipation if he wants to obtain the valuable effects of expectancy and surprise, fear and hope, disappointment and relief.

SUSPENSE

Suspense is a scarecrow for most moviemakers. If there is anything wrong with a picture, it usually is attributed to lack of suspense. If a picture lacks construction, if the story is dull and the line confused, the usual advice is: add some suspense. Great hopes are based on suspense, as if this word contained some magic medicine, as if it had all by itself sufficient power to help us overcome all deficiencies of a narration. Yet few people seem to know exactly the characteristics of suspense and how to achieve this effect.

Despite its importance, suspense is only a secondary effect deriving from other dramatic elements. Suspense becomes possible only with a strong and correct structure. It can never exist by itself, it cannot be added, and it can hardly be corrected or improved by itself, because it depends too much upon the other elements.

Suspense is not an element of the story, but a reaction of the spectator to the story. If it is said that a story has no suspense—it is meant that the spectator is unable to feel suspense when the story is told to him.

Suspense is the doubt of the spectator as to the outcome of an intention of an actor in the story.

Therefore the first necessity in order to achieve suspense is the intention. A story without intentions cannot possibly cause any suspense.

The intention sets a goal. In the absence of any difficulties, there is no doubt that the intention will attain the goal. Because there is no doubt, there is no suspense for us. The story will move quietly toward a goal which has been set by the intention.

In order to create a doubt, the intention must hit against difficulties. In the resulting struggle between intention and difficulties lies the doubt as to whether the intention will be frustrated or fulfilled, and whether the goal will be attained or not. And as long as the spectator doubts the outcome of the intention, he experiences suspense.

It seems as if this were fairly easy to understand. But it is amazing how many different ways are tried to achieve suspense. There is, however, no other way of achieving it than the one described.

One of the frequent mistakes results from the fact that a story without difficulties for its intentions moves quietly toward the goal. Obviously, the spectator cannot experience any suspense. From this, people conclude that the lack of suspense is a result of the clearness of the goal. They think that the spectator does not experience suspense because he knows exactly where the story is heading. They attempt to repair this absence of suspense by withholding the goal. In doing this, they do not create suspense but confusion, because suspense is not blindness but uncertainty.

Lessing in his *Hamburg Dramaturgy* states, "By means of secrecy, a poet achieves a short effect, but in what enduring disquietude could he have maintained us if he had made no secret about it. Whoever is struck down in a moment, I can only pity for a moment. But how if I expect the blow, how if I see the storm brewing about his head?"

The spectator must know where the story is heading, but he must be uncertain whether the goal will be attained or not. And in order to create this uncertainty or doubt, the spectator must know of difficulties standing in the way of these intentions.

Very often, suspense is confused with curiosity. This confusion is understandable—if not pardonable—because the reaction of the spectator is similar. In both cases he asks the same question, What is going to happen? Curiosity, however, results from our lack of knowledge of what the actor wants, while suspense results from our lack of knowledge as to whether the actor's intention will be fulfilled or frustrated. The resulting reaction from our side is similar but the causes for it are different.

Curiosity is our desire to find the goal, while suspense can only exist if we know the goal. Therefore the two are opposed to each other; both cannot exist at the same time. The exposing of the goal which destroys curiosity is the preliminary step for suspense, and the absence of the goal which is necessary for curiosity makes suspense impossible.

Curiosity can be a very good preliminary to suspense. If we are first led to ask, What is the goal? we are more interested in the goal than if we were told right away. After the answer to this question is given, that is, after the goal has been exposed, suspense begins to work if there are difficulties in the way of attaining the goal. Curiosity in relation to the main goal can only exist in the beginning, while suspense can continue throughout the narration. But before each auxiliary goal we can have the transition from curiosity to suspense, if we desire it.

It is easy to make the difference clear by way of an example: A terrorist puts a time bomb in his bag. We know that he wants to blow up something. But we do not know what. We are curious. Later we learn that he wants to blow up a ship. Now we know the goal, but we do not know as yet whether he will attain his goal. We experience suspense: will his intention to blow up the ship be fulfilled or frustrated?

Because the definition of suspense means simply that it is the doubt as to the outcome of an intention, suspense can be achieved in thousands of different ways. For instance, a fugitive is hiding in a barn. A peasant enters the barn. Will the fugitive's intention to hide be fulfilled or frustrated? Or a man wants to catch a train. He is held up by traffic. Will his intention to catch the train be fulfilled or frustrated? Or a jockey intends to participate in an important race. He is locked up in a room by the villains. Will his intention be fulfilled or frustrated? Or a villain is about to commit a crime. Will the hero arrive in time to prevent the fulfillment of the villain's intention?

Suspense is not necessarily bound to blood and murder. A tender love story can have suspense as long as it adheres to the same principles of intention and opposing difficulty, thereby creating a doubt in the mind of the spectator.

Thus intention and difficulty are equally essential in creating a doubt in the spectator. Primarily, it does not matter how strong and powerful each of them is. But it does matter what the balance of strength between them appears to be. For if the strength of the intention appears to be much greater than that of the difficulty, its chances for success and victory are uncontested. Consequently, there can be no doubt as to the outcome. Furthermore, if the strength of the difficulty seems to be considerably greater than the one of the intention, its chances for success are obvious. We cannot doubt that the intention will be frustrated.

In order to achieve a doubt, and thereby suspense, the chances for the success of the intention or of the difficulty must be nearly equal.

Let us assume that you are on an ocean liner. The ocean liner has powerful machines, great resistance against storm and waves; it has instruments of navigation and a trained crew. Its chances for success, that is, crossing the ocean, are far better than are the chances of the ocean—as the difficulty—to resist. We have intention and difficulty, but the chances for success are not equal; therefore we cannot experience suspense. If, however, the ocean liner is torpedoed and the people get into the lifeboats, the chances of success are about equal. The chances of the difficulty lie in the vastness of the ocean, in storm and waves, in the lack of drinking water and so on. The chances of the intention lie in the fact that the survivors may be picked up by passing boats or that the wind will drift them to an island. The equal chances make it possible for us to experience suspense.

Likewise, this applies to an airplane flying from Los Angeles to Honolulu. The chances for the airplane to reach its goal are much better than those of the difficulty to prevent it. This was proven in dozens of previous flights. But let us assume the pilot suddenly discovers that the gasoline tank is leaking. Will the gas last until they reach land? It is the leakage which makes suspense possible, because now the chances for fulfillment and frustration are nearly equal.

Let us assume that you go to a prize fight between the heavyweight champion and an unknown boxer. You will not be able to experience suspense, because you cannot doubt that the champion will win. But if he fights against a well-known and indomitable opponent, the stadium will be full and the crowd will be tense and excited, because the chances for both opponents are about equal. In both cases, the champion may put up an equally vigorous fight, but in the first instance we are not able to experience suspense, and in the second we can.

Translated into story terms, it means the following: two men who want to kill each other offer good suspense, because you have intention and counterintention, or intention and difficulty. If you characterize these two men as strong and ruthless, you have better suspense. A courageous, but resourceless man who wants to kill a coward who is very powerful offers excellent suspense.

Although this seems very obvious in a clear analysis, mistakes of that sort often happen, mostly because of the writer's enthusiasm to make his hero wonderful, and the opponent a combination of all bad and despicable qualities. The latter vilification is permissible as long as the opponent is powerful, and his badness is not identical with weakness. If his despicable qualities are represented as ruthlessness and villainy, and at the same time are combined with power, then suspense is achieved, because the chances of success are about equal. Alfred Hitchcock expressed it like this: "I always respect my villain, build him into a redoubtable character that will make my hero or thesis more admirable in deflating him. . . ."

It was said that the strength of the difficulties which are tackled expose the strength of the intention. Simultaneously, they expose the chances for the success of the intention. For instance, an army of five thousand men defends a bridge. It is not likely that an opposing force of two hundred men will tackle the five thousand men, because the chances of success are too unequal.

It is possible that a cop will single-handedly burst into a nest of gangsters, though it appears as if the odds were all against him. But by the simple fact that he dares to brave such odds, we assume that he must have some reason for doing it; that is, he must have some other chances for success which are as yet unknown to us.

The realization that such situations contain very powerful suspense has led some writers into grave mistakes. They allow the hero to face an obviously desperate situation. Afterwards, he is not saved by some assistance which he was anticipating—a fact which would correspond to the law of the equal chances of fulfillment or frustration—but by some accidental help. This is downright silly. A hero who goes to a place where he knows a dozen criminals are hidden is not a hero but an idiot. If the hero is then saved by the accidental arrival of police, he was not worth saving, and the writer insults the intelligence of the audience.

The spectator weighs the chances subconsciously. But motion pictures have spoiled the natural feeling for weighing the chances to a large extent, because they made a practice of letting everything come out well at the end. We were so used to the hero's victory that we did not give up hope, even though things seemed to be absolutely hopeless. We still felt suspense, even though there seemed to be no possible doubt that the hero's intention would be frustrated. This is false suspense, however, because it is based upon hope and confidence in the kindness of a producer who would not disappoint us by letting things come out in a bad way. The following example will serve to illustrate the difference between true and false suspense: A train carrying the hero and the heroine heads toward a bridge which has been destroyed. The train travels at a speed of seventy miles an hour and there is no warning. Consequently, we should not feel any suspense, because there is little doubt that the train will plunge into the river. But because we like the hero and the heroine, we shall not give up hope that something will prevent the train's intention to fall into the river. This is false suspense. However, if a guard who discovered the fallen bridge, runs as fast as he can toward the train in order to warn the engineer, then we have true suspense. Will the guard warn the engineer in time? Will the train's intention be fulfilled or frustrated? Obviously, true suspense is much more exciting and powerful, and we should search the script carefully for equal or unequal chances. It is very simple, at times, to insert a reason to make the chances equal, as was shown in the above example.

The reasons determining the chances of fulfillment or

frustration of an intention may exist whether the spectator knows about them or not. But we must realize that the spectator cannot experience suspense until he is informed of the difficulties opposing the intention, as we have seen in the example of the train and the guard. From this we derive the demand that the information be given at the opportune moment in order to obtain the best values of suspense.

Let us consider this example: The villain has lured the girl into his home and intends to kill her. We cannot doubt that he will fulfill his intention, for he is stronger than the girl. However, the lead is on his way to the villain's house. If he arrives in time, he may be able to save the girl. Now let us consider when the information about the lead's intention should be given? If we are not informed about this intention, the lead's intention exists nevertheless, but the spectator is not capable of experiencing suspense. All of the villain's preparations for the murder are without suspense. When the lead arrives, his arrival is unexpected and not effective for the spectator. Instead, the information about the lead's intention to go to the house should be given at about the same time that the villain's intention to kill the girl is exposed.

During the progress of the story, the chances for fulfillment or frustration may change and, with them, our doubt. If the difficulty is an obstacle, it may be overcome gradually by the intention. Our doubt or our suspense is subject to very rapid changes. This is desirable because it makes the outcome unpredictable. The victory of one side over the other may either happen gradually or rapidly. This rapid change in the chances for fulfillment or frustration is identical with Aristotle's conception of the reversal: After the chances for both have been equal for a long time or even favorable to one side, suddenly one or the other gains decisive superiority. We say decisive superiority, because there must be one point where the doubt about victory or defeat of the intention must be replaced by certainty. And this decision is the climax.

If suspense is the questioning about the outcome of intentions, the climax gives the answer. After the climax there is no more doubt possible about whether the intention will be frustrated or fulfilled. An answer dissolves a question. The climax destroys suspense. It is therefore clear that the climax should be as near the end of the picture as possible in order to make use of suspense up to the very end. The climax is not identical with the end of the story. It simply represents the decision as to victory or elimination of the difficulty. The progress of the story from climax to attainment of goal is without interest because it lacks suspense. We can even go as far as to imply the actual attainment of the goal, because there is no doubt left that it will be reached. This is the case in many love stories. After all the difficulties have been eliminated, we need not show the lovers married.

This completes our investigation of the nature of suspense.

THE FORWARD MOVEMENT

Moviemakers are very much concerned with the forward movement of a picture. They will exclaim enthusiastically that it moves at a rapid pace or they may sigh in dejection that it is slow. This may be the case with the entire picture, or only with certain parts. "It drags in spots." Thereupon, the slow spots are cut shorter and shorter, until hardly anything is left, which makes other parts of the picture difficult to understand. The mystery of the slow or fast forward movement of the picture can seldom be solved by cutting.

Of course, it is not the picture which moves fast or slowly, because the picture is driven forward by the electric motor of the projection machine at a steady speed. It is the mind of the spectator which must be moved forward from the beginning of the story to its end.

The mind and the imagination of the spectator are fundamentally inert. They sit down with the spectator in the seat of the theatre. They have no forward movement of their own. But they have the faculty for certain reactions. By arranging the story elements in the right order the writer is able to attract the mind of the spectator to move forward. If the story fails to contain these elements, the verdict of the spectator is that the picture was slow, long, and boring.

The forward movement is something new—brought about by the form of motion pictures—and moviemakers have good reason to be concerned about it. The theatre is not so interested in the forward movement, because its time is uninterrupted. Each second of its scene or act represents a second of actual time. Therefore it cannot move faster or slower, and the movement of the mind of the theatre spectator is identical with the movement of the play, neither slower nor faster. The novel does not know this kind of forward movement, because the reader can put the book away at any time he likes and does not have to sit through from the beginning to the end. Furthermore, the novel has the connecting sentences which lead the reader smoothly forward, while the interruptions after each scene in the picture are felt very harshly. It must be realized that the lapse of time between scenes interrupts the smooth flowing of the forward movement.

Each scene represents an even forward movement because the time in each scene is identical with actual time. But the lapse of time—being of different length—represents a very dangerous discontinuation of the forward movement.

We must understand that the form of the motion picture is not a continuous entity; instead, it is a conglomeration of blocks, represented by shots and scenes. These blocks have the tendency to fall apart, thereby interrupting the continuity of the story in a decisive manner. In order to overcome these breaks we must search for connecting elements within the story. If these elements of the story overlap the breaks caused by the technical subdivision, we can achieve connection. With this in mind, we understand the predominant importance of the forward movement in motion pictures compared to that in other forms of storytelling.

We must search for the elements in the story which cause our imagination to move forward. In order to find them, it is necessary that we understand the elements of dramatic construction very thoroughly. Only a moviemaker with very definite knowledge of the laws of dramatic construction is in a position to make a motion picture which "moves fast."

If we were to compare our mind with that of a man who walks on a highway, we would undoubtedly believe that he knows where he is going. He must have a goal, otherwise he would not walk, but stand still or sit down. And this is exactly what the mind of the spectator does during his march along the story if he is not told what the goal is.

In order to cause any kind of forward movement a goal must be set. The setting of a goal is the preliminary condition for the forward movement. Without it, the spectator will not move, and the picture will be slow, and uninteresting.

As soon as the goal is set, the spectator anticipates the possibility of its attainment. This anticipation expresses itself as a desire to arrive at the goal. And this desire causes the forward movement in the mind of the spectator.

In general, our anticipation works so strongly that we want to attain the goal immediately and resent the actual execution of the intention before attaining the goal. The delay caused by necessary but time-absorbing actions appears as a hindrance of the forward movement.

In order to eliminate this impression of hindrance we have to insert doubt, that is, suspense, because then the attainment of the goal which is desired by our forward movement is not merely hindered by a delay but made altogether uncertain. Suspense is fundamentally an unpleasant feeling from which the spectator would like to escape. This sounds strange because we know that suspense is very desirable for the movie script.

Being an unpleasant feeling, suspense helps the forward movement. We would like to obtain certainty. It is often said that the certainty of something bad is preferable to uncertainty which leaves open the chance for the happy outcome. It is said that the certainty of the death of a relative is less tormenting than if he is missing. Therefore, in order to run away from the uncertainty which is felt as suspense, the spectator moves forward toward the goal and toward the decision which makes clear the outcome of the intention.

As such, the forward movement of the mind of the spectator is a product of his anticipation and his suspense. For anticipation, we need a goal, which, as we remember, can only be set by an intention. And for suspense, we need a doubt as to the outcome of the intention, which, as we remember, can only be created by a difficulty.

It is our desire to create a smooth and fast forward

movement of the mind of the spectator. Now that we know its causes, we can proceed to arrange the elements of the story in such a manner that we may obtain the best possible results.

We find that the main goal of the story should be set as early as possible in order to cause anticipation; this means that the intention setting the goal should start very near the beginning. At the exact moment at which the intention begins and the goal is set, the forward movement starts, because anticipation makes us desire the goal. Before the goal has been set or before the main intention has been exposed or caused, the story will slouch along at a slow and reluctant pace; it will only gather speed after the main goal is clear. Previous to that, we have no desire to get anywhere—we sit still.

As soon as the anticipation begins to work, we begin to resent all further actions as a hindrance if we do not experience any doubt as to whether the goal will be attained. Again we feel that the picture is slow.

In order to make our speed identical with that of the picture, we have to insert the doubt. The difficulty opposing the intention and making the attainment of the goal uncertain must be exposed soon after the intention has been set. If the time elapsing between the exposition of the two is too long, we have the disagreeable feeling of being hindered in our forward movement.

It was said that the climax dissolves our doubt or suspense. This being the case, we must take care that the climax is near the end of the picture, for after the climax, or after the destruction of suspense, we begin to experience the same feeling of hindrance if we cannot attain the goal shortly.

Lastly, it must be said that the main goal must coincide with the end of the picture. Our forward movement stops the moment the goal is attained. If the picture proceeds further, that is, if it moves forward after the goal has been

attained, we are unable to follow. The rest of the picture—
from the moment that the main goal is attained to the end
—ambles along or dangles in the air.

In looking back, we already find four definite reasons
for creating or hindering the forward movement. And
furthermore, we see that the speed of the forward movement is subject to changes. It can be slow in the beginning, then take on speed, then become slow again, then
gather speed, then lose it again, and stop completely before the end, according to the time when the main intention begins, when the difficulty appears, when the climax
takes place, and when the main goal is attained as compared to the actual ending of the picture.

Now we are ready to find further determining factors
for the forward movement. The main goal is attracting
the mind of the spectator. But it must be realized that
much of its strength of attraction is being lost in the
distance. The further away we are from the main goal,
the more its power of attraction is weakened. Obviously,
we are furthest away in the beginning of the story. The
more we proceed, the closer we come.

We could compare the main goal to a powerful magnet.
In order to overcome the weakening of the power of
attraction because of the distance, we can put up smaller
magnets along the road which attract us forward. As soon
as each one is reached, its magnetic power is extinguished; thereby our forward movement is continuous
and gathers momentum toward the main goal.

These magnets along the road are represented by the
auxiliary goals. Since they are goals, they can be anticipated by the spectator, and if they are anticipated, they
cause a forward movement. If they are wisely arranged,
they contribute greatly to our forward motion until the
main goal becomes powerful enough to attract us by itself.

There is no fixed rule or ratio which would guide their

distribution. They should be chosen in accordance with the necessities and requirements of each individual story. Each story contains innate auxiliary goals, and even though their distribution is irregular, it may be satisfactory and does not demand any correction. However, if there are large spaces without any auxiliary goal, our forward movement slows down. These large spaces without auxiliary goals are so-called slow spots or dull parts of the picture although much may be happening in these parts. But we are not led to anticipate anything—therefore we do not move forward. Frequently, the cutter is supposed to correct these deficiencies in the completed picture by cutting out sections from these dull spots. Yet this correction was the duty of the writer, who should have inserted or created auxiliary goals.

It is a fundamental principle that it is the anticipation of an auxiliary goal which causes the forward movement, and not the briskness of the dialog or the swift action of a scene. Imagine, for instance, a scene in which a man visits a woman. He talks brilliantly, his dialog is brief and precise, and the scene ends before any apparent dull moment could occur—yet the scene is without forward movement, as we do not anticipate any auxiliary goal. Imagine now that we know this man came to see the woman in order to kill her. He comes in and begins to talk about the weather. No matter how dull and slow the dialog, no matter how many uninteresting things may be said, the scene will have an uncanny forward movement, because an attracting auxiliary goal exists. As a matter of fact, the hindrance caused by the slowness of the actions and dullness of the dialog makes us all the more conscious of our forward movement. It makes us impatient and this impatience strengthens our will to get somewhere—it strengthens our forward movement.

Thus the experienced writer can exploit the attraction

of a good auxiliary goal even further. The strong forward movement will help to alleviate the hindrances caused by much exposition and unavoidable information. Even the best writer cannot escape giving certain expositions which are less interesting than the rest of the story. But he may give them in this way: A person approaches a man in an attempt to learn something which is extremely interesting. The man, either through stupidity or ill will, talks about everything else, but not about that particular subject. "Everything else" the man talks about, is of course exposition and information which we would hardly want to listen to if it were not for our forward movement caused by the anticipated auxiliary goal. The writer has transformed a deficiency into an excellent dramatic effect. Not only does he give us the exposition, but in doing so he accentuates our anticipation by making us impatient. The auxiliary goal as a magnet draws us over the slow spots. Our forward movement is hindered by the difficulty which—in this case—only intensifies our will to arrive at the auxiliary goal. Let us consider for a moment how far we have already advanced: not only are we able to cause the forward movement, but we can even dare to hinder this forward movement, thereby gaining a new effect.

In order to obtain the smoothest forward movement, we must be aware of the following fact: the auxiliary goal has the capacity of attracting us until it is reached. But as soon as it is reached, it loses its attraction. The extinction of the attracting power of the auxiliary goal has a tendency to stop our forward movement. It has the tendency to let us slump down. As soon as one auxiliary goal is eliminated, the duty of moving forward the mind of the spectator rests upon the following auxiliary goal or goals, and of course upon the main goal. It is clear that this duty can only be transferred if the following auxiliary goal exists already and not if it must be set after the preceding goal was extinguished. In order to guarantee a smooth forward movement, the following auxiliary goal must be set somewhere in the middle of the previous intention. Then it takes over automatically where the first goal leaves off. But if the new auxiliary goal is set only after the preceding goal has been eliminated, our forward movement will result in jumps and halts and not in a continuous flow toward the conclusion of the story.

To make this appear more clearly, we can represent graphically the correct and the wrong appearance of the auxiliary goal. Let us assume that the entire picture is represented as a straight line. The main intention should begin with the beginning of the picture, and the main goal should be attained at the end. Underneath, we can show the subintentions as smaller lines, beginning with the motivation and ending with the auxiliary goal. Not only is it necessary to have a fairly even distribution of the auxiliary goals, but the beginning of the subintentions must overlap each other.

Motive	Main Intention	Main-Goal
M		G

	motivation	auxiliary goal			
m	g				
	m	g			
		m	g		
m			g		
			m	g	

In the graphic description, we are able to distinguish clearly the connecting power of these overlapping subintentions. We must remember that the closer we come to the auxiliary goal, the stronger its power of attraction. After the one is eliminated, we approach the succeeding

one, which in turn begins to attract us more and more.
Now consider a representation of faulty connection:

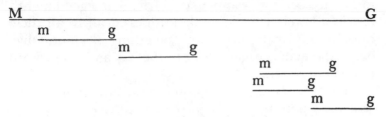

It is apparent that after each auxiliary goal, we are left
without attraction. Our forward movement stops. Then
suddenly a new auxiliary goal is set, which makes us rush
forward. After it is eliminated, we are let down again.
Our progress is similar to that of an old automobile—a
series of jerks and stalls and not the smooth forward
movement of a modern engine.

It may seem that our conclusions are very abstract.
However, after these factors are thoroughly understood,
their application is fairly simple. It is not too difficult to
recognize the essential subintentions in a story. After they
have been recognized, it is a simple matter to find where
they are revealed, that is, at what moment the spectator
begins to anticipate an auxiliary goal.

Thereafter one recognizes at once whether there are
large spaces of story time without subintentions, and
therefore without forward movement, and whether the subintentions are overlapping one another or not.

It is necessary that we compare the capacity of the
auxiliary goals and of the main goal in their relation to
each other. First we must recognize that the goal may
arouse the anticipation of something pleasant or of something unpleasant. And these two different types of anticipation affect the forward movement.

Let us again compare our mind with that of a man who

walks on a highway toward a distant city which is his goal. The man may anticipate a wonderful dinner after he gets to the city, or he may anticipate a friend or a good night's rest in a hotel or a profitable business deal. In all these cases his anticipation contains something pleasant. Obviously, the man is eager to get to the city and his forward movement is fast.

However, it may be that the man anticipates a jail sentence upon his arrival in the city or that he expects a beating from his enemies. We are safe to assume that he will refuse to move forward, unless he is compelled by some powerful reason.

These examples refer to the anticipation caused by a main goal. The anticipation of pleasant or unpleasant things with respect to the auxiliary goals affects the forward movement in a different way. If the main goal is to get to the distant city, and the main anticipation contains something pleasant, like the union of two lovers, the auxiliary goals can be unpleasant without disturbing the forward movement. Auxiliary goals are unpleasant if the man has to suffer cold and hunger, has to sleep in hard beds, and becomes tired from the strain of his voyage. All this, however, will not make him stop, because the main anticipation is pleasant.

Translated into motion picture terms, we understand that the mind of the spectator will move forward more eagerly if he anticipates a happy ending. It will not move forward if it has to expect " a beating" upon arrival. The auxiliary goals may be unpleasant and terrorizing. But their terror will not disturb the forward movement, because they are only stepping stones on our way to attain something pleasant. As a matter of fact, this terror of the anticipated auxiliary goals may be a new cause for accelerated forward movement: we want to get it over with in order to arrive at the pleasant main goal.

Let us again consider the example of the man on the highway: We notice that he is standing before a road sign. At the bottom of the sign he reads the name of the distant city—the main goal—in large letters. Above, in much smaller type, he finds the name of three or four towns which come before this main goal. The main goal is made clear by the size of its lettering.

Let us assume that a sailor who is easily persuaded comes ashore in San Diego. He wants to go to his home town, which is thirty miles beyond San Francisco. The auxiliary goal as represented by San Francisco is much more attractive and much more important than the main goal which is his home town. There is every reason to suspect that this particular sailor will remain in San Francisco and get drunk and never reach his home town. This can be very easily altered by reminding the sailor that his best girl, whom he has not seen in two years, is waiting for him in the home town. Immediately, all the attractions and seductions of San Francisco lose their power over him, and the big city becomes an unimportant station before the great goal of seeing his girl again.

May we be permitted to compare our imagination to a drunkard who has very little resistance against any kind of temptation. Our intelligence can be very adult and full of will power. But our imagination remains childlike. It is intrigued by the slightest sensation; it is aroused by the lightest temptation, and then it is very difficult to control. Should one of the auxiliary goals become more attractive or more interesting than the main goal, the imagination, like the drunken sailor, will only reluctantly move on. The result is that from this attractive auxiliary goal on, the journey to the end of the story becomes uninteresting because the forward movement is hopelessly reduced.

Frequently, the author fails to make clear which is his main intention and which his subintention. Then the spectator may falsely assume that a subintention is the main intention, believing that the end of the picture is reached when the auxiliary goal is attained. To his astonishment, the picture drags on until what the author believes to be the main goal has been reached.

The attraction of the main goal must be the most powerful of all. However, a comparatively unattractive auxiliary goal in the beginning will still be able to attract us because the powerful attraction of the main goal is so far away. The closer we approach the main goal, the stronger the auxiliary goals must become in order to exert any kind of attraction.

This is the dramatic graduation of values. A light love scene at the beginning of a picture may be very good. The same scene before a bullfight which may cost the life of the matador, would seem ridiculous. The love scene must become important, tragic, or poignant.

Thus every following event must be more attractive in order to move us forward, in order to make an impression upon us. This graduation must be applied to every part, to every element of the story. Every characterization must grow toward the end. Every emotion must be gradually strengthened. Every decision must become graver. Every event must become more interesting. This represents no small problem. If the writer fails to achieve thorough graduation of all the elements, he will be confronted with effects which he had not intended. Those parts which he fails to graduate will remain stagnant, losing interest and value because the others have progressed.

If well handled, the uneven graduation may become an effect. For instance, a battalion of soldiers passes, on its way to battle, a farmer who is tilling his soil. On the way back, the soldiers meet him again. In the meantime, they have gone through hell, they have fought, they have suffered, their friends have been killed, but the farmer is still there, working his soil as before.

Professor George Pierce Baker, in his *Dramatic Technique,* writes that it is the common aim of all dramatists to win as promptly as possible the attention of the audience. This unquestionably correct demand has often been misunderstood. It is true that the interest of the audience should be aroused immediately, but not by events which are so impressive as to prevent a subsequent graduation.

While it is desirable to begin with interesting events, impressive events should be saved for later on in order to obtain a steady graduation. It requires discipline, restraint, and wisdom to arrange the events in such manner as to obtain an even graduation. Many pictures achieve a terrific beginning—which is desired by most producers—but are unable to continue. They throw the spectator into forward movement with a jerk but are unable to keep up the speed. Most of these pictures are disappointing toward the end, for no other reason than the fact that the powerful beginning cannot be graduated. If the beginning were less impressive, the rest of the picture would become more interesting. In Hollywood one speaks of a school of first act writers. Their "first acts," that is, the beginnings of their stories, are very powerful, but the rest is disappointing. At times this first act serves its purpose: it induces the producer to read a script, instead of discarding it after a few pages. But it does not serve the purpose of making good pictures for the audience. Such stories are topheavy, and no effort of rewriting can balance them, because no graduation is possible.

Television has aggravated this danger by its demand that the viewer be "hooked" at the very first moment. Years ago, the filmmakers could count on a captive audience in the movie theaters, so that they developed their expositions at a more leisurely pace. But today, when a nervous switching to another channel may bring about the demise of a series in the rat (ing) race, the viewers have been conditioned to beginnings that pack a wallop. And the moviemakers, aware that their theatrical films will end up on television, have increasingly speeded up their openings, to the point of capturing audience interest before the main title.

A startling or dramatic opening does not necessarily preclude a subsequent crescendo of emotional and suspenseful clashes. The gimmick at the beginning, no matter how explosive the impact, does not yet affect the audience as strongly as a less forceful scene after we have become involved with the protagonists of the story.

Nevertheless, it becomes clear that we should only choose emotions and characterizations which will allow graduation. They must be planned in such manner as to make the gradual strengthening possible. Many a script, in a natural desire to graduate its intentions toward the end, permits them to outrange their motives and characterizations. The result is ridiculous: we may remember the example of the engineer who finds himself fighting for his life while all he wanted was three hundred dollars a week. The result of graduated intentions from weak motives is a giant on baby feet. It may also happen that the subintention is more powerful than the main intention, which again is ridiculous. In order to overcome such dangers, the writer should choose his characterizations and main motives for strength; then he has ample possibilities of strengthening the subintention toward the end without disrupting the proportion between the elements of the story.

The climax of this development comes when no further graduation is possible. This means that graduation should be distributed over such a space that its highest point coincides with the end of the picture. If this moment is reached earlier, the remainder of the picture becomes stagnant. If the picture ends at a time when we are still able to anticipate a further graduation of its elements, the end comes unexpectedly and unsatisfactorily.

Graphically, correct graduation would look like this:

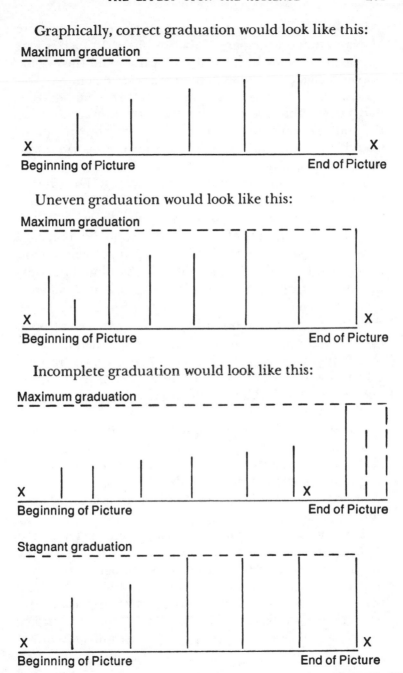

Maximum graduation

X   X
Beginning of Picture   End of Picture

Uneven graduation would look like this:

Maximum graduation

X   X
Beginning of Picture   End of Picture

Incomplete graduation would look like this:

Maximum graduation

X   X
Beginning of Picture   End of Picture

Stagnant graduation

X   X
Beginning of Picture   End of Picture

Graduation seems to require an extremely subtle sense of evaluation on the part of the spectator. In fact, it may appear that the realization of such values and the evaluation of the general strengthening of each element requires a sensibility which is far beyond the average audience. It may appear that the possibility of further graduation at the end of the picture could not be realized by the public. Could this mean that graduation is an unimportant and uncertain principle?

This assumption would be entirely wrong. The subconscious mind of the public has a judgment which is infallible. Its instinctive evaluation is by far superior to the concentrated thinking of the writer. It could be compared to a photographic film. A camera with its lens almost closed will leave hardly any trace on the film. The same film will record further designs if the lens is opened further. Even though we may photograph another subject, the film will always record other contours should we open the lens more and more. This can be continued until the sensitivity of the film is exhausted. However, the reciprocal process is impossible. After an exposure with a fully opened lens any feebler photographs will not be recorded on the film.

Our subconscious receptiveness acts with the same precision as the photographic film. It records the values of each scene with a precise sense of graduation. If there is stagnation or even reversion of the progress, it will leave a blank on our receptive mind. Our reaction is uninterest, boredom, impatience or forgetfulness.

The forward movement represents an exertion and therefore contains the danger of fatigue. If we analyze the fatigue of a human being closely, we recognize that it is only partly caused by actual exhaustion, and for the other part it is a result of the misconception of the task before us. Whether we have physical or mental exertion before us, in either case we appropriate a certain amount of

psychological energy for the task, according to our estimate of the need. If our estimate was wrong, that is, if the
task is more difficult than we expected, we shall feel
fatigue, because the energy that we appropriated was not
sufficient. If, however, our estimate was correct from the
beginning, then we shall feel less fatigue despite the fact
that we are confronted with the very same exertion.

Again let us use the example of the man on the highway. If the distance before him is two miles, he will be
able to walk faster without fear of exhaustion; if it is
thirty-four miles, he will have to cut down his speed
considerably, in order to save his strength. If he did not
know the distance, he might use the wrong speed and fall
down exhausted before reaching his goal.

Translating this into motion picture terms, we find the
following principle: If fatigue is only partly caused by
actual exhaustion, and for the other part by a miscalculation of the task, we must enable the spectator to make a
correct estimate of the distance before him. The actual
exhaustion of the spectator results from the strain on his
eyes and ears, and from his mental processes, as experiencing emotions, anticipation, suspense, evaluation. But this
actual exhaustion is infinitely smaller compared with the
fatigue through miscalculation.

It is not easy, in the motion picture to let the spectator
estimate the distance. The stage play which is divided
into two or five acts of about equal length lets us clearly
distinguish the time of its ending. In reading a novel the
number of pages left lets us recognize the exact distance
which has yet to be traversed. Besides, the element of
fatigue does not exist in the novel because the number of
pages we read in one sitting depends upon our energies.

But the moviegoer can only estimate the distance if a
goal has been set. Once he knows the main goal, the
spectator has a continuous feeling for the distance which
has yet to be traversed. He can estimate the difficulties in

the way of the main intention. If the picture exceeds this estimated ending point, the spectator feels fatigue. If the end of the picture comes too early, he is left with superfluous energies which cause dissatisfaction. If no goal has been set, there is no distance which could be estimated.

After these investigations, we are in a position to balance the progression or sequence of events in the story with the forward movement of the spectator.

First of all we must cause the forward movement. But then we must arrange the sequence of events and scenes of the script in such manner that they will satisfy the forward movement which was caused.

It is true that the sequence of events must be logical and consecutive on the basis of cause and effect. But it must also be such as not to interrupt or interfere with the forward movement of the spectator.

In most pictures one can change some scenes around without any apparent damage to the action, and without any violation of the consecutive progress of time, particularly if we interpose scenes of two different story lines. Very often, scenes are changed around at the last moment; sometimes they are even reversed after completion of the picture. At times, this can be done without distorting their meaning, but it may disturb the forward movement of the spectator.

In order to guarantee a smooth forward movement, the sequence of events and scenes has to follow the interest of the spectator. The same principle was established when we found that the camera had to follow the shifting interest of the spectator.

Failure of the story to follow our interest gives us the impression of a chopped-up script. This feeling does not result from a large number of scenes, nor does it result from the fact that these scenes occur in many different places. It simply results because the sequence of scenes does not follow our interest.

Of course, if there is no forward movement, there is no interest, and the sequence of scenes cannot follow anything. All the scenes will hang loosely together without any arrangement. So the first step is to create interest and thereafter follow it.

Primarily, it is the intention of an actor which causes our anticipation and forward movement and interest. An intention necessarily prepares a following scene where this intention will be executed or frustrated. These intentions cause us to believe that the following or one of the following sets will show us the anticipated place. As common an intention as "I'm going to bed" need not be followed up because it does not create any interest. But in no event is it possible to show a man in Singapore who says, "I'm going to New York," unless you give extensive explanation. Any intention which creates interest must be followed up.

However, it is not necessary that a scene which is prepared should follow immediately. Instead, it may follow at a later moment. But this delay cannot be chosen willfully.

Our immediate reaction is to anticipate that the scene which is prepared by the intention will follow immediately. But an intention may be connected with a certain lapse of time. In that case, we are relieved from the necessity of letting the execution follow directly.

If the time element does not relieve us of the necessity of following up the interest immediately, the sequence of scenes must be immediate. Should the script writer—for some reason or other—give us another scene which may possibly represent another story line, he is hindering our forward movement. This may be used on the basis of attraction and hindrance in order to make the spectator impatient. But if he fails to realize that intention or motive have thoroughly prepared another scene, and if he puts two or three other scenes in between, he may interfere with our forward movement. At the same time, he takes away all the strength and power of the interfering scenes because our interest lies in another direction, and this prevents us from concentrating upon these other events. It is very dangerous to hinder the attraction of one anticipation by interposing equally important scenes; that results in a splitting of our interest.

The knowledge of all the facts creating or hindering the forward movement makes it easy to find and correct any possible faults in the script. The strange behaviour of motion pictures with respect to their speed has lost its mystery.

Chapter 6

Television, Cable and Pay TV, Video, Satellite Broadcasts

Technology develops rapidly, but the psychological and emotional make-up of people changes only imperceptibly. Therefore the effects on the viewers, described in the previous chapter, cannot be altered by satellite broadcasts, laser beam systems, or wall projections in your own future "home entertainment center."

Whether the spinners of yarns may some day be called cassette-creators, pay-television dramatizers, or computerized story-relay technicians, they will have to tell a story.

Throughout this book, film and television techniques have been described simultaneously, unless they were specifically differentiated. Now, some particular aspects of television must be examined.

The intimacy the small screen provided is no longer an exclusive television attribute, as the diagonals keep growing larger. Big budget features are now seen more frequently on cable TV than low-cost "movies-of-the week."

Conversely, the same film may affect you differently, when seen in the privacy of your home or in the large movie palace. This is especially true of comedies; the laughter of the public around you is infectious. TV's laugh-tracks are inadequate substitutes for the indefinable subconscious communication within a group. In fact, even professionals, watching a comedy in a studio projection room, may consider it less funny than the hilarity of theater audiences later demonstrate.

THE TELEVISION SERIES

Paradoxically, the modern series has its roots in the outdated movie serials. The TV series has become the most popular viewer attraction on the tube. For the writer who creates a long-running series, it is financially most rewarding.

The two-hour TV movie must establish its characters from scratch and complete their development in the relatively short time allotted to it.

The series can familiarize the audience with the leads in weekly episodes. The characters become friends or enemies, sometimes better known to the viewers than their next-door neighbors. Gradually, they become more than acquaintances. We are aware of their traits, their habits, and their quirks. We look forward to our next meeting with them at the appointed time. The are part of our TV family.

FORMAT AND PRESENTATION

Since the creation of a TV series can be so lucrative, I am often asked how an idea should be presented. First, the idea for a series must have the potential for a continuous supply of story material. A dramatic incident or one comedic situation may be excellent in themselves. But if the overall concept does not project the potential for a series that could run two, three or more years, the network may not consider it worth the risk of a pilot.

After describing the basic concept, the merit of the series format should be demonstrated by several story springboards. They need be no longer than one paragraph. They may be preceded by a one-page outline, involving the lead characters in a sample episode.

Brief character sketches of the continuing leads should be included. Usually not more than four or five are necessary. After a series concept has been acquired by a production company or network, the do's and don'ts regarding a series are worked out in detail. The parameters are fixed for outside submissions as well as for staff writers. If the series flags in the ratings wars, some anxious shifting of the parameters begins.

Brevity is essential for the initial presentation. Busy executives abhor reading. A basic dilemma in the entertainment industry remains the fact that bustling decision-makers do not find enough time to read, while their "readers" can only make negative decisions.

If possible, the first paragraph should capture attention, spark interest, and incite the wish to find out what follows. The initial presentation need not be longer than ten pages. More can be attached to the basic proposal. But it is in that first summation where the battle is often won—or lost.

SOME PRACTICAL HINTS

It is often believed that some people are creative and others are not. Fundamentally, this distinction is a fallacy. Everybody daydreams at times; this free play of imagination is a form of creating. Some talented artists are creative beyond the ordinary. Still, it is a matter of degree.

Inspiration, as was said earlier, can be trained. Imagination can be stimulated. For instance, let us assume you wrote the name of your lead character: "Paul." Now visualize the color of the suit he wears. After imagining several colors, you may settle on jeans and a checkered shirt. You see him walking down the street; he stops to talk to an acquaintance. Even as you read this, you can't help evoke in your mind his tousled hair. By now you enjoy inventing traits of his character—whether or not you will use all of them in your script.

Not only will it vitalize your imagination, but it is helpful to learn everything about the leads in your script. In the course of "fleshing them out," nothing is superfluous. Any detail you write down about them will help to uncover contradictions you overlooked. Whatever you ferret out about their youth, their relatives and friends, and their living habits contributes to bringing them to life. Although you will only find space to use highlights in the script, their motives and actions will be convincing, their dialog will ring true.

The more you dig into the motion picture language, the dramatic structure, and the methods of story telling, the more you will be interested in your own reactions to the movies and TV shows you watch. As you progress toward professionalism, you will make a conscious effort to remain partially outside your total involvement in the drama. Thereby you will confirm the application of what you have already learned, you will practice by observing the example. Most likely, you will also detect mistakes.

Afterwards, you may find it useful to sketch a brief resume of the filmed story for your own examination. Perhaps, the inner workings of a structure will come to the fore; secrets of the trade will be exposed. You can take advantage of the fact that abundant study material is constantly at your disposal.

PROTECTION

It is advisable to protect your manuscript, which you can do in one of two ways. If it is a novel, a complete screenplay, a stage play, or a musical, the Library of Congress will copyright it for you.

Write to:

REGISTRAR OF COPYRIGHTS
LIBRARY OF CONGRESS
WASHINGTON, D.C. 20559

They will send you the appropriate forms (for a nondramatic literary work or a performing arts work) with instructions on how to fill them out. After you send them the "Work" with a check of about $10, you will obtain the legal protection of copyright.

If your manuscript is a format, outline, synopsis, storyline, or script specifically intended for theatrical motion pictures or television, you can register it with the Writers Guild of America, either in New York or Hollywood:

Writers Guild of America, East
555 West 57th Street
New York, New York 10019

Writers Guild of America, West
8955 Beverly Blvd.
Los Angeles, Calif. 90048

The Writers Guild will not read, judge, submit, or sell your script for you. But upon receipt of a clean copy and $10–$15 for nonmembers, it will seal your "Work" in an envelope, date it, and preserve it for 10 years, after which an extension can be obtained.

The effect of this procedure is that you can furnish proof on which date your work existed. In case of conflict, proof of priority can be legally helpful.

PART III

THE DRAMATIC CONSTRUCTION

Chapter 1

From Idea
to Final Form

A WRITER is frequently asked about the basic ideas from which he develops his stories and scripts. The original concept seems to arouse as much interest as its subsequent growth. Often, almost magic powers are attributed to the truly creative notion, as distinguished from one that is unproductive; indeed, it is often assumed that the "good" idea appears full-blown in the writer's mind, replete with the capacity to grow of itself along inherent and foreordained lines.

Nothing could be further from the truth. Any writer looking back upon his completed works will recall that the first ideas have come to him in a rudimentary or fragmentary form, in a variety of ways, and, more often than not, in a completely unpredictable manner. Even the most disciplined creator cannot control or willfully produce the moment of inspiration, though he may have otherwise trained his imaginative powers to be at their peak during certain working hours, or in a given set of circumstances, or under the prodding of habit and idiosyncrasy. Further, at the instant of their first appearance, some of his best ideas may have gone almost unnoticed; only in retrospect can he recognize which seed fell on fertile ground, which spark could be fanned to creative flames, which notion was productive of results, fulfilling an earlier, uncertain promise.

Since the fundamental concept determines the outcome of the whole, it is of the utmost importance for the writer to choose wisely among many possible ideas before committing himself to the time and effort involved in full development. Yet in the beginning, when he has to make this selection, he has insufficient material upon which to base his choice.

Being incomplete, the initial notion cannot yet be "good"; indeed, many a promising idea may have been squashed, or rejected by an outsider, because it was offered too soon, submitted to impersonal view before its potential had been given a chance to manifest itself.

The very nature of the primary impulse is such as to elude definition. It is not identical with the subject matter, though this may be part of it; nor with the theme, though this may be found in it. It may be a childhood memory, a dominant character trait, even a glimpse of landscape or a fragment of dialog.

The teeming brain never ceases to produce images, thoughts, ideas. Of these, many are so fleeting as to escape our attention almost entirely; some are briefly examined and rejected; others are considered, perhaps tested and worked on for a while, but ultimately forgotten. And then there are those which, for some reason or another, have a unique effect upon us and are not to be dismissed, no matter how hard we may try; they sometimes return to us over a period of years.

In its embryonic stage the ultimately successful idea

seems to offer no other criterion than this intuitive affinity the writer feels for it. It has the peculiar capacity to stir his imagination and to remain in his memory until he has given it form.

Nor is it surprising that the initial selection should be made on this very personal basis. If a character, a situation, or a background has the power to affect us in some way, to linger on or to return to us over a period of time, it indicates some special, perhaps unconscious, appeal or meaning to us. In the arduous labors of developing the script, all our creative energies are then likely to participate; we have "our heart in it," we are more than rationally interested, we take pleasure in giving it form.

It stands to reason, therefore, that the subjective, rather than the objective, choice of the basic idea is likely to lead to the best results. Since no objectively valid value standards can be applied in the rudimentary stage, our individual involvement is likely to prove the decisive factor.

Thus the original concept represents the most personal contribution of the writer. At the other end of the creative process is the final script, directed at a mass audience; to be understood, the personal must be cast into objective language—the subjective into a universally valid form.

It may be said, therefore, that the creative process begins in the subjective and ends in the impersonal. Individual emotion must be expressed in terms of the commonly identifiable experience. Only in this manner can the dramatist achieve the desired effect of evoking in the individual spectator the emotions he intended to stir. The poet can largely dispense with this detour, aiming directly at the heart of his reader. But the screenwriter has to follow the full span from the subjective to the objective in order to reproduce in the individual spectator the subjective response once again.

In developing his basic idea toward this goal, the writer

finds that the final form foreshadows its demands upon the earliest stages of growth. On the one hand, the primary concept remains the seed around which the crystal conglomerates; it continues to be the mainspring which powers the story and script. On the other hand, we must soon ask ourselves which direction to take in order to reach the objective of the particular form we have selected, if indeed the fundamental idea lends itself to that objective.

As the various outlets for the writer's creative efforts change in nature, it becomes increasingly important for him to learn how to evaluate the potential of his idea at the earliest possible stage.

The strong situation which had promised to provide all the conflict and drama for a feature film reveals itself as too introverted a character study in its final resolution. Conversely, the idea which had seemed so right for a half-hour television show may really require an hour, or perhaps even ninety minutes, for full development.

By necessity, if not by choice, more and more writers are becoming experts in different forms. Consequently, a writer no longer has to reject an idea because it happens to be unsuitable to the specific medium in which he is working at that moment. Instead, he can jot it down, file it away for future reference, and take it out again when it has either ripened to the point where he feels impelled to work it out or when it can fulfill the demands of an outside request.

Since the creative mind produces ideas spontaneously and without much regard for the length of stories required by a certain magazine, or the running time of a particular television series, the writer cannot promptly coax, prod, or force his brain to deliver what he needs at any given time. He can, however, train to recognize in himself the flow of ideas, their hidden or potential merit, and thus to build up a backlog that becomes not only the storehouse, but the fundamental wealth of any writer.

At what point, from what portion, and in what manner we draw from this storehouse depends on so many variable and individual factors that no general rules can be drawn. Inner or outer impulses beyond the writer's control may play the decisive role; all he can consciously and willfully do may be to match the right idea to the desired objective.

The interplay between the creative impulse and the strictures of the form poses some of the most fascinating problems confronting the writer. At times, particularly while struggling with some of the harsher restrictions imposed by the medium, it may be well for us to remember that completely unfettered creation is impossible and has never existed; that the mind, in order to escape chaos, has always sought form in spite of, or because of, its strictures. We cannot express an abstract thought without fitting it into an orderly sentence structure and submitting it to the rules of syntax. And throughout the centuries, even the poets vacillated between the extremes of the sonnet and free verse, between voluntarily imposing upon themselves the strict forms of regulated rhythm and rhyme, and then, at other times, seeking to escape their confining rules.

Ideally, the writer who can afford to disregard all economic considerations would obey only his creative impulse; overcome and compelled by an idea, he would decide which form would best lend itself to fulfill its inherent potential—novel, stage, screen, television. In practice, however, a majority of writers must give serious, if not foremost, consideration to the outlets for their work. If an idea chances to match the demand to perfection, the writer can proceed without difficulty. At the other end of the scale is the need to produce ideas exclusively on request, without any regard for the creative impulse.

In this interaction between the creative impulse and the demands of the form, the latter seems to play the decisive and determining role. For one thing, its theoretical needs are quite clearly established, derived, and conditioned by its very nature; they can neither be circumvented nor changed; they must be obeyed.

And in a practical sense, the producer, editor, or publisher can be equally definite in his demands. He may request a story for a certain star, a script for a specific television format, a novelette aimed primarily at the woman reader. He prescribes the length, he knows the budget, and, not infrequently, he knows the preferences of his star or sponsor.

Opposed to this, the creative impulse seems vague, groping, indecisive at times, and uncontrollable at others. A basic idea, still unformed, seems malleable enough to be guided in any desired direction. There seems to be no reason why the story material cannot be developed to suit either the necessary length or any other demand.

But it soon becomes apparent that the basic story material has its inherent projections that are at least as stubborn as, and often even more incontrovertible than, the fixed demands of form and assignment. Anyone who has ever struggled with certain given story elements knows how deceptively pliable they may seem at first and yet how iron-willed they actually are. At some stage of development the flaws or inconsistencies are bound to come to the fore; the closer the final script, the less adequately can they be concealed or patched.

In the course of our creative labors, therefore, we have to look forward to our goal and go back to our basic ingredients; we must be aware of the demands the final form we have selected will impose on us, and we must examine the projections of the elements with which we are working. Only by a perfect blending of the two will we achieve the dynamic progression characteristic of the successful story and script.

The creative process, from the inception of an idea to the final form, is a striving for total awareness. Along the way, we are hindered by a lack of foreknowledge of the future and hampered by an insufficient awareness of the meaning of past decisions.

Only the completed work can give us the full view, the full realization of intent and result, the full consciousness of idea and form—and that joyous moment of liberation known only to the creative mind as one of its singular rewards.

Chapter 2

How to Choose Story Material

Variety

At first, it seems impossible to find any general rules concerning the basic material. Stories are as varied as life itself. Everything that can be imagined can also be told. A story can deal with a Sherpa mountain climber or with the Queen of England, it can dramatize death and agony, or it can describe an idyllic planting of flowers.

Instead of attempting to impose a narrow definition upon such bountiful freedom, we proceed to make this very variety our first demand: stories *must* be different from one another. The audience constantly wants new stories, the public desires to hear new things. Thus variety is an essential attribute of the story.

Still, in all this multitude and variety, there are elements which all stories have in common.

Since the primary subject of storytelling is the human

221

being and his actions, all stories are in accord with the principles investigated in the chapters on dramatic construction. Consequently, these rules are the skeleton of any story since they are general enough to be applicable to most living beings and to most actions about which stories are told.

Let us consider a few examples: Love for a divorced woman prompts a king to abdicate his throne. A child-wishes to get a toy. A gangster attempts to rob a bank.

All stories with intentions, like the gangster's attempt to rob a bank, are subject to the relations between motive, intention, difficulty, goal, no matter how different from each other they appear to be.

Now let us propose two alternate stories about the same person: (1) a grocer competing with a supermarket; (2) a narrative description of the grocer's married life. The difference is that in the first instance there is the dramatic drive of an intention, and in the second there is none.

Some kinds of stories, such as "a chase" or "revenge" or "ambition," invariably contain a built-in propulsion. Others lack any basic intention. As a result, there are erratic filmmakers who, to their own amazement, produce good pictures as well as bad ones. The inconsistency of their output stems from the fact that they have no real knowledge of their craft. Occasionally, however, they are fortunate enough to get a story with innate dramatic qualities so that it need not be revamped by an expert adapter.

At first, we may be blinded by the variety of the story material, but after a while our mind achieves the faculty of the X ray looking through the outward layer of flesh, blood, and muscle in which a specific happening is clad. Inside, we find the bones of structure and the invisible nerve fibres through which the dramatic impulses are relayed.

In no event should this structure be confused with what is commonly known as the "formula." The laws of dramatic construction apply to any action or combination of actions, whereas the formula is a whole system which is never changed. Although the formula may be clad in new clothes every time, it is the death of any creation. It is the aid of the weak writer, who is incapable of looking into the depths of the dramatic laws; instead of using his knowledge, he works on the basis of tried-out schemes. Obviously, this limits the field of his story material considerably. Besides, the formula violates the essential attribute of the story—variety. Soon the spectators recognize the same scheme in different clothing and become uninterested. But if the writer possesses a thorough knowledge of the dramatic laws, he can combine an unlimited number of schemes, and his stories will be of limitless variety.

Considerations of Form

Generally, the selection of story material rests with the producer and studio executives: the screenwriter is engaged later. But the free-lance writer, particularly in television, must choose his basic material very carefully before investing a great deal of labor on writing it, since sale or rejection may depend on a correct choice.

But apart from these practical considerations, the choice of material is of decisive importance, because it predetermines the success or failure of the final script to a large extent. It is true, however, that many a good picture is based on most insignificant material; an expert screenwriter was employed to develop it. It is also true that many a time the bad material cannot be improved, and the story is shelved after months of fruitless attempts to improve it.

Since we are forced to base our primary choice upon

material which is still raw and incomplete, we can be misled to overestimate its potentialities; or we may overlook the obstacles for further development in a treatment. But we might also fail to recognize valuable seeds in a short story, just as we might throw away a diamond before it has been polished. Indeed, how many timid souls would have been as perceptive as Frank Capra, who used the text of a Christmas card by Philip Van Doren Stern as the basis for *It's a Wonderful Life?*

After our initial response to the material, we should proceed to examine each element and evaluate it separately. To say "I like it" or "I don't like it" may be too rash a judgement in accepting or discarding a story. Instead, we ought to consider whether it qualifies to meet some of the preliminary requirements of the film medium, such as are demanded by its form, for instance.

Not all stories are equally adaptable to motion pictures even though they were eminently successful in other forms of storytelling. For one thing, the material must fit the limitations of space, which means that it is suitable to be compressed into a restricted time of performance. Therefore, it cannot be too much or too little. It is better to choose too much than too little, because too much can be condensed, while too little, if it has to be stretched, becomes thin. An enormous novel, if it is to be translated to the screen, must be of such nature as to allow simplification and reduction to essential lines. There are but few novels where this is not possible. Tolstoy's *War and Peace* has been filmed more than once, the last time by the Russians in a huge film that had to be shown on successive nights. On the other hand, Robert Bolt and David Lean successfuly condensed *Doctor Zhivago.*

Next it must be realized that the camera's photographic realism affects the story and thereby the choice of material. The lens shrinks the realm of fantasy and imagination for the spectator to a considerable degree: the events are visualized for him by the camera. On the other hand, no matter how vividly the novelist designs and paints with words, each reader must use his own imagination to translate these words into pictures. But the photographic certainty of the camera limits his mental concept of, say, *a medieval knight*. Instead, it shows him an actor clad in armor. To conjure up and preserve illusions under these circumstances is difficult: historic pictures often depict characters and events that are larger than life so that *style* and élan overcome the earthbound realism of what is seen on the screen.

Fantasy, parable, and allegories are more easily accepted in the legitimate theatre, where the limitations of the stage necessitate a partial suspension of disbelief. We know full well that in reality people would not enter or leave a room in a precise succession which precludes any stage waits. If only intuitively, the audience grants the playwright permission to overcome the immobility of his set by resorting to various devices which could be rejected as dubious or downright creaky upon literal scrutiny.

Indeed, the theatre has continually sought to escape from realism, vacillating throughout the centuries between a declamatory and a naturalistic style. The exaggerated masks of the ancient Greek actor and the stylized conventions of the Japanese Kabuki or Noh plays matched unreal appearance to the other factual shortcomings of the dramatic composition.

Reality, photographed in close-ups, has made it more difficult for the moviegoer to accept the improbabilities that are not only permissible but sometimes desirable in the theatre. Watching a play, we are prepared to go along with the symbol-substitutes of the stage: our skepticism is pacified by the tacit agreement that what we see is "as if" and not "what is or was."

Nevertheless, this symbol-substitute has the same exactness—without being fully true—that a map has in comparison with a landscape. The map represents a scientifically exact transcription of the landscape; nobody could doubt its correctness, yet it is not the landscape. If that "likeness" remains consistent, as has been achieved in some of the allegories by Kurosawa or Fellini, a gauze seems to be draped over the harsh stare of the camera. That same consistency makes the writing of Franz Kafka so effective: his fantastic allegories are conceived and executed with a chilling realism. On the other hand, erratic and undisciplined symbolism in pictures multiplies the difficulties of overcoming the fundamental opposition of the medium, which, in any event, tends to return to realism after its sporadic flights of fancy.

Though comedy seems to be the exception, it also proves the rule. Unlike the drama, which has much less leeway in its truthful representation of life, there are dozens of different kinds of comedy, ranging from broad farce to sophisticated wit. A whole new set of requirements and responses comes into play that appear to escape the evaluations of logic or the scrutiny of a spectator comparing implausible events to his own experiences. Coincidences or misunderstandings that would be judged outrageous in a drama become permissible in farce. Indeed, unrealistic exaggeration has the same illuminating effect as the comic distortions of caricature and is equally desirable.

Yet it would be wrong to believe that "in comedy anything goes." For one thing, once the kind of comedy is selected, its style must be preserved. It would not work to alternate between Rabelaisian ribaldry and Shavian wit. Oscar Wilde would not have been the ideal scripter for Laurel and Hardy, nor could the Marx Brothers have done justice to Philip Barry's *Philadelphia Story*.

Beyond this adherence to a certain style, the writer should not assume that he can expect a total suspension of disbelief on the part of the audience. "Deuces wild" presupposes that other cards retain their normal validity, or the game would become too confusing. Similarly, suspension of disbelief is best expected of only one essential premise—from which all other comedic situations arise.

Considerations of Dramatic Construction

Since it is the story content which is of primary interest to the audience, one might assume that the requirements of dramatic structure are not to be considered in the initial selection of the material. But because the story's dynamic potential becomes crucial in the development, the dramatic elements must be evaluated in their still latent stage.

In some instances, the basic substance simply does not lend itself to dramatization. There may be no way to establish a main intention that will vitalize the entire drama. Then again there may be too many separate intentions which would confuse the basic story line. In such cases, one can explore which single intention would prove to be most productive; the others can then be either eliminated or suppressed. Having chosen the dominant flow, it is often possible to link the others in a subsidiary confluence. Thus material that does not seem promising at first glance can be "whipped into shape" like a lumpy clod of clay by a sculptor's molding hands.

The quality of the dramatic elements embedded in the material will come to the fore more plastically as the script is developed. Despite hackneyed dialog and stale situations, many Westerns owe their popularity to clear and strong intentions: the rustler sets out to steal cattle and the sheriff wants to get him behind bars. On the other hand, the same simple setting can enhance a powerful clash between clear-cut determinations.

While some inexpensive pictures provide little burden for strong motors, many a big film has placed a heavy load on weak propulsion. We find the feeblest and most uninteresting intentions among some "colossal, stupendous, spectacular" productions.

Dramatic construction has taught us that all happenings occur on the basis of very intricate relations and interconnected proportions. It is perilous, therefore, to pick out one element and strengthen it so markedly that it unhinges the others. However, a careful evaluation may serve to recover a balanced structure that has been twisted out of shape.

Chapter 3

Understandability, Probability, Identification

Understandability

First, the story must be understood.

The novice is inclined to forget this necessity in his enthusiasm. He concentrates upon the things he wishes to express, the emotions he wants to arouse, the messages he has to deliver, and he is liable to forget that none of his desires will be fulfilled unless the story is understood. The spectator cannot believe in a story, he cannot experience fear or hope, terror, or joy, he cannot feel sympathy or aversion, and he cannot be moved to relief or anguish unless he understands the story.

A writer intent upon making a personal statement might not care how much of it is understood. But if he proceeds without regard for clarity, he must be aware that the emotional responses of the audience will be proportionately weakened by the degree of obscurity.

It is happily true that today's audiences are much more sophisticated than the early picture makers would have believed possible. Years of movie going and television watching have made people alert to every plot twist or subtle hint. They become quicker and sharper and require less information every year.

At one extreme, they may grasp a telegraphed story point sooner than the writer would like and hoot its arrival. At the other extreme, they may be mystified by opaque films or incomprehensible sequences that reflect either a surrealistic filmmaker's sincere intent or a charlatan's fear that his shallowness might be seen too plainly if he were clearly understood.

To navigate a true course between these reefs and shoals is no easy task. Even the experienced novelist and the playwright may waver. The language of film is itself not overly articulate, and this hampers the understanding.

In the last analysis the motion picture expresses itself by means of some sort of hieroglyphical language similar to that of the ancient Egyptians who told their stories by expressive picture symbols. We know how difficult it is to read hieroglyphical language. We know how difficult it is to decipher charades. And though each image may be easily understood, their succession jumps facts and implies meanings which require swift interpretation of the fragments speeding by.

Since the story must be grasped in one uninterrupted sitting, without any chance for "rereading" or pondering over certain passages, it may be advisable to remind the spectator of certain facts which he could have forgotten or misunderstood. But because space limits the amount of information, much that the writer would like to add must forego elaboration.

What further complicates comprehension is the fact that the information given should be universally expressive and universally understandable. If a man looks at his wrist watch, all civilized people know that he wants to see what time it is. But people in foreign countries may not understand the strange manipulations of a customer at Horn and Hardart's automats. Nor does every American understand why shoes stand outside hotelroom doors in French motion pictures. Therefore we must be sure that all information is understandable to everyone.

Understandability is particularly important in the motion picture because it shows us only parts of the story in accordance with the selection of information; it banks upon our ability to supply, understand and anticipate the missing parts. We must remember how much we expect from the spectator: we expect him to anticipate, and for that it is necessary that he understand the characters, their actions, and difficulties. We expect him to conclude from motive to intention to goal; but if the quality of the character and the nature of the intention are beyond the reach of the spectator's understanding, he will be unable to do so. In his mental jump from conclusion to conclusion, the spectator will fall by the wayside. And the story will be without anticipation, without suspense, and without forward movement. Furthermore, we expect the spectator to evaluate, a process which does not only concern the chances for intention or difficulty so necessary for suspense, but also for graduation. For all these activities, the spectator must be able to "understand." What are called "highbrow" pictures are unsuccessful not only because the single factors are beyond the comprehension of the average spectator, but also because their vagueness destroys all the story functions which we found so necessary. It is this kind of pretentious picture which drives the audience to the primitive but strong intentions of the Western and makes the producers smilingly say: "See, the masses don't want any good pictures."

In order to make the story content understandable, it would seem necessary to choose factors which are well known to the spectator. But this is a fallacy. In the very first part of this book, it was said that the primary desire which forces a person to listen to stories is the wish to partake of the lives of others or to get information about the way others live. This desire is in direct contrast to understandability based upon his knowledge, because he wants to learn things which he does *not* know.

This apparent dilemma has led to much confusion among producers. In order to satisfy understandability, they would make pictures about average people and, more or less, average events. Although the audiences understood these pictures, they were not interested in them, because they wanted information about things which they did not know. It seemed that the audience preferred to see emperors, adventurers, exotic people, or freaks on the screen rather than to see themselves portrayed. If a producer then went to the other extreme, he found very often that outstanding personalities or extraordinary events were beyond the reach of the average audience; they could not be understood and therefore were not successful.

To illustrate this confounding difficulty, we need only think of a classic picture like *The Bicycle Thief,* which was a success everywhere except in its country of origin, Italy, where the events were too familiar, and its neorealism too close to home.

The solution for this problem is not simple: the audience wants to learn new and interesting facts that should contain the measures and values which are universal knowledge. Few people are in a position to evaluate and understand the conflicting diagnoses of two brain surgeons. But everybody will be able to understand exuberance or fear. Few people will be able to evaluate an investment banker's decision in a stock issue. But everybody will be able to understand the conflicts resulting from a gangster's violation of law and justice, because the law is universal and all people are subject to it.

Therefore the problem must be solved by giving new information which can be measured and evaluated on the basis of universal knowledge. And the most universal knowledge among all human beings is the experience of emotions.

If we tell a story about a king or a tycoon or a famous dancer, we surely give a lot of new information, since such persons are different enough from the average moviegoer. We could not understand the problems of state with which the king is confronted, or the decisions with respect to corporate mergers confronting the tycoon, or the questions of success with which the dancer has to concern herself. It would not be possible for the moviegoer to understand these factors intellectually. But the king and the tycoon and the dancer are human beings, and as such they have only a limited range of emotions no matter how different their lives are. These emotions, ranging from joy to sadness, from terror to happiness, from satisfaction to dejection, from motherly love to passion, are caused by different factors in the lives of different people, but the emotions themselves are the same for everybody. Therefore they can be recognized by the spectator as his own feelings, and as such they can be evaluated, measured, and understood.

It does not matter whether the mother is a queen or a scrub woman. Each will feel a similar pain when she gives birth to a child, regardless of whether the one brings her child into the world in a palace, and the other one in the slums. Their feeling is similar, for it is the love of a mother, not the love of a queen or the love of a scrub woman. Therefore the scrub woman is able to understand the feelings of the queen. On the other hand, a picture about average people, if it lacks emotions or exposes unknown feelings, will not be understood by the audience, despite the fact that the sets, the actors, and the happenings portray such people as make up the audience.

By way of contrast, consider a full length picture by Walt Disney: you find elephants and mice and horses and other animals, living under circumstances which are not immediately recognizable or understandable to every one of us. But the picture would never strike us as bewildering. Why is it that we understand the doings of animals which are certainly different enough from our own? The explanation is that we understand them emotionally: the elephant mother who loses her baby is believed to experience a feeling as our mothers would. And a mouse which feels pity experiences an emotion similar to ours. And a ferocious lion fills the rabbit with the same terror as our own.

It is of the utmost importance to know that the understanding of the audience is emotional. A picture which is based on intellectual facts with characters who are unable to feel emotions, and without causes to feel any, is not understandable. Not only are these emotions the only common ground for all people, but it is also true that the audience has no time for intellectual digestion of the material. The emotional understanding is a subconscious process which requires no time.

Therefore the filmmaker should carefully select one of the three possibilities which enable him to reach and absorb the audience:

1. A story of unfamiliar happenings with familiar emotions, instead of familiar happenings with unfamiliar emotions.
2. Familiar people involved in an unfamiliar situation, such as the friendly undertaker abducted in *Bonnie and Clyde.*

3. If the uncompromising filmmaker wishes to depict average events in the lives of average people, he
ought to contribute his original style, thereby adding novelty without diminishing realism.

In all these alternatives, the audience's wish for both
the new and the familiar is fulfilled.

Understandability, however, is only a precondition—not
the ultimate goal of the picture. Although we must endeavor to facilitate comprehension, this alone will not
make the picture good. Indeed, producers have too often
chosen empty, flat, insipid material which is understandable over material which is intelligent, interesting, but less
easily explained.

Reproached by critics, these producers answer that the
moviegoer in "the sticks" must be able to understand the
picture. Using this as an excuse for incompetence, they
will go so far as to claim that they intentionally make bad
pictures to suit the tastes of a mythical audience.

It is, of course, not true that only platitudes, clichés,
stock characterizations, and insipid formulas can be made
understandable, while interesting and worthwhile stories
must remain beyond the range of comprehension by vast
audiences.

All it means is that we must bend every effort to make
interesting, valuable, and even complex stories understandable to millions of people. Certainly, this is not an easy
task. Anyone who ever watched a Hollywood film in a
third-run movie house in Singapore will realize what exotic audiences the commercially oriented studio hopes to
include in its mass appeal—culturally diverse and unedu-
cated audiences that are watching unfamiliar events en-
acted in foreign countries where alien languages are
spoken. And yet, some of the truly great pictures were
equally successful in Norway and Bangkok, in the United
States and in Peru.

To achieve this objective requires all the skill and

ingenuity and knowledge of the movie creator. The better he handles the means of expression and the film's dramatic construction, the more profound and complex is the content he can project to the simplest audiences.

Probability

The next demand which we must make upon the material is that it be probable. It is true that the spectator in the movie house is inclined to be a trusting soul, that he has the desire to believe what is told to him, and that he seldom stops to analyze intellectually whether the happenings occurring on the screen are probable or not. However, his belief can be of varying strength, and the degree affects his attention to and appreciation of the story. The more he believes in the story, the more seriously he will take it and the more raptly engrossed he will be. If the story is improbable, he will be reluctant to go along. And even if he does, because he reacts unconsciously to many elements, he will have the feeling of being fooled and will resent it.

To the surprise of many writers, experience has shown that simple and unsophisticated people have a much more strict judgment of what is probable and true to life than educated and sophisticated people. It seems as though the latter are more accustomed to deal in fictitious values, that their apparatus of thinking is better fitted to the philosophy of "as if." Time and again, I have accompanied "sophisticated people" to see an improbable movie and have seen them enjoy it in spite of its improbability. But the people around us—to our astonishment—thought it was silly on account of its improbability, and when the audience renders such a verdict, it refuses to partake in the action. The only time when it relaxes the strictness of this judgment is in comedy or fantasy.

The writer is often tempted to use improbable material because it opens entirely new fields for him, whereas the demand of probability restricts him in his imagination. Consider for instance Walt Disney: without attempting to minimize his wonderful imagination and fantasy, we must recognize that many of his best ideas were made possible by the fact that he was not bound to any real world, that many of his persons or speaking animals were not true to life. The elimination of probability has also opened unlimited new fields to creators like Fellini and to the young experimental filmmakers. By way of contrast, the writer of true-to-life stories must restrain his imagination. If he exceeds the boundaries of the probable, he may gain attractive and excellent situations. But much of their value will be lost in the mind of the spectator who refuses to believe in them.

Very often a story arises from false premises, but thereafter is absolutely true to life. There are stories of twins who look so much alike that they cannot even be recognized by their own wives. It is improbable that persons so close to the twins could not distinguish between them. But the rest of the story may be very likely and probable and true to life. There are stories of a tramp who is mistaken for a millionaire. Except that it is not probable that the tramp would not soon be discovered, all the rest of the story is very truthful. So, too, for stories of the sales girl who "busts" the Bank of Monte Carlo and obtains a lot of money. Such false premises open a new field of possibilities for story material. Since all the rest of the story proceeds truthfully, we are led to believe in it, except that the false premises put something like a veil of untruth upon the entire story.

We remember that the dramatic construction can either be right or wrong, but the story can be true or false. And this decision as to the truthfulness of the material is not simple, because it is not necessary that the story which is told should actually have happened. All a story needs to be true to life is that it *might* have happened or, you can even go as far as to say, that it is *likely* to have happened. Strangely enough, this demand of probability eliminates a great many stories of events which actually occurred because they are not probable, despite the fact that they are true. Truth is stranger than fiction. Events of that kind are not useful story material, because, although possible, they are improbable. The spectator will not accept them as true since they are not likely to have happened. This is particularly dangerous if the writer uses them for his own benefit—that is, to solve a difficult story problem. The audience resents such accidental solutions. Thomas H. Uzzell in his *Narrative Technique* says: "A coincidence which is part of the generating circumstances of a story is allowable, but one which solves the plot in a story intended to emphasize character is not allowable."

The law of probability does not prescribe that the writer should only choose events and people which are average or commonplace. To the contrary, the spectator is interested in specific instances, specific happenings, specific persons. A crazy woman, although not average, is true and probable. But a man with five eyes is not true, nor is a hero without any fear whatsoever.

The modern trend has been toward probability. It is as if the age of the Cinderella story and other motion picture fairy tales had passed, as if the audiences had progressed from credulous childhood to a more critical, adult attitude. Improbable stories that seemed interesting and exciting in the past would hardly arouse a smile of contempt in present days.

Though far less stringent standards are applied to comedies, frequent failures result even there from an excess of improbability that makes the jokes silly rather than amusing.

Identification

Let us assume that by now the spectators understand the picture. They also believe in the story. But this is still not sufficient cause for them to indulge in all the activities which are demanded of them.

For it is wrong to think that the spectator remains inactive during the picture show. If you go into a movie house and see the long rows of spectators gazing with blank faces upon the screen, you might assume that they are passively absorbing what is told to them, you might think that the only activities take place on the screen. But if you continue to watch them, you may hear them laugh suddenly, or you may see them cry, or you may notice general sighs of relief or groans of disappointment. And these noises are only the outward signs of intense activities going on in the mind of the spectator while he watches the happenings on the screen in an apparently passive manner. We remember that the spectator anticipates, evaluates, moves forward, feels suspense, experiences emotions, hopes and fears, is joyful and depressed, satisfied and disappointed. In order to cause the spectator to undergo all these pleasant and unpleasant reactions and feelings, he must be interested.

Every one of us has used this word "interest" lightly and frequently. Motion picture people are continually referring to a story as interesting or not. But you seldom hear a clear explanation of what makes a story interesting.

It is not the story which is either interesting or uninteresting, but it is the spectator who decides whether he feels interested in a story or not. Therefore the very same story can be interesting to one spectator and uninteresting to another. If we attempt to write interesting stories, we must search for human qualities in the story which are more or less universally interesting.

Nor should interest be confused with anticipation, suspense, and forward movement. A story without these three elements is boring, slow, and static; but interest depends upon other qualities.

Let us imagine that you are watching a football game between two teams, both of which are unknown to you. No matter how exciting the game, you will not feel interested—at least not until you know something about the teams. The very same game, or even a less exciting game, if played by your home town team, will become intensely interesting. The interest cannot lie in the quality of the game, but in the relation which you have to the game.

Likewise, we are less interested in the struggle of a stranger than in the fate of our next-door neighbor. To a certain degree our acquaintance with the star forms the same sort of relation that we would have with our friends across the street. As a matter of fact, for readers of fan magazines Elizabeth Taylor, Paul Newman, or Jackie Kennedy are more familiar than their neighbors.

But "acquaintance" is nothing more than helpful at best. The essential reason the story is interesting is the relation between its content and the life of the spectator. If he recognizes his own struggles, yearnings, conflicts on the screen, he follows the story with interest.

This conception embraces much more than the actual life of the spectator; it concerns primarily his thoughts, his desires, his fears. As such, the interest must not necessarily be represented in a story about automobiles for a car dealer and not about stables for a jockey; but the facts of the story must correspond to their thoughts and wishes. And these thoughts and wishes may be directed toward general abstract goals like success or the survival of a loser, happy love or a reward for the underdog.

If a relation between the spectator and the story has been formed, the way for the activities of the spectator has been cleared, and his very first step in this direction is to identify himself with certain characters of the story.

This process of identification is a curious phenomenon. It occurs in real life as well as in motion picture audiences.

Identification is caused by the desire to partake in other people's lives. This desire is particularly strong in people whose own lives are dull and empty, while people whose lives are full and rich will be much less desirous of identifying themselves with others, which means that they look after their own business and are less curious than others.

The motion picture audiences consist to a large extent of people who are dissatisfied with their own lives, whether their lives are unhappy or whether they are empty and dull, or whether they are simply unsatisfactory in comparison with their hopes and desires. And these people have a strong wish to identify themselves with other people even if it is only for the short duration of a movie show.

This desire of the spectator must be helped and facilitated by creating characters in the story which permit this identification.

Principally, it can be said that the spectator will only identify himself with persons who correspond to his tastes, to his wishes and desires. This being the case, there need be no identity of character between the actor of the story and the spectator. An old woman in the audience can easily identify herself with a young and beautiful actress because youth and beauty may correspond to the old and ugly woman's yearnings. A young girl in the audience can identify herself with an old woman on the screen as long as the old woman has some admirable qualities. A justice of the peace in the audience can identify himself partially with a gangster on the screen as long as this gangster shows some good qualities, such as outstanding courage or pity or kindness to the poor. Primarily, of course, you will find identification with the leading man and woman, from the male and female element of the audience respectively, regardless of age or beauty. But the identification is not limited to the protagonists, nor is it limited to only one person of the story. The spectator may identify himself for short moments with one or two of the supporting cast, just as soon as this person is in some relation with the spectator or with the spectator's wishes or desires.

The Greek word *sym-pathos,* from which our word sympathy is derived, means "sufferance together with," that is, together with someone. It is not possible for the spectator to suffer with somebody "unsympathetic." The spectator cannot identify himself with somebody disgusting or lying or detestable, because the spectator does not think of himself as being horrid or lying or detestable, even if he has all these qualities, nor does he wish to be nasty or cowardly. So audiences will prefer to identify themselves with somebody who embodies sufficient desirable qualities, or who helps them to sublimate self-pity. Thus the actor becomes sympathetic. In fact, even the worst gangster, while watching the average crime picture, is likely to feel sympathy for the hero instead of for the picture-gangster as would seem natural. He would have to be very detached and capable of conscious, logical thinking to sympathize with the criminal in the motion picture.

Once identification has been effected, it prevents the feeling of inferiority which the average person experiences when confronted with an "idolized" human being. Instead of resenting the larger-than-life protagonist, the spectator who has identified himself with him loves all the superb, desirable attributes as though they were his own.

But it is not necessary that the person with whom the

spectator identifies himself have nothing but splendid characteristics. If there are flaws and weaknesses, it makes the characterization all the more sympathetic, because then it is not too far distant from that of the spectator, a fact which facilitates identification. Thus the spectator is pleased by weaknesses in the hero's character which correspond to his own.

Inconsistent characterization, however, is extremely dangerous. Then the spectator who has identified himself with the character finds himself doing things which he does not wish to do. Disgusted, he wants to dis-identify himself. When the hero becomes acceptable again, the spectator grows confused; his feelings become mixed and uncertain. The inconsistent sympathy of the story is like a shower alternating hot and cold water.

If the weaknesses of a person with whom the spectator has identified himself are presented in a pleasant manner, it causes unending satisfaction. In a scene where Katherine Hepburn attempted to cook (in *The Woman of the Year*), some of the women in the audience recognized their own clumsiness; others had the satisfaction of comparing their own ability with her inefficiency.

Continuous comparison is an unconscious function of identification. For instance, we compare ourselves favorably to the villains. Considering ourselves so much better than they are, we feel relief and satisfaction.

For the same reasons, we like comedians who enable us to feel superior. Charlie Chaplin, Buster Keaton, Laurel and Hardy, made us realize how much more resourceful and intelligent we are, as well as how much less persecuted by bad luck. We are enchanted by clowns in the circus, not because we admire their bulky noses and baggy pants, but because they are helpless, awkward, and perplexed by trivial difficulties that we could easily overcome.

Through identification and comparison, the spectator

comes into closest contact with the actor. Thereafter the performer acts out the spectator's secret wish-fulfillments, whether related to aggression or fear or other latent desires. Thereby he produces pleasure or else relieves the spectator of suppressed pain by way of catharsis.

For this the spectator is grateful; he likes the actors who project his frustrations and achieve vicarious triumphs for him. This emotional bond plays a considerable part in creating stars. Even Boris Karloff was popular and one might say well liked, although he played horrifying parts. Audiences liked him because he focused and sublimated their terror.

All in all, then, the villain and the silly comedian and the unlucky fellow are as important as the sympathetic hero, because these despicable or unfortunate characters allow a favorable and satisfying comparison with ourselves. On the other hand, many a well-made picture has failed because its characters left the audience "cold."

Once identification has been established, the spectator takes sides. Primitive audiences go so far as to love the hero and hate the bad man. They may even cease to distinguish between the actor and the part he plays. Mark Twain tells the story of a showboat troupe giving a performance somewhere on the Mississippi, when suddenly one of the spectators began to shoot at the villain of the piece because he manhandled the innocent girl.

At a race track, you are likely to watch with greater interest if you have bet on a horse. As mentioned, the most expertly played football game will lack emotional excitement, unless you root for one team or the other. But once you have identified yourself with one team, the entire struggle appears in a different light. For one thing, you may notice at the end of the game that you remember only the passes of your team, while those of the others are hardly recalled and if they are, only as hindrances and difficulties to the actions of your side.

Thus the results of identification are manifold. It is as if you got "an angle" to the story from which to look at the happenings. For one thing it is no longer a struggle of strange people but a struggle between us and others. The things done to the actor with whom we are identified are things done to us. We experience fear and hope, love and hate, happiness and misery, as if we were going through the same things as the actor. At this stage it is not even necessary to ask, "How would I feel in such and such a situation," in order to follow the actors' emotions, because we actually are in his situation. Through empathy we became part of the story; we partake personally in the struggle. Unconsciously, we may feel: There but for the grace of God go I.

Previous to this participation, the story appears to us as a maze of intentions which we consider impartially and objectively. But as soon as we have identified ourselves with one actor, we hope that our intentions will be fulfilled, whereas we fear that the others may be successful. As a consequence, we are relieved or disappointed, depending on the outcome.

By dividing the total amount of intentions, we make it easier for our mental eye to discern the progress of the story. The happenings become simplified, the events more perspicuous. It is as though the story were reduced in scope, and therefore easier to be conceived.

Furthermore, suspense becomes exciting only if we are identified with the intention; we must feel sympathy with the actor whose intention concerns us. Our doubt about the chances of the intention becomes exciting only when we personally want it to succeed. Our sympathy can even lead us so far as to disregard the odds against an intention, which ordinarily destroys suspense.

And even the forward movement is made possible by identification. Since it is partly caused by anticipation, as the desire to reach the goal, we will be much less eager to get there if it is the goal of someone else. But if it is "our" goal, we are eager to move forward. As for the other cause of the forward movement, suspense, which drives us forward to escape uncertainty, it only becomes sufficiently unpleasant and thus effective after we have taken sides so that we are anxious to know that "our" intentions will be fulfilled.

Of course, the identification of the spectator with the actor is never complete. The only time when this becomes apparent is when the spectator has different information than "his" actor. For instance, the spectator knows that "his" actor is walking into a trap, a fact which is not known to the actor. In this case the identification becomes split in an almost schizophrenic manner: the spectator sees himself walking into a trap. The effect is peculiar and very interesting: the spectator would like to warn the actor; he would like to prevent him from going there; he would like to tell him the information which the actor lacks. This desire became so strong during the performances of the play *Angel Street* that the spectators actually called out to the detective on stage not to forget his hat, which would have betrayed him.

In view of all the beneficial results of identification, the author should take great care to make it possible. If the story tells of a struggle between two detestable persons, the audience cannot take sides. Being disinterested, the most they can summon up will be some sort of detached curiosity.

Conversely, it is also hazardous to make all the contestants sympathetic. In a struggle between two sympathetic persons, the possibility of taking sides is eliminated. Both being equally well liked, the audience cannot favor the victory of either one. Furthermore, such a story entails certain dissatisfaction because one of the sympathetic characters is bound to lose.

Chapter 4

Story Content

THE QUESTION CONTINUALLY HAUNTS the industry: Why does a particular picture become a success, though it may be flawed? And why does the one playing across the street, though equally well intended and sometimes more perfectly executed, turn into a failure?

Costly experience has taught that glossy mounting adds little to the enjoyment of the audiences. Expensive stars have ceased to insure tremendous box office receipts. A well-done picture will certainly attract more people than the same subject ineptly filmed; but in the last analysis it is the story content that outweighs all other attributes. Or, as might be proper to say in this context, the "meat" of the story.

A man goes to a restaurant because he wants to eat. A person enters a bar in order to get a drink. And when people go to see a movie, it is to satisfy some mental craving.

This basic need is often obscured by superficial motivations. The moviegoer says he wants to get out of the house, has to kill time, or is seeking escape from worries by distraction. But along with the ostensive purpose, there is a concurrent expectation that the picture may still a psychological hunger which is unconsciously or perhaps only dimly felt.

The picture which best responds to that need will "appeal." Certainly it is crucial to understand or sense what the audience craves. But there the difficulty arises: a picture addresses itself to audiences that are far from homogeneous. And even the same spectator may have different hungers at different times.

When you open a newspaper to the movie page, you may select a title as you would choose a dish on the menu of a restaurant. One evening you may be in the mood to see a comedy, and another time to watch a detective story or a love affair, although in general you favor one or the other kind.

Since pictures have to satisfy variable appetites, it would be a mistake to keep serving the same kind of food. Too much of anything would saturate audiences to such an extent that they would sicken of it, as they would from overeating; besides, it would leave dissatisfied all those who hunger for other things. It is therefore necessary at all times to have a wide variety of stories, even though one or the other kind may be more in demand temporarily. Fortunately, different kinds of movies play at the same time in one city so that the spectator may choose which to attend.

Psychologists and sociologists could learn a great deal by studying and comparing the receipts of pictures. For the public, by its response—that is, by showing interest—betrays its latent desires, problems, and difficulties. Not only do these fluctuate from year to year, but they vary within different countries or even cities, in different strata of society, or at different levels of education. Thus the same story may be successful at one time and unsuccessful at another, as has been proven by many a remake of earlier hits. Some pictures made during World War II rode an emotional crest; revisited today on the "Late Movie", they leave one wondering how they made such an impression. On the other hand, Harold and Maude, originally released to limited success, has gradually won renown in later years.

Outguessing the audience is difficult at best. A perceptive filmmaker once told me that anybody who claims to know ahead of time "what the audience wants" is either a fool—or a billionaire. The audience is not conscious of clearly expressible desires. Sometimes a "lucky hit" picture will rack up huge grosses. Then again, one and the same film may be successful abroad, but not domestically, where it may be "spotty." Or it may "click" in the big cities like New York, Chicago, San Francisco, and fail in the suburbs.

Since the audience's inner quests are opaque to analysis, and since so much depends on a right choice, it is not surprising that studios resort to imitating the most recent success. No sooner has a new film demonstrated its appeal than story editors and agents frantically search for "another"—another beach party, another motorcycle gang story, another *Star Wars*.

Yet most imitations have not won the acceptance of an original. Since the lead time from conception to completion and release of a picture is anywhere from six to eighteen months, the audience's interests may change substantially. Moreover, other imitations, completed sooner, may have dulled a once vivid story.

If there is any link between box office success and the *climate of the time*, it is certainly not plain. For instance, it is noteworthy that during the worst period of the Great Depression some of the best—and successful—American comedies were filmed, including those with the light "Lubitsch touch," which contained no trace of biting satire or bitterness. Conversely, in the prosperous sixties a succession of heavy dramas of despair, which stressed the sordid and ugly, were served up, granting the viewers no relief or reprieve.

The idolized character is also subject to fashions. For instance, the ancient Greeks admired not only a man who was brave, but also one who was cunning. They exalted every little ruse Odysseus put over. Today we are inclined to despise a cunning hero. There were times when mediocrity was admired, other times the adventurous spirit. Later, the courageous or successful leader was defeated by the loser, the beat, the anti-hero.

Overall, simple classifications such as comedy, tragedy, suspense drama, horror picture, or spy yarn do not clearly reveal the content. For instance, a comedy may make people laugh because they are made to realize how absurd their sense of importance is. Or if somebody's dignity is upset, they may laugh because of a subconscious desire to retaliate against domination. Then again, they may laugh because they are fooled by something they believe in. Obviously, there is little connection between these causes; the comedy that causes the laughter can satisfy many different types of mental hunger.

The seemingly shallow escapist picture may hide much sadism beneath its serenely blue lagoon. And drama, involving the spectator in different kinds of conflicts, affects him in many ways. Aristotle said that the purpose of tragedy is the catharsis from pity and fear. For a modern audience, his concept could well be enlarged to the psychological purging of aggressions, erotic fantasies, frustra-

tions; to the redemption from the humiliations and re-
pressed rages caused by "the slings and arrows of outrageous fortune, the heartache and the thousand natural
shocks that flesh is heir to."

Identification with the protagonist makes this catharsis
possible. In two hours the spectator lives through events
that would take years in real life. Primarily, he performs—
together with the actor—intentions that he is prevented
from executing in real life. Witnessing the motion picture,
he has a chance to act out these deeds, as Walter Mitty
did in his daydreams. Thereby he gains relief in a dimension beyond the obstructions of reality.

This identification is also capable of clarifying the spectator's inner and outer problems. If the motion picture
story places the protagonist in situations comparable to
those confronting the spectator, he sees his difficulties or
indecisions elucidated in the third person. It may be
sufficient if the story states the problem in a clear and
definite form without providing a pat solution. Entangled
in the facts of his own life, the spectator may not even be
able to recognize the problem; but if it is presented in the
more perspicuous form of the motion picture story, it is
easier for him to resolve his own conflicts. And for that
very reason many a writer has discovered that in working
out the destinies of his characters on paper he has gained
most helpful insights into himself.

Being "timely," the motion picture has become a source
of teaching for vast numbers of people. The tremendous
changes of the last decades shattered much of the super-
structure erected in the course of millennia by philosoph-
ical and religious thought. Deprived of the cultural shel-
ters which art and literature had provided, people groped
once again for answers to the perturbing questions of the
human situation. The proverbs and sayings on calendars
and in almanacs seemed no longer applicable, or only

partially so. Relentlessly swept ahead by new developments, the average person is confronted with an avalanche of unprecedented problems for which he finds no precepts or rulings in outdated teachings. For better or worse, the "accelerated literature of the screen" is capable of keeping pace with rapidly changing times.

No polls can reliably determine what bothers, troubles, puzzles, or moves an audience in a specific period. To recognize underground currents, trends, or latent needs, one would have to cut open all the locked homes and apartments and look in and listen to inaudible thoughts and amorphous feelings. That there are no scientific or statistical guide rules makes creation such an exciting exploration. In the long run, the honest writer is more likely to be in tune with the audience than the slick purveyor of sure-fire formulas. If he expresses what is stirring in his own heart, he is likely to give voice to what lingers unsaid in millions of other hearts. In this sense, the young filmmakers are right to seek self-expression even in a mass market—provided that their deeply personal experience is not so unique as to be severed from the universally relevant.

Although producers tend to seek stories with the most general appeal, a picture directed to a specific, but limited, audience may reach that audience more successfully. This became increasingly apparent in recent years as the generation gap and other factors began to splinter audiences. No longer was there a monolithic mass to be reached, but limited groups with specific tastes, artistic or otherwise. As a result, the financial operations of the studios were thrown into disarray.

From the commercial point of view, a picture is successful when people pay more money to see it than the producers paid to make it. Thus, although Picture 1 may be seen by fewer people than Picture 2, it may be successful if it costs only $3,000,000, while the other one is a losing proposition if it costs $20,000,000. Therefore the balance sheet of the studio is no true reflection of audience tastes.

Monetary considerations do not demand that every picture should gross as much as *The Sound of Music* or *Raiders Of The Lost Ark,* only that cost and appeal stand in a reasonable proportion. The writer who wishes to address himself to a limited audience will have to bear that in mind: it would not be advisable to tell his story in lavish production scenes. Conversely, some stories should not be filmed unless the size of the production matches the scope of the content.

Chapter 5

The Writing
of the Script

HERE WE ARRIVE at the chapter that might have stood at the beginning of this book. Because everything that precedes it is really part and parcel of the writing of the script.

There is no short cut to this final objective, just as there is no system to beat roulette. In order to know how to write a script, the reader must first acquire a knowledge of the craft.

It would have been useless at the beginning to explain that the screenplay contains dialog and descriptions of the things to be filmed. It would have been premature to divulge merely technical facts, for instance, that the shooting script has an average length of 130-150 pages in which the shots are numbered consecutively. Although this knowledge is necessary, it would not have sufficed; for the reader would not have known what to write in these 130 pages, nor how to subdivide the scene into set-ups, nor what to say in dialog and what objects to describe in the visual representation. Any book about motion picture writing that is limited to the explanation of technical facts will fail in all vital respects.

Motion picture writing is not only a creative art, but also a craft. Whether we like it or not, this is a fact to which we must reconcile ourselves. It means that nobody— no matter how great his talent or even genius—can get along without having intuitive or conscious knowledge of structural elements; it means also that somebody with little talent but adequate knowledge may turn out satisfactory scripts—particularly if they are adaptations of novels or plays. The outstanding talent will be resentful of this fact, whereas the less gifted writer will be grateful for a medium which permits him to achieve success as an artisan without the need of being an artist. Hollywood was often suspicious of the great artists without knowledge; it prefers the artisans with knowledge.

Art cannot be taught, but technique is less abstract and can be conveyed by one person to another. No amount of teaching will make Mr. X a second Leonardo da Vinci, but even Leonardo da Vinci had to learn throughout his life. And the later plays of Shakespeare were more expertly crafted than his earlier ones. The creative power of the mind has never been fully analyzed. It has never been proven with certainty which qualities cause the imaginative power. Creative imagination cannot be taught, nor can it be learned. But knowledge and technique can be acquired by the creator. And even the greatest work of art of an inspired genius consists of creative ideas which are brought into form by his experience or knowledge or technique.

Thus there is a difference between "having ideas" and "writing the script." No sure method exists to coax ideas from a reluctant brain. And yet most professional writers have their own idiosyncrasies to break the dams of inspiration, whether candlelight, or a favorite tobacco, or a particular desk. Yet all these peculiarities go to show that inspiration can be trained to come forth by certain customary adjuncts or at definite hours. The writer who waits for inspiration to strike him like a thunderbolt, at any time of night or day, will soon fail to experience the divine spark. But the creator who goes to his desk at the same hour, patiently offering himself up to the sublime visitation, will gradually do his most inspired work during those fixed periods. Whether he works best in the morning or after midnight (as John O'Hara did) does not matter; it is the regularity that invites the spontaneous. Indeed, most productive writers have done a daily amount of work. Beyond that, there is no rule which would bring equally good results for all writers.

Inspiration is not altogether the flash of lightning out of a clear blue sky that it is often assumed to be. Intense concentration on a problem may lead to its continuation by the unconscious. After having been processed beneath our conscious thoughts, the solution may surface "spontaneously." In this sense our mind is like a computer into which we have fed certain questions. Personally, I have found it beneficial to concentrate on a problem before going to sleep. The next morning, what had seemed insoluble before is suddenly clear. There is wisdom in the saying that one should "sleep on it" before making a decision.

Maurice Maeterlinck, a man whose creations earned him a Nobel Prize once told me: "To have ideas is paradise—to work them out is hell."

Nobody can conceive the script directly in its ultimate form. It must be gradually developed since one cannot overlook the entire body in the beginning. Novelists like Balzac or Zola can extend their material through many volumes. But dramatic writing must be very precise. We cannot afford to proceed accidentally, since the developments must be focused to achieve a compact intensity.

Instead of writing haphazardly, we must adhere to the method in which we develop the story. Instead of beginning with the final screenplay, we must proceed from a rough structure through various stages to the ultimate form. This is painstaking work, unwelcome to the impatient creative mind. But the great sculptors had to work months and months before anything like a human figure would take shape in the stone.

Practically speaking, there are three principal stages of development: the outline, the treatment, and the screenplay (or shooting script).

First, we must realize the advantages of the gradual development. From stage to stage, unsafe elements can be eliminated or corrected. Additional material can be added. The leaps from stage to stage are smaller; consequently, they make smaller demands on the imaginative power. By slowing up the process of fixation, we are sure to obtain a smoother and more natural narration. If we do not have to jump to distant conclusions, we can find safe conclusions. In building the script gradually, we may find details which might otherwise escape our attention. We must be sure that no mistake has slipped by. As a matter of fact, it may be advisable to go backward and write a synopsis of an already finished screenplay because the more elaborate form may contain seductive attractions which might be exposed as illusions if the narration were reduced to its essentials.

Since the slow development contains so many advantages, we cannot go wrong if we subdivide the transition into additional stepping stones. We may begin with an outline of about 6 pages which we can develop into a treatment of about 30 pages. Thereafter we can proceed to a continuity of about 60-100 pages from which we derive the screenplay with a length of about 130 pages. This screenplay is to be elaborated to the finished shooting script.

It might be expected that an impulsive writer would be disgusted with such calculated methods of construction and creation. He might feel that it is preferable to write spontaneously instead of making abstract detours. He might feel that a scene which flows immediately from his pen or typewriter is more realistic and more true to life than one which has been turned back and forth by his creative and by his critical thoughts. He might feel that the intuitive impression is preferable to the structural effect.

It is possible to write a short story in one fortunate streak of creative power. But no literary work of any extent can be executed without considerable work on the structural elements previous to the actual writing. The author who begins to write the script by conceiving fresh and vivid dialog may find to his surprise that the scene which was very realistic, sounds distorted, false, and unbelievable in the entirety of the picture.

Great artists are not those who think that they have sufficient talent to proceed without knowledge, but those who have so completely mastered craft that they do not seem to have to grapple with this problem. Great writers have a conscious or unconscious knowledge of structural requirements.

Only through correct placement does the single scene become truthful, logical, and realistic. Blood can never circulate in a mutilated body. And there is even more to the perfect dramatic construction than just the fact that it is correct and contains no mistakes. It is as if music originated from the symphonic combination of all parts. It is as if the story came to life.

The Outline

Before the writer starts to develop a story, he must know what it is about. Offhand, so obvious a statement appears to be superfluous. And yet, just try to remember how often you left a movie house without really knowing what the story was all about.

It is of the utmost importance, therefore, that you should question all the aspects and ramifications of your material. Sometimes the initial exploration can make you aware that this is not what you actually meant to tell. You have time for correction: a basic shift in emphasis may set matters straight and give you the desired results.

The outline states the salient facts of the forthcoming screenplay. It need not yet contain all the facts; but those that are given should suffice to describe a full and complete story, without holes or creaky developments. Some of the missing elements may be inserted later, provided their absence raises no crucial questions; other facts may be altered in the subsequent development. But the importance of the primary layout cannot be overestimated. It is as if you were a builder selecting a lot and surveying its size, shape, grading. The ground you stand on will decisively predestine the building you have in mind.

The Adaptation

The material you set out to adapt may be before you in different forms. Whether it is a conglomeration of your own ideas, memories, and inventions, or whether it is a novel or a stage play that you wish to transform—the approach in all these cases is alike: you must first reduce the existing material to a simple and clear line.

If you are adapting an original story of your own, you may have had the idea in mind for some time. During the period of gestation, related but fragmented scenes or events clustered around the kernel. Once you have started to work them out, you may begin by giving your imagination free rein. At the same time, you may jot down realistic notes about the locale of your story, about the job or profession of your characters, their hobbies and tastes, their neighbors. Though you may not be able to use more than a fraction of such information, it may be most helpful in creating real people and events, instead of cardboard characters and contrived plots.

From this wealth of material, the basic outline has to be selected. The skeleton has to be recognized before the script is fleshed out.

Similarly, any completed book or drama must first be condensed to its basic facts and then redeveloped. There is no easier or more direct way of adapting a novel or a play to motion pictures than to reduce it to those elements from which the novelist or dramatist started to develop the story into a novel or into a play respectively. It is not feasible simply to cut or re-arrange the material, nor is it possible to photograph entire scenes from the novel or from the play. Since the physical characteristics of the different forms have different requirements, the very same scene may be inexpressive if it is not properly integrated into another form. The smooth continuity may be completely disrupted by false transformation, one which does not go back to the facts of the material.

In the early days of motion pictures the transformations of novels or plays produced the most horrid violations of the author's work. These brutal distortions caused a reaction of disgust on the part of the audience. Today, the transformation seems to have swung to the other extreme: producers are ambitious to be as loyal to the original work as possible. But this is not always beneficial to the picture or to the author. Many an author would be better off if his work were changed considerably; as long as the meaning and the essence of his story are reproduced, it is in his interest that such liberties be taken with his work as will result in the best possible transformation to the screen. In the introduction to Sidney Howard's *Dodsworth,* Sinclair Lewis said: "Actually, portions and sometimes all of a dramatization are valuable precisely as they depart from the detail of the original fiction."

Extreme, stubborn loyalty to the original material may be harmful; the writer who proceeds to copy diligently entire blocks of the material into the new form may find that, regardless of his fidelity, the adaptation gains an entirely new spirit and fails to do justice to the original. In other instances, an adaptation which represents a less literal transformation is much more faithful to the original.

When I adapted *The Bridge of San Luis Rey* to the screen, Thornton Wilder kept urging me to depart from the text of his Pulitzer Prize novel. Since the motion picture had its own form, he said, I would do him no service by adhering too faithfully to scenes conceived to be read rather than spoken. And in a letter to John Ford he wrote, "It is your own work which to a large extent has shown me the degree to which a motion picture has its own way of telling a story and brought me to see the extent that a picture may, and must, take extensive liberties with the text of a novel or a play."

It might be best to understand the process of transformation by this example which the director Lewis Milestone told me: "If you want to produce a rose, you will not take the flower and put it into the earth. This would not result in another rose. Instead you will take the seed and stick it into the soil. From it will grow another rose." Similarly, you cannot transplant entire scenes from a play or from a novel to the picture; they will fade. It is better to speak of transformation than of adaptation, because adaptation sounds more like shortening, cutting, and rearranging. But transformation means to extract the content from one form and pour it into another.

Adapting a great and enduring masterpiece for modern audiences often requires deft compromises. Dated conventions and stilted expressions may unnecessarily mar the vital impact of the content. Yet any attempt to modernize even the outer trappings is likely to be criticized by purists. Delbert Mann, who alternated between modern classics like *Marty* and such literary perennials as *Jane Eyre*, successfully brought out the innate human qualities that overcome time and space.

The Treatment

The treatment tells the full story, but not yet in fully crystallized scenes. Just as the motion picture occupies an intermediate area between the novel and the stage play, the treatment may be considered a narrative description of the future script.

There is no prescribed length for the treatment. It may be as short as 30 pages or extend over 200 pages. Jean Paul Sartre once wrote a film treatment of 800 pages. As far as I know, nobody ever reduced it to a practical screenplay length.

The treatment is an elaboration of the outline. It may contain rudimentary scenes or full dialog. Often, inconsistencies or unforeseen difficulties become apparent in this further development. Most producers prefer to see a treatment rather than let the writer go directly into screenplay. Since the material is still in a more or less fluid state, it is an opportune moment for correction. All further progress does not so much concern the basic development of the content as its presentation and expression in motion picture terms.

We may have started out from an outline which did not

contain all the facts of the story. Since the treatment demands the full information, additional facts have to be added in order to tell the complete story. The creative process is a continuous series of choices; the average executive does not reach as many decisions in the course of a busy day as the dreamy artist.

But gradually the areas of the creator's free will decrease. As soon as a limited number of facts is established, others are automatically created; they exist although the writer may not have paid any attention to them; sometimes they are even unwelcome to him. He may be concerned only with certain facets of his main characterizations while being inclined to overlook others. But these others will contribute to the play of forces as the story develops. Sometimes, the writer is only interested in the relation between two people, but if other relations exist between one of them and others, these other persons automatically come into a relation with the second person of the first combination.

Fortune-tellers have made this calculation one of their essential means of predicting the future. Without resorting to supernatural aides, without looking into crystal balls, without evoking spirits from the other world, they can predict with reasonable certainty some of the developments that will arise from a few known premises. Certain characters in certain circumstances will act and interreact in a certain manner. A married couple who at the beginning combine affinity and repulsion will progress through various stages until they divorce or until they have become adapted to each other; both cases amount to adjustment. We all know old marriage partners who have become so similar to each other that they are almost alike. On the other hand, 90 per cent of all divorce suits might have been predicted at the marriage ceremony by a person who knew sufficient facts to realize that affinity was inferior to repulsion.

Similarly, the writer in the beginning of his work should practice some fortune-telling with regard to his story. For he must be aware that from a certain point on, it is not he who tells the story, but the story which tells itself. After he has established a number of facts, these facts will exert their power, and all that remains to the writer is to listen to these demands and carefully feel along the path which the story demands. If he starts out from certain premises and would like to get to an end which is incompatible with these premises, he will find that his story has just as much energy and will power as he himself possesses. In the process of working, he will be more and more sidetracked and led away from his original goal to the goal which his story tells.

He will be surprised time after time when he arrives at results and situations which were neither planned nor desired by him. No matter how much work he wastes afterwards, he will not be able to bend the story to his desires.

This occurrence is very frequent. The outline, because of its vagueness, may tell a story which seems plausible. But as the writer develops the story with more and more details, he finds that the outline was full of impossible developments and that other developments have to take their place if the story is to be probable. He arrives at what the story wanted to tell and not at what he wanted to tell. Very often the screenplay is so different that it must be abandoned because it does not correspond to the original idea. In other instances it may be only one characterization which had seemed perfectly interesting and which then turns out to be ridiculous. It is not the writer's development which is wrong, since he may have followed the lines prescribed by the story with great diligence; it is the fault of the facts which were badly chosen in the beginning. All further patchwork and building-up will not help. Sometimes it only serves to make the characterization more absurd, like the police sergeant who was intended as a sympathetic hero but ended up as a ridiculous idiot. It is often attempted to smooth out these adverse results, but no amount of pretty speeches and no amount of nice gestures can help. Sometimes it is desirable to make one character unsympathetic and another one sympathetic. But the facts of the story may be such that our sympathy falls with the wrong person, while we have nothing but contempt for the one who is supposed to be sympathetic. It happens frequently in pictures where the story demands that the hero get the girl in the end although he has played a most inane part throughout the picture. Toward the end the writers begin to ask themselves, How can he be made a hero despite the fact that he has made a fool of himself all along?

This, however, must not be confused with a definite change of a person from good to bad, or vice versa. Such a change is a fact of the story and not a violation of the story which tells itself. Nor should the conception of the story which tells itself be confused with the story which "telegraphs its ending." In the first case, the story tells itself to the author, whereas in the second case the story tells itself to the audience. Of course, if the audience could know all the facts the author knows, they would have the same knowledge about later developments as he must have. But the knowledge of all the facts is only gradually exposed to the audience, while the author knows them before he starts to tell the story. In a good story, the audience is unable to predict the outcome, not because the story is unpredictable, but because the spectator lacks the knowledge of all the details making such a prediction possible.

In order to choose the right facts, we must recognize the nature and quality of those which are accepted. For this it is necessary to observe them without any illusions as to their outward appearance. The inexperienced writer may become enthusiastic over an idea, only to discover after a long period of work that this idea has no possibilities of development. The unsuspecting writer may be charmed by the quality of a scene, by the excellence of a characterization, by the loveliness of a feeling, by the originality of a twist. He will make his story a series of such wonderful material, and then he is greatly surprised if the whole thing put together doesn't work.

As his experience grows, he will begin to look at the facts with more detachment. He will dismantle them of their outer appearance, considering only their inner qualities, for he knows that the specific form in which they appear—no matter how tempting and brilliant it is—has only a momentary effect, which vanishes in the progress of the structure. There, whether desirable or undesirable, only the true nature and the essential qualities of the facts come into effect.

We should endeavor to consider the material from the abstract point of view of the dramatic structure. Instead of the beauties of a love affair, we should think of it as an intention which is or is not prevented. Instead of considering the excitement of an automobile accident, we should try to find out its appearance as a dramatic cause or goal or motive. Instead of enjoying a humorous situation, we should ask whether it is connected with a progression, for jokes alone do not make good pictures. Only after we have seen through the flesh to the bones of the dramatic body are we able to recognize whether the story can live, or if it must break down.

It is not easy to x ray the material in this manner, but it is absolutely necessary. For the material does not betray its merits and mistakes except through the abstract consideration of the elements reduced to the structural necessities. It may be almost impossible to understand what is wrong with a certain part of the story if you do not look at it from the abstract point of view. In doing this, the understanding becomes very simple: the variety of developments can be understood as motives, intentions, goals, difficulties. The impenetrable maze of happenings becomes perspicuous in terms of lines. And these lines betray their qualities almost graphically. We can see whether there is a main intention and where it starts and where it ends. We can see when the difficulty in the way of the main intention arises and where it ends. We can see where the climax takes place, where the goal is reached; we can see whether the counterintention is pointed to the same goal or not, we can see whether the subintentions have unity of purpose or whether they are separate main intentions, we can see whether the motivation is dependent upon the motive, whether the graduation is faulty, and whether an auxiliary goal outranges the main goal.

By this simple process, the virtues and faults of the material appear very clearly. At this point it is not too late to remedy the flaws. By questioning every aspect of the material, the writer will be prepared to answer the questions which the producer or director is likely to ask later.

The writer can also perceive in the treatment where the elements are diffuse. Older moviegoers will remember the days when the operator in the projection cabin would fuss with the lenses of the projector in order to focus the picture on the screen. The audience would boo and yell until the objects became clear. It would be unthinkable to force people to watch an entire picture, the faces and objects of which are diffuse. But they are often forced to watch pictures with a diffuse story and with a dramatic construction which is out of focus.

The focusing of the story material is comparatively easy. Sometimes it is sufficient to change some of the characteristics of a person in order to create powerful affinity or repulsion. Sometimes it is sufficient to prevent characterizations from clashing which have no adequate reason for conflict. It is easy to recognize that people with affinity who are united cannot possibly struggle. They can easily be separated. Then the intentions should be carefully investigated. In the South, people say, "I aim to go home." Or "I aim to buy a gun." This "aiming" is nothing but an intention. The interesting part is that the dialect—which everywhere has the best feeling for essential language—expresses the fact that an intention "aims" at a goal. Now this aim may be diffuse; it may not hit the bull's-eye.

The diffusion of the material makes the story sluggish or ineffectual. It is impossible for any powerful situations to arise from such a story. Through the process of focusing we "aim" the intentions at the right goal. It is interesting to notice with how little effort most stories could be improved considerably by this simple process.

In this way the material becomes precise and powerful. So the last thing to be considered is the distribution, for it may be that long portions do not advance the story while others may be overcrowded. In order to achieve perfect distribution, we must first contemplate the beginning of the main intention and the beginning of the difficulty, the location of the climax, and the location of the main goal with respect to the end of the story. After we are satisfied that they are distributed effectively, we can consider the distribution of the auxiliary goals. They let us clearly foresee which parts of the story are going to be dull and slow and which parts will be confusing and overcrowded. If the distribution appears to be uneven, we still have time for correction.

The novel is essentially a narrative which the author can condense into scenes at will. The screenwriter, starting with the descriptive outline, gradually crystalizes the material into the scenes required by the motion picture language.

If we visualize the story as a line, the scenes appear as blocks or rectangles separated by intervals. What is contained in these scenes must be expressive enough to convey what took place during the mute intervals. The scenes can be compared to cornerstones holding up the story, backward and forward. Or a writer enamored of his work might think of his scenes as "pearls" and imply the string that holds them together.

The novelist can fill the gaps between scenes by descriptive or explanatory sentences. The more ingenuity the screenwriter applies in implying gradual developments, the more compelling and rapid becomes his sequence of scenes. For that reason, he will rarely open the picture with the "beginning" of the story. Instead, he will start at a crucial point and imply or inform the spectator what preceded it. For instance, he is not duty-bound to dramatize how two partners became enemies. He can begin by showing one partner setting out to punish the other one for treacherous embezzlement. Or a former relationship can be projected in the first minute, when an escaped convict arrives to confront a pal who has turned stool-pigeon.

A persistent difficulty arises frequently when boy meets girl. As thrilling as falling in love may be for the involved couple, it is a tedious process for the innocent bystander. Nevertheless, it taxes our credulity when the writer introduces boy to girl, and in the next scene we are asked to believe that they fell in love forthwith. One of the solutions practiced by experienced writers is to imply a prior acquaintance or even a prolonged relationship which is picked up at the point where it becomes intensified or disturbed.

Obviously, this makes the story interesting right from the start. But throughout the picture a good writer will strive to dramatize only the highlights of implied developments, whereas the pedestrian scripter is liable to spell out tedious progressions and then be forced to skip climactic happenings, because he does not have enough time left for their dramatization.

The Screenplay

The screenplay completes the task of expression in terms of scenes.

If the story has been developed carefully up to this point, the writing of the screenplay is no radical departure from the previous stages, but merely a final crystalization of the material.

The last elimination of narrative passages may require further changes of the story. Since the literary technique can no longer be relied upon, we must be sure that all information necessary to the understanding of the story is contained in scenes. We must so employ the means of expression at the disposal of the motion picture as to convey all the facts of the story to the audience.

To achieve this purpose, we must make use of dialog, noise, action, sets, props, objects, music. We must ask, Is everything clear to the audience? Thereafter we must investigate whether we have repeated ourselves. If so, the superfluous information must be eliminated. The space which is available to the motion picture is desperately short. Utmost economy is essential; this economy has the added advantage of creating more powerful situations. If two scenes are used to express two developments, we should ask if both these developments could be expressed in one scene that is more revealing. We have seen that many elements reveal information about one another;

therefore we shall have to decide which one can be exposed most advantageously. In almost every instance, we can ask, Should we expose the motive or the intention or the goal? How shall we handle the division of knowledge between actors and audience? At what moment is a certain bit of information most effective? Shall we arouse curiosity or suspense? Shall we make use of a misunderstanding? Shall we cause contrasting anticipations, expectancy or surprise, fear or hope, disappointment or relief? To explore all the possible variations of constructing a story is indeed an interesting and intriguing task.

Furthermore, the sequence of scenes should be examined with regard to variation, change, or contrast. If the author wants to give his audience comedy or tragedy or excitement, he soon realizes that he will attain his end better by an occasional interruption of the mood rather than through a steady following of the same trend. Not only is this necessary because contrast highlights the extremes, but also because the psychology of the audience demands this variation. If a tragic story contains no moments of comic relief, the spectators may laugh unexpectedly during serious scenes just to find release from their aroused emotions. On the other hand, the truly great comedians insert touching and earnest moments into their stories, because the continuous connection of one joke to another may soon destroy a funny mood.

From the point of view of the story mechanics, it is desirable that the meetings of the main characters, who are likely to be united in many scenes, should be more or less evenly distributed. They should not be combined in many consecutive scenes and then sink into oblivion for a long time. Moreover, if at all possible, every main character should have at least one scene with every other character so as to bring out their respective characteristics to the fullest extent.

Since the scenes are separated by lapses of time, connection of scenes is a particular problem of the screen-play. We have seen that the intentions carry the main burden of connection insofar as they arouse our anticipation and cause the forward movement. In many instances, however, we may want to add connecting elements. For instance, somebody wants to deliver a briefcase. Obviously, the delivery is an intention, but, in addition, by its simple appearance in many scenes, such an object can effectively act as connection. Or we may end a scene with a specific object and begin the new scene with the same object. We may even end with a close-up of an actor's face and begin with the same close-up in another place. However, we must take care that the transition from one shot to the other is held together by an intention.

Not all scenes need equally strong connection. We may collect blocks of scenes which are especially strongly connected. Between the blocks of scenes we may need less direct connection; we can compare these to the chapters of a novel. However, this is only a comparison and not a parallel, since the form of a novel is different. And for the same reason we cannot see why a motion picture story should be divided into three acts like the stage play although this conception persists among many screenwriters. The division into acts is a characteristic of the theatre determined by its physical form, whereas the motion picture, which does not have this characteristic, requires no such division.

The Shooting Script

The shooting script contains all the technical descriptions necessary for the director, the editor, the cameraman, the art director, the production manager, and the musical director. Although it is likely that the director has collaborated on previous stages of development, the shooting script is predominantly his responsibility.

The director will indicate the kind of shots which will render justice to the means of expression or to the combination of means capable of revealing information at a certain time. He will also indicate where the set-up is to be changed. These set-ups are numbered consecutively. After giving the kind of set-up, the director mentions what is to be seen in the field of the camera. These indications must be clear enough to inform the art director of the kind of set needed, the prop man of the props required, the assistant director of actors and extras needed, the cameraman of the camera angle and also of the lighting, the musical director of incidental music, and the sound engineer of the need for mixing or dubbing which should be known before the recording. The editor works from the shooting script in assembling the different shots into one consecutive picture.

At this stage the pressures of impending production make themselves felt. To estimate the running time of the finished picture, the script is often given to an expert who is familiar with the director's pace. It may be found that the script is substantially too long. So the writer, with bleeding heart, has to cut scenes and effects which by themselves are good and valuable; it is better, though, to do it at this stage than to find them subsequently on the cutting room floor.

Not infrequently it is felt during rehearsals that a scene does not play as well as it looked on paper; then the writer may be asked to rework it. And just when he thinks that he has at last a perfect shooting script, unexpected overruns in the budget may require a belt- and script-tightening. The sickness of an actor or a stretch of bad weather can enforce rewrites beyond anyone's wish or control. To the last shooting day, the words on the paper remain more eradicable than the images and sounds on the celluloid.

Nor is the final wrap-up the end of the changes to

which the script is subjected. During post-production there may be cuts, or additional lines may be dubbed in; sometimes a scene is transposed. And finally there comes the evening of the first preview, sometimes a rather traumatic experience.

The audience sees the picture for the first time. Their reactions are often very unexpected. They may laugh in the wrong places or, in a comedy, anticipate a laugh too soon. They may get restive or bored in what had appeared to be a taut sequence. Finally, the preview cards filled out by the spectators on leaving often reveal additional reactions.

Thereupon the stage of experimentation begins: a scene is cut here, a long sequence shortened there. But there is no end to the bewilderment: a long scene is not long because of its running time, or because nothing is said, or because nothing happens, but because of some structural deficiencies. There may be other long scenes where nothing happens, yet they may be intensely dramatic, as for instance: the silence of a person who has just received some traumatic news. Sometimes retakes become necessary; or cutting may improve faults. But at so late a stage, there is no essential remedy or way of correction. Therefore it is all the more important to subject the screenplay to a thorough examination before it goes into production.

Analysis

Whereas creation is a process of building up, analysis means the dissection of more or less finished material.

Comparatively few people believe themselves capable of creating a story; but nearly everyone assumes the ability to criticize. Unlike criticism, analysis is not a reaction based on personal taste. As the reverse of the creative process, it requires an equal understanding of the dramatic elements.

The first step in the analysis of a screenplay is to recognize the individual factors in the material. While criticism judges the film as a whole, analysis peels out the single elements, evaluates them, and thereby enables us to render a diagnosis which is the sum of our judgment of all the parts.

Analysis is used for many different purposes. One of them is to guide our choice of material as discussed before. Another one is to find mistakes for purposes of correction. This analysis for correction takes place at practically every stage in the development of the script.

To avoid confusion, we must realize that the symptom is not identical with the disease. A doctor who wants to cure a patient will not try to stop his fever, but will rather endeavor to eliminate the cause of the fever. Even though someone feels pain in his eye, the pain may not be caused by the eye but by a tooth. A good tailor may not alter a coat where it appears to be faulty, but lift the shoulders and so automatically eliminate the fault in the waist. Likewise, it is seldom possible to correct the mistake in a motion picture script at the place where it becomes apparent. This may merely be the symptom, not the cause. The actual deficiency will frequently be found in a different place. Let us remember the chapter concerning selection of information, where it was shown that the very same scene may achieve an entirely different meaning by changing previous information relative to the scene. Therefore correction may be necessary, not in the scene which seems unsatisfactory, but in previous scenes. Almost all pictures which grow dull or boring toward the end can be corrected, not by changing the second half, but by improving the first.

It is generally assumed that analysis of the script is only practiced by story editors, producers, executives, rewriters or script-doctors. In fact, many people are inclined to distinguish between analytical minds and persons with creative power. Many artists despise analytical or critical people. But this is unjust, since the artist needs a certain amount of analytical perception. The truly great artists are not a prey to uncontrolled and unbridled creative talent. More often than not, their greatness is a result of both qualities.

In order to develop a story, we must interrupt the progress of creation at various stages and pause to analyze the existing material, not only to discover its faults, but also to find the future steps to which the story will force us. We might call this analysis for development. And this is in no way destructive criticism, but something which is most creative. It is as if the creator paused to see in which direction the story is progressing. It is as if the creator were listening to a story which tells itself.

This analysis can be compared to the perspective sketching of an artist. In order to check the exactitude of his perspective, he can extend the lines of the bodies to the horizon where they have to meet in two fixed points. In the same way the writer should attempt to extend the lines of his story to the end. This will help him to perceive where the story leads.

Once you possess sufficient knowledge, the process of analysis is actually very simple. You merely have to ask questions. And the story gives the answers to these questions. Thereby the almost hopeless task of evaluating an impenetrable entanglement of story elements is reduced to finding a number of simple answers to simple questions. Once the writer knows the nature of his material, he can develop those elements which are important while suppressing those which are less substantial. In this way the story takes on a clear and shapely form and through simplification facilitates understanding for the writer as well as for his prospective listeners. It may show up the falseness of a situation which otherwise might not become apparent until the author starts writing the dialog, which may sound silly—simply because the situation is impossible.

Our knowledge of the dramatic laws teaches us what questions to ask. Where does the main-intention begin? Is the motive equal to the strength of the main-intention? Does the content of the story satisfy a latent hunger of the audience? How are the auxiliary goals distributed? How much information does the spectator need to understand a certain development?

Instead of giving a complete list of questions to be asked, it is preferable to give a list of the most common mistakes from which the questions necessary for analysis can easily be derived. In looking over this list of possible mistakes we recognize how difficult it is to make a perfect motion picture and how often everybody is bound to fail, at least in some respects. Whoever is without fault, shall throw the first stone.

Mistakes in Regard to Content of the Story:

1. Lack of recognizable content.
2. No relation to the audience's interests at a certain time.
3. Cost in no proportion to appeal.

Mistakes in Regard to Identification:

4. Lack of relation between facts of story and life of spectator.
5. Lack of sympathetic characters.
6. Inconsistencies in sympathy of character.
7. Lack of characters who make favorable comparisons possible.

Mistakes in Regard to Probability:

8. Lack of probability.
9. Temptations to interesting but improbable situations.
10. False premises.

Mistakes in Regard to Understandability:

11. Lack of variety.
12. Use of exhausted formulas.
13. Insufficient information.
14. Use of incomprehensible symbols.
15. Preventing evaluation by use of unfamiliar factors.
16. Familiar characterization and happenings with unfamiliar emotions.
17. Lack of universal emotions.
18. Insipid picture because of the inability to make interesting material understandable.

Mistakes in Regard to Forward Movement:

19. Main intention is exposed too late.
20. Main difficulty is exposed too late.
21. Climax too early.
22. Main-goal attained before end of picture.
23. Slow spots because of lack of auxiliary goals.
24. Stops and jumps because subintentions are not overlapping.
25. Subintention misunderstood as main-intention.
26. Lack of graduation.
27. Material which does not allow any graduation.
28. Uneven graduation.
29. Story beginnings which are too impressive.
30. Graduation which is not carried to the extreme.
31. Stagnant graduation.
32. Fatigue because of wrong estimate of distance.
33. Dissatisfaction caused by remaining energies.
34. Choppiness because sequence of scenes does not follow interest.
35. Failure to follow up intentions.
36. Interposition of scenes hindering forward movement.

Mistakes in Regard to Suspense:

37. Confusion because of lack of information concerning goal.
38. Unequal chance for success.
39. False suspense which is based upon hope.
40. Failure to expose difficulty at the correct time.
41. Gradual slackening of doubt toward the end.

Mistakes in Regard to Anticipation:

42. Anticipation of author's intention. (Telegraphing ahead)
43. Lack of knowledge for anticipation.
44. Lack of information for anticipation.
45. Lack of surprise.
46. Attempts to create suspense without sufficient anticipation.
47. Failure to end anticipation.

Mistakes in Regard to Main-intention and Sub-intention:

48. Lack of main intention.
49. Weak main intention.
50. Parallel or diffuse main intentions.
51. Main intentions which do not extend over the entire length of the story.
52. False subintentions not furthering the main intention.
53. Subintention without motivation.
54. Motivation which is not dependent upon motive.
55. Strength of motivation exceeding strength of motive.
56. Subintentions which have no concentric directions.
57. Failure to fulfill or frustrate subintentions.

Mistakes in Regard to Disturbance and Adjustment:

58. Descriptive story without disturbance.
59. Combinations without characteristics.
60. Combinations without affinity or repulsion.
61. Failure to separate parts with affinity.
62. Failure to unite parts with repulsion.
63. Failure to prevent splitting of parts with repulsion.
64. Failure to prevent unison of parts with affinity.
65. Motives without resulting intentions.
66. Intentions without motives.
67. Inadequate goal for intention.
68. No proportion between strength of intention and motive.
69. Failure to oppose intentions.
70. Attempt to obstruct intention by difficulties which are not in opposition.
71. Failure to fulfill an intention which is not obstructed.
72. Failure to focus counterintention to the same goal.
73. Sole opposition of main intention by obstacles or complications.
74. Failure to make strength of intention manifest.
75. Inadequate strength of difficulty.
76. Failure to recognize mutual exposition of strength in attack and resistance.
77. Lack of final decision.
78. Clash with difficulty reveals stronger intention than the motive did.
79. Unnecessary exposition of conclusive factors.
80. Failure to imply execution of unopposed intention in lapse of time.
81. Failure to show execution of intention which is opposed.
82. Rapid change in characteristics.
83. Inadequate preparation of adjustment.

84. Adjustment which falls back upon undisturbed stage.
85. Unacceptable adjustment.
86. Unhappy end which has possibility of later adjustment.

Mistakes in Regard to Characterization:

87. Lack of psychological knowledge.
88. Lack of characterization.
89. Negligence in exposing obligatory factors.
90. Inconsistent choice of factors.
91. Willful designation of factors.
92. Inconsistent actions.
93. Inconsistent reactions from other people.
94. Neglect of details capable of characterization.
95. Uneven distribution of characterization.
96. False choice of characterizations.
97. Duplication of characterizations.
98. Lack of color scheme.
99. Neglect of bit parts.

Mistakes in Regard to the Selection of Information:

100. Unessential information.
101. Too little information.
102. Repetition of information.
103. False distribution of information.
104. Lack of necessary explanation.

Mistakes in Regard to Division of Knowledge:

105. Failure to inform actors.
106. Boring exposition of information to actors.
107. Failure to inform audience.

Mistakes in Regard to Place and Time:

108. Indifferent choice of place.
109. Wrong choice of place.

110. Disregard of effects of place upon scene.
111. Indifferent choice of time.
112. Disregard of consecutive time.
113. Disregard of progression of time.
114. Disregard of effects of lapse of time.
115. Omission of exposition of place.
116. Neglect of exploiting characteristics of place.
117. Choppiness because of unfulfilled preparation of place.
118. Insufficient exposition.
119. Disregard of exposition of time through action.
120. Irregular intervals in lapse of time.

Mistakes in Regard to Enlargement and Composition:

121. Photographing the wrong sector.
122. Wrong choice of set-up.
123. Pointing to unimportant factors.
124. Failure to show essential factors.
125. False composition of factors.
126. Delay in following interest.
127. Unwarranted movement of the camera.
128. Lack of connection between shots.
129. Harsh change of set-up.

Mistakes in Regard to the means of expression:

130. Expression without meaning.
131. Uneconomical use of the means of expression.
132. Use of the wrong means of expression.
133. Too much dialog.
134. Actions without adequate sound.
135. Disregard of expressed information.
136. Contradiction in different means of expression.
137. False reminiscence.
138. Lack of elaboration.

139. Absurd duplication.
140. False symbolism.

Mistakes in Regard to Space:

141. Too much material
142. Too little material.

Chapter 6

The Young Filmmakers

THE YOUNG FILMMAKERS are here to stay—to grow older and more experienced and, in time, to give way to the next wave of inspired firebrands.

If today's unfettered, exuberant experimentation permits no other predictions, at least the above can be anticipated as surely as that there will be a continuing demand for filmmakers in the foreseeable future, even though technological progress may change their names. Indeed, to be on the safe side, let us note here the clause inserted in writers' contracts, which encompasses all presently known technical devices as well as the future ones yet to be invented.

For the interest in storytelling is sure to persist; curiosity did not come to an end when the listeners gathered in a cave to hear the latest report of the Mammoth-hunter it is likely to be equally spellbinding when returning

284

astronauts relate their explorations of a distant universe by means of thought-transference—for which a startling new form of copyright protection will have to be invented.

No doubt the technical innovations will continue to speed ahead faster than the changes in the sensory, mental, and emotional capacities and responses of the audiences. While the mechanical advances will not cease to alter the forms of storytelling, there will remain at the other end the more or less immutable recipient to whom the content is addressed.

For many years the stable studio structures preserved the technical status quo of moviemaking. But when the decay of static studio systems permitted new freedom and spurred greater ingenuity, improved equipment was invented and utilized. Portable cameras, high-speed film, smaller lights, directional mikes, and more flexible sound equipment opened new vistas of production, unheard-of possibilities in location shooting, and reduced costs. And this technological revolution has not run its course as yet; perfected tools are continually announced.

Coincidentally and fortunately, many young filmmakers have come to the fore, enthusiastically exploring the unprecedented facilities. In colleges and universities, a highly motivated generation of students is working with the new materials at hand, investigating the original effects to be achieved, while learning the established techniques.

In due course, the thrill of innovation will pass from the mechanical to the dramatic, to the inventive presentation of human relationships, the fresh view of basic situations. Much that became stale and hackneyed will be discarded by the creative impetus, and replaced by the artistic perception which sees the world day after day as if it had never been observed before.

Novelty per se, however, has as little staying power as

any fad and fashion. While the latest wrinkle attracts fleeting attention, it is in a sense the reverse of the old-time producer who tried to keep abreast of the times by telling the writer, "What I'm really looking for is—a new cliché."

It can hardly be denied that much screenwriting in the past was eclectic: elements from successful pictures would be cannibalized and installed in new vehicles. I have been in many story conferences when a past picture would be mentioned: "Do you remember how people laughed at that scene?" Or someone might say: "Put a police chase in. That's always good." But the portions that have proved their worth in other films are likely to fall apart in the new combination. Better to build from scratch than to ransack the files.

Yet, as necessary as experience is, in the past it was difficult, if not impossible, for the young filmmaker to come by. Almost every other major industry allocates large sums to research and development; the studios were mortally afraid of experimentation. Large corporations have extensive training programs and devote considerable effort to attracting and selecting the most promising candidates; the studios did not search out young filmmakers, but employed talent scouts only to replace actors and actresses whose youthful looks could not withstand the ravages of time forever.

Fortunately, this has changed in recent years. Excellent film courses are offered in many universities and colleges. In Los Angeles, California, the American Film Institute's Center for Advanced Film Studies provides a unique context in which young filmmakers can make films and work in close tutorial relationships with the finest practicing film artists and craftsmen. The Center's program is open to professional filmmakers and scholars in the early stages of their careers and to university graduates of special promise. Equipment, film, and other resources are allocated according to the requirements of each project. The Film Institutes's Intern Program has made it possible for young filmmakers to work with such major directors as Marty Ritt, Peter Yates, Mike Nichols, Elia Kazan, Robert Wise, Robert Mulligan, John Frankenheimer, Arthur Penn.

A significant new development is the decrease of specialization among the young filmmakers—in contrast to its rapid increase among, say, physicians or chemists. Opposing the decentralization of the human being, the artist reasserts his individuality. Against the studio's concept of teamwork, the young creators advocate the concept of the total filmmaker. Few will disagree that it is a healthy assertion against the principle of creating by committee— because it is too often true that "a camel is a horse designed by a committee." Yet as laudable as the striving for artistic individuality may be in theory, in practice filmmaking is a many-headed Hydra that seems to require an assortment of resourceful trainers.

The concept of the "auteur" (one man, such as Charles Chaplin or Orson Welles, writing and directing and producing and sometimes acting) has become increasingly attractive to many filmmakers. But it is not likely to perpetuate itself as easily in motion pictures as in novels, traditionally written by one author. Even such strong personalities as Fellini or Hitchcock, no matter how unmistakably they impress their individuality upon the film, have to work with writers, composers, cameramen—not to mention the substantial contribution of their cast. In short, the *auteur* in films is to be admired not so much for his achievements as a lone wolf, but as the brilliant conductor with a gift for eliciting the best orchestration from his team.

Moreover, the most individualistic of total filmmakers

will be forced to realize sooner or later that he cannot ignore, much less fire, his one silent and even absent participant—the audience. It demands that his "personal statement" attain a degree of universality. Making pictures to please *only* oneself, perhaps to aggrandize one's own insecure ego, is an expensive hobby; it will not be indulged in very long. Modern poets can seek self-expression in esoteric symbols which nobody else understands. But the filmmaker can hardly extricate himself from the interrelationship with his audience.

Nor should this be considered a cause for regret. That the average moviegoer has the mentality of the twelve-year-old has been disproved more often than proved. To insult the intelligence of the public is hardly a good idea; other merchandisers, no matter how they may evaluate the tastes and intellects of their fellow men, prefer to flatter the customers.

Being a democratic art, motion pictures have the beneficial and the imperfect aspects of a democracy, the advantages and the drawbacks. Among the dangers are the tendency toward vulgarity, platitude, commonplace banality. Since it addresses itself to the mass psychology, it may become the vehicle for mass seduction, a phenomenon which we have experienced too often in the last decades. Among the beneficial aspects is the sound and healthy judgment delivered by the multitude, in contrast to the verdicts of a few self-appointed arbiters who may be given to excesses, wrong beliefs, artificial feelings, false emotions, snobbish lies. The vast jury of ticket buyers, while not infallible, safeguards a sound measure of justice in the courts.

The majority of the young filmmakers, whether idealistic or not, are concerned with the state of the world and the shortcomings of society. The work of the others, though they may reject any involvement, influences their contemporaries just as much. For the truth is that all storytelling cannot help but instruct as well as interest or entertain. No matter how selfish or opportunistic a movie-maker may be, he cannot escape the fact that he is also an educator.

By his selection of facts from the multitude of life, and by his attitude toward them, the film creator inevitably projects a world view. Consciously or unconsciously, he teaches what he believes. And although, today, that indirect education may be obscured by the great output of trash, by the heaps of sensational or insipid films, the writer fundamentally descends from a long line of illustrious ancestors—from the ancient prophets, from the inspired poets guiding their people, from the visionaries, seers, and teachers.

No matter how hard he tries, he cannot shirk this basic responsibility—today less than ever, because the mass media multiply the effects of his words. Oscar Wilde said that life imitates art more often than the other way around. And that certainly holds true nowadays, when a new hairdo introduced by a star immediately spreads to millions of girlish heads from Azusa to Zanzibar.

Thus the movie creator affects civilization by weaving his views into the cultural context. For better or worse, he alters, shapes, damages, or nurtures the environment in which we live. Though he may strenuously resist this link and seek to isolate himself, he is nevertheless inextricably embroiled with his fellow men, with the fate of the world, in a mutual interplay in which he not only absorbs and expresses, but influences as well.

Though unintentionally, the young filmmaker may imply how things ought to be—by revealing honestly "where it's at" or "what it's like, man." And that there is a great need for their clear vision is expressed by a character in my novel *The Thirteenth Apostle:* "It is the artist's duty to explore an ever-changing world, to re-discover and re-create it for each generation. His function in a nation's body is to experience life as it then exists and to communicate it to his contemporaries as the eyes, ears, the senses as well as the emotions, do for the individual. Never before had the need for a constant re-discovery of our lives been so great, because never before had the environment changed so rapidly. The world tends to become a stranger to us with each passing hour, growing as it does, from day to day, in a million separate places. It keeps moving away from us in steps so small that we do not notice them. And yet, if we do not recapture it at intervals, we are bound to end up, before long, without a true sense of being, trapped by withered petrified notions from previous world climates, leading phantom-lives in imagined surroundings that were true once, but no longer exist."

Chapter 7

The Daring Conviction

THE WRITER who starts his screenplay in the quiet of a small room may be thrilled by the thought that the words which he conceives will be heard by millions of people. Such an unimaginably powerful rostrum inspires him to do his very best: he hopes that success, artistic or commercial or both, will crown his efforts.

A journey of a thousand miles starts with a single step. At the outset, the traveler may invoke his favorite lucky charm, whether he prefers rubbing a rabbit's foot, touching wood, or crossing his fingers. In fact, if he were not too embarrassed, he might consult a tea-leaf reader to ascertain whether he will reach his goal.

Since the dawn of time, men have sought oracles to predict the course of events; they have tried to discover magic with which to manipulate that course; they have yearned for rules by which the gods could be forced to do one's bidding. And the kings that ran studios placed their

291

hopes in a succession of chief sorcerers, wrathfully firing them when they failed to produce the promised miracles.

From the amulets of the tribal priests to the latest pronouncements of motivational research pundits, the same human desire for certainty manifests itself. The sense of fearful helplessness, engendered by the lack of control over audience responses, prompts networks and film studios today to try any device that will predict or enforce a success.

Nowadays, of course, when the dances and sacrifices of ancient medicine men are mentioned, we readily offer a supercilious smile. But we knit our brows in serious thought when we study the completely contradictory findings of two competing television rating systems.

By responding to our modern needs, superstition has managed to survive—it has merely changed its terminology to a statistical and pseudo-scientific vocabulary and methodology. And as long as our human situation continues to generate the same needs for some sort of control over life's bewildering unruliness, magic and oracles are bound to invade our thinking.

Some time ago, I took part in a panel discussion dealing with various phases of the entertainment industries. In the course of the evening, some widely divergent opinions were expressed. A motion picture producer, affirming his faith in the star system, was questioned by a director, who pointed out that two features starring the same actress were released in one year; one was a great box office success, the other a total failure.

The motion picture producer, while conceding the existence of such inexplicable discrepancies, remained firm in his adherence to the star system. "When you risk so much money in a production," he exclaimed, "you must have *some* insurance—even if it doesn't always pay off."

No one pointed to the slight contradiction in the concept of an insurance which does not have to pay off, because by then the argument had raged on to the question of pleasing an audience. A story executive lauded the merits of pre-sold properties, such as hit plays and best-selling novels. Whereupon a critic cited examples of fine plays and novels that had been turned into bad motion pictures—and vice versa. An exhibitor, paraphrasing Pontius Pilate, asked: "What is good?" And he quoted a review by the critic who had praised a certain motion picture, which had been condemned by another equally distinguished critic. At that point the producer emphasized, very wisely as well as sadly, that such disagreements on quality were not limited to individual critics or viewers. For a motion picture is directed to the same mass audience, which—in a presidential election—is just about evenly divided in the appraisal of the respective candidates' merits.

As yet, the discussion had not discovered any reliable principles. The situation became still more confused when a sponsor of television programs was questioned on his method of buying shows. He readily admitted that he had no faith whatsoever in the value of the rating system to which he subscribed.

"Then why do you keep renewing it?" he was asked.

"I must have something to go by," he protested.

"But if you don't believe in it?"

He shrugged. "It's better than nothing."

A paradox?

Of course. But one which expresses the dilemma of men who must make decisions based on intangibles.

Indeed, it is perfectly understandable if the executive who is forced to make his choices in a welter of elusive values and volatile factors ultimately reaches for any kind of yardstick, for any kind of measuring device, even when he does not believe in it. In his despair, he may prefer dubious rules to none at all—simply because it is "better than nothing."

But show business, though often accused of irrationality and unbusinesslike methods, is not alone in this paradoxical situation. The same applies to the stockmarket, where a vast number of investors are guided by the predictions of influential and respected advisory services—though a close study of the record might reveal that their analyses and prophecies are about as reliable as a medieval sorcerer's incantations. And a close look at the disagreements of hard-headed bankers and economists might cause us to wonder whether our practical affairs, involving the measurable quantities of hard dollars, are quite as securely embedded in a dependable realism as we assume. And, last but not least, gigantic industries, before staking enormous sums in new products, have applied every conceivable device of audience research—as did the Ford Company, before designing the Edsel.

There is something cussedly ornery and unpredictable about the consumer, the audience—about people. There is still that area of mystery in the human being which the poet can grasp more easily than the statistician. And for that reason the creator remains in control of his field. Instead of succumbing to despair after he recognizes the inevitable failure of all measuring devices, statistical crutches, whimsical insurance, and untrustworthy precedent, the creator, forced to rely on his own judgment, can once again experience the fascination of his work.

In most of us operate two conflicting drives—the wish for security, the safe, the predictable—and the adventurous spirit, the wish for the challenge, which gives us the thrill of feeling alive.

The creator— whether we apply this term collectively to the author, playwright, screenwriter, to the management and staff of a company, to the combination of artists and technicians involved in a production—is continually advancing into uncharted territory.

Unlike the trader or cautious investor who can acquire a store or a going business on the basis of past earnings, the creator starts each new project from an unformed potential, from malleable materials, from seeds which do not reveal their future growth. Nor can he repeat past successes. For the audience, though accepting and even insisting on a reassuring measure of the familiar, also demands the new—which evokes in the viewer the same thrill that had previously excited and inspired the creator.

Unable, therefore, to perpetuate precedent, the creator, driven toward the new, must be guided by a daring conviction.

Since it is a conviction—and not a proven law—it is subject to doubt. And further, since it is daring—it is subject to fear. Both insecurity and fear, therefore, are inseparable from the creator.

But so is courage, for he would not long remain a creator, if he lacked the spirit to fling out a daring conviction. And so is good judgment, for without the capacity for critical evaluation, his courage would soon be exposed as foolhardiness.

In contrast to the graphs and charts that facilitate decisions in other fields, the creator finds his imagination sparked by an idea, by the excitement he experiences in reading a book or story, by his emotional response to a play. On the basis of so volatile a reaction, he must make his initial decision.

A poet, sparked by an idea in the middle of a night, can complete his verses within minutes, or he may polish them over years. But in any event, no costly or far-reaching decisions are involved.

The creator in show business, however, though the initial spark may be equally fleeting, must decide to set in motion the enormous apparatus of production. He must evaluate his primary emotional and rational response in the light of the cumbrous burden, the vast effort, risk, labor, and devotion it will have to sustain. Is it surprising, then, that no basic material seems quite strong enough to endure this comparison—unless it is bolstered by pre-sold qualities, by stars, or by some sort of unfathomable trade axioms?

And yet, even this groping for support does not obviate the need for the daring conviction. For after the first decision, there begins the task of realization, a long road of which each step defies prior guarantee. Indeed, nothing less enduring is demanded than to carry that initial spark and emotional response through sound stages, laboratories, cutting rooms, projection booths, theatres—right into the hearts of the audience, where it must flare up once again after having been extinguished, battered, obscured; after the emotion has long vanished from the experience of the creators, has slipped from their grip, has grown stale by endless repetition.

All creators need daring conviction. In the case of the poet, the circuit from heart and mind to the pen is so brief as to grant safe passage to the tender and gentle and wisp-like impulse. But a Michelangelo needed a burning and compelling vision to sustain him in the titanic labors of painting the Sistine Chapel. And the motion picture, because of its singular nature, requires its own brand of conviction. The creator's incipient vision must be implemented by a whole caravan of artists and technicians, treading on a rainbow, lugging all their heavy equipment over the radiant, multicolored and utterly insubstantial bridge across the air—toward the distant image, the distant emotion, the distant pot of gold at the end of that rainbow.

And their hazardous journey is first imagined, and then fulfilled, by the will of the writer. Their entire trek over the luminous span of the rainbow is conceived by—his daring conviction.

INDEX

ABOUT THE AUTHOR

EUGENE VALE is the highly respected author of more than sixty film and television scripts and over a dozen novels. His experience in all phases of the motion picture industry—although principally a writer, he has worked as a laboratory worker, cutter, stage manager, director and producer, and in distribution, publicity and finance—is brought together in *The Technique of Screen and Television Writing*. Originally published in 1972, the book was completely revised and expanded by the author in 1982, and is widely used as an authoritative text.

Mr. Vale's novels include the best-selling, prize-winning *The Thirteenth Apostle*, which has by now achieved the status of a classic, and *Passion Play*. Among his screenplays are *The Bridge at San Luis Rey* and *Francis of Assisi*. He is an active member of the Writers' Guild of America and the Academy of Motion Picture Arts and Sciences, and has taught screen writing on a number of campuses.